Doing What Works
in Brief Therapy

Doing What Works in Brief Therapy

A Strategic Solution Focused Approach

Ellen K. Quick

Kaiser Permanente
San Diego, California

 **Academic Press**

San Diego   New York   Boston   London   Sydney   Tokyo   Toronto

Cover graphics credits: 10099, Eric Wunrow; 10094, Carlye Calvin; 10064, Carlye Calvin; copyright © 1993, ColorBytes, Inc

This book is printed on acid-free paper.

Academic Press, Inc.
A Division of Harcourt Brace & Company
525 B Street, Suite 1900, San Diego, California 92101-4495

United Kingdom Edition published by
Academic Press Limited
24-28 Oval Road, London NW1 7DX

Library of Congress Cataloging-in-Publication Data

Quick, Ellen Kaufman.
    Doing what works in brief therapy : a strategic solution focused
approach / by Ellen K. Quick.
            p.   cm.
    Includes bibliographical references and index.
    ISBN 0-12-569660-4 (alk. paper)
    1. Brief psychotherapy. 2. Solution-focused therapy.
3. Strategic therapy. I. Title.
RC480.55.Q53   1996
616.89'14--dc20   95-25308
                                               CIP

PRINTED IN THE UNITED STATES OF AMERICA
96   97   98   99   00   01   BB   9   8   7   6   5   4   3   2   1

The author earned her undergraduate degree from Wellesley College and her doctorate in clinical psychology from the University of Pittsburgh. She has practiced psychology for over twenty years, specializing in brief psychotherapy. Since 1981, Dr. Quick has worked at Kaiser Permanente in San Diego.

Contents

3

Amplifying the Solution: Variations on the Miracle Question

4

Evaluating Attempted Solutions: If It Doesn't Work, Do Something Different

5

Designing the Intervention: Validation, Compliment, and Suggestion

6

Therapist Decisions: Clarifying, Amplifying, or Interrupting

7

Couples: Problems and Solutions

8

Coping with Difficult Situations

9

Medication and the Model

10

Brief Therapy: Problems and Solutions in Managed Care

11

Case Examples: Intermittent Care

12

Excerpts: Single-Session Therapy

13

Excerpts: Brief Therapy

Preface

*D*oing What Works in Brief Therapy: A Strategic Solution Focused Approach is a description of strategic solution focused therapy—its development, its theory, and its techniques. It meets a need for a step-by-step presentation of the procedures, outlined in sufficient detail that the reader can apply them in his or her own practice. At the same time, the book repeatedly emphasizes that *no* techniques, including those described here, can be applied in all situations. The need for flexibility, clinical decision making, and for tailoring the therapy to the individual is one of the central guidelines.

The primary audience for this book is the practicing psychotherapist. Those practitioners already familiar with brief strategic therapy and/or solution focused therapy will recognize how the current model applies, integrates, and extends the models. Therapists of very different orientations will appreciate the discussion of issues that emerge in therapy of all kinds. Balancing client needs for change and stability, speaking the client's language, and dealing with uncertainty and life dilemmas are universal therapist concerns addressed in this book. For beginning therapists, most often graduate students in psychology, social work, nursing, and medicine, this is a guidebook. It not only discusses the procedures but describes just how to use them, with numerous and specific clinical examples.

Managed care administrators and health care planners will be interested in seeing how brevity is frequently a natural consequence of using a strategic solution focused approach. Rigid adherence to specific protocols is not required for efficiency; on the contrary, flexible construction of interventions for individual situations produces maximum efficiency and relevance. Finally, psychotherapy researchers and social scientists interested in outcome research and accountability will recognize that psychotherapy models need to demonstrate their efficacy. Systematic outcome research on strategic solution focused therapy still remains to be done. This book can become a starting point for the development of a treatment manual for strategic solution focused therapy.

The book begins by introducing the model. The theory and techniques of the two parent models, Mental Research Institute (MRI) brief strategic therapy and Brief Family Therapy Center (BFTC) solution focused therapy, are reviewed in Chapter 1. The current approach combines brief strategic therapy's emphasis on clarification of *problems* with solution focused therapy's emphasis on amplification of *solutions*. It further integrates solution focused therapy's emphasis on *doing what works* with strategic therapy's focus on *changing what does not*. The chapter reviews the literature on combining models in systemic therapy and outlines the current approach.

Chapter 2 discusses problem clarification, a first and important step in strategic solution focused therapy. The essential idea is that understanding exactly what happened that is problematic and *how* something is a problem will lead to increased precision in the treatment. The author further describes how problem clarification can itself become an intervention, leading to significant normalization and reframing.

Amplification of solution scenarios is the focus in Chapter 3. This chapter reviews how to use de Shazer's "miracle question" to transform goals to specific solutions, some of which may already be present. Variations on the miracle question that involve "specific miracles," "multiple miracles," deliberate *avoidance* of the word "miracle," and coping solutions are discussed.

Chapter 4 concentrates on attempted solutions: identifying them and evaluating their efficacy. Common sense attempted solutions that frequently do *not* work well enough are reviewed, and some alternatives are considered. There is discussion of a variety of "restraint from change" messages.

In Chapter 5 the focus is on planning and delivering feedback to clients. This chapter describes how to develop a "three part intervention" that includes validation, compliment, and suggestion components. The suggestions emphasize amplification of emerging solutions that work and interruption of those that do not.

Chapter 6 addresses the question of when to emphasize which component of the model. The author proposes some guidelines about initial selection and subsequent shifts of focus. Doing the most straightforward thing first, the therapist attempts to find procedures that "work;" when they do not, the therapists "does something different."

Working with couples from a strategic solution focused perspective is the subject of Chapter 7. This chapter presents a format for an initial conjoint session that elicits separate problem descriptions and miracle scenarios from each partner. Indications for conjoint versus individual follow-up are suggested, and ways of dealing with animosity, secrets, and infidelity are discussed.

Chapter 8 presents a strategic solution focused approach to therapy in difficult situations. The author suggests that clients may not need to wait to eliminate all uncertainty and discomfort from their lives in order to make things better. The chapter reviews the use of "coping questions" and ways of transforming unattainable goals to achievable solutions. What therapy *cannot* accomplish is also addressed.

Chapter 9 examines the topic of psychotropic medication and how it relates to strategic solution focused therapy. Clients' "positions," which may be strongly pro-medicine or anti-medicine, are considered. In the spirit of doing what works and changing what does not, it is suggested that *both* medicine *and* psychotherapy sometimes work, alone and in combination—and that both can also become unsuccessful attempted solutions.

Managed care and brief therapy are the focus of Chapter 10. The author points out that brevity is not the primary aim of this approach, but it can result from precise clarification of problems and solutions. There is discussion of single session therapy, brief threatment, and intermittent care, with consideration of ways of discussing benefit limitations with clients. Cautions and potential problems in managed care are addressed as well.

Chapters 11, 12, and 13 present case examples in strategic solution focused therapy. Chapter 11 gives examples in intermittent care: a woman with a "difficult husband"—before and after his death, a man who comes only when his doctor and employer tell him to, a woman with longstanding "rage," and a couple—before and after marriage. Chapter 12 presents two single session therapy excerpts that illustrate different components of the model. Chapter 13 consists of excepts from brief therapy, two from first sessions and one from a final session.

As all the chapters emphasize, the critical elements in strategic solution focused therapy operate at two levels simultaneously. Working with the client, the therapist attempts to clarify the problem and to facilitate the client's doing what works and changing what does not. At the same time, the therapist selects techniques tailored to each situation, shifting to something different in response to problems or obstacles as they arise. *Clarifying problems, doing what works, and changing what does not:* that is the recurring theme throughout this book.

The ideas presented here are not original. I have been strongly influenced by the important work done at MRI by Gregory Bateson, Don Jackson, Richard Fisch, John Weakland, and Paul Watzlawick. The thinking and writing of Steve de Shazar and Insoo Kim Berg at BFTC have also been central in the development of the ideas described here. I have been influenced by the thinking of Milton Erickson as well.

I am particularly grateful to Richard Fisch for the many ideas he has shared with me, in the context of telephone case consultation over the course of several years. I also want to acknowledge Scott Miller, who on several occasions tailored training to our needs in San Diego. I am grateful to Jon Pinter, whose description of work in Milwaukee led to my initial attempts at combining the models.

I want to acknowledge my fellow members of the San Diego Strategic Solution Focused Therapy Professional Interest Group: Linda Brown, Nancy Haller, Robert Mashman, Lisa Peterson, Marian Richetta, and Mark Schlissel. Our case sharing and discussion have been instrumental in the development of many of the concepts described here. I also very much appreciate the input provided by Kaiser co-workers and trainees in seminars we have shared.

I am grateful to Marvin Yelles at Academic Press, who suggested developing my ideas into a full-length book. I also appreciate the assistance of Naomi Henning at Academic Press. Nicole Mestler, Emelyn de la Peña, Mary Lee, Andrea Henrahan, Dai Robertson, David Bernard, and Barbara Scarantino all participated in the preparation of the manuscript, and I appreciate their assistance.

I owe special thanks to my clients. Their ability to construct solutions continues to impress me. Finally, I want to thank my husband, Frank, and my daughter, Melissa, for their companionship, support, and humor. Frank's assistance with the computer was a tremendous help.

My thanks to all of you.

The Model and Its Origins

This is a book about a specific way of doing psychotherapy. The approach is strategic solution focused therapy, a model that combines the principles and techniques of two other models, brief strategic therapy and solution focused therapy.

The reader might legitimately question why the field of psychotherapy needs yet another therapy approach. Are there not already enough models, too many, perhaps? The author's answer is an outgrowth of her experience working in managed care settings, including community mental health centers and a group model health maintenance organization, for twenty years. During this time, demands for service skyrocketed, while financial resources dwindled. Practice guidelines were increasingly implemented by insurance companies and mental health administrators, and frequently these standards limited the number of times clients could be seen.

In attempts to accommodate to the external changes, therapists searched for models that would allow them to work more briefly. Short-term psychodynamic therapy (Mann, 1981; Strupp and Binder, 1984; Bauer and Kobos, 1987; Sifneos, 1987), cognitive therapy (Beck, Rush, Shaw, and Emery, 1979), and interpersonal therapy (Klerman, Weissman, Rounsaville, and Chevron, 1984) were among the approaches used. All too often, however, therapists who used these models became frustrated because they found themselves trying to squeeze "watered down" versions of a model into too few appointments. As the author experimented with brief strategic therapy and then solution focused therapy, she discovered that some of the frustration with external limits seemed to diminish. Brevity became a natural result of conducting therapy with these models.

But questions remained. If both models were useful, when should the therapist use which? Were the two models fundamentally different? Clinicians[1] in the field seemed to disagree about these issues. Gradually it became clear that a number of therapists who were familiar with the two models were using both. The combined model was emerging. As discussion about managed care increased, therapists using the combined approach were frequently asked to describe what they were doing and to teach the approach to others. As concepts were put into writing and articulated to others in terms of specific procedures used, the integrated approach was being described more clearly. Strategic solution focused therapy was similar to the two parent models in many ways, but it was not identical to either. It seemed to combine "the best of both."

In informal discussions, therapists remarked that it seemed possible to do what the model described in a busy, varied setting and still feel invigorated and creative. This reaction was strikingly different from the chronic sense of frustration experienced by many therapists when they think that "treatment could help this person—if only the system gave me the time to do it right."

This book has been written in response to multiple requests for more extensive guidelines on how to conduct strategic solution focused therapy. It should be noted that the efficacy of this approach has not been empirically investigated; perhaps these guidelines can serve as a preliminary "treatment manual" for such investigation in the future. This book simply describes how to do strategic solution focused therapy. The present chapter describes each of the "parent" models and introduces the combined approach.

The Model

The principles that guide strategic solution focused therapy can be summarized as a three-part theory:

1. What's the trouble?
2. If it works, do more of it.
3. If it doesn't work, stop doing it. Do something different.

The first and third points come primarily from brief strategic therapy, while the second comes primarily from solution focused therapy. (The word "primarily" must be stressed here, because strategic therapy often addresses "what works" and solution focused therapy often addresses "what doesn't" and the nature of the problem.) The difference is what is *emphasized* in each of the models.

[1]Positions taken by specific clinicians are elaborated later.

Brief Strategic Therapy: The MRI Approach

Brief strategic therapy was developed at the Mental Research Institute (MRI). (The letters MRI, as used here, have nothing to do with magnetic resonance imaging brain scans.) The Mental Research Institute, located in Palo Alto, California, is a multidisciplinary corporation founded in 1959. Some of the original participants included Don Jackson, Virginia Satir, and Paul Watzlawick. All of these people had a grounding in psychoanalytic theory, followed by an interest in family therapy and systems theory. The MRI therapists were also exposed to the work of Milton Erickson, psychiatrist and hypnotist. Erickson's concept of "utilization" would be important in the MRI approach. As Rossi points out, Erickson "utilized problem behaviors, thoughts, and feelings as part of the solution" (Erickson, Rossi, and Rossi, 1976). Erickson also utilized the patient's mental processes and expectancies in different ways when he presented suggestions in language the patient had introduced.

In 1965, a group of MRI therapists began a research project called the Brief Therapy Center. This project was designed to investigate what could be done in a time-limited period, up to ten sessions, by focusing on the chief complaint. Interventions would include a variety of procedures. The project, assumptions, techniques, and conclusions have been described extensively in the book *The Tactics of Change* (Fisch, Weakland, and Segal, 1982).

One important premise of the approach is that multiple views of reality exist. Rather than seeing reality as "one fixed truth," the MRI theorists emphasize that "views" of reality are all we can know, and perhaps all that exist. This has been described as the "constructivist perspective" (Watzlawick, 1992).

A second premise is that behavior is constantly shaped and maintained by social reinforcement. MRI therapists generally downplay physiological predisposition to behavior disorder. They have further emphasized that even when biological factors exist, how they are viewed and dealt with makes a considerable difference in how problematic they become (Fisch, et al., 1982). Current interactions are examined, not "deeper roots of pathology" (Weakland, Fisch, Watzlawick, and Bodin, 1974). Thus, MRI brief strategic therapy is an *interactional* model. Problems are not entities that exist within a single individual; rather, they result from interactions between individuals.

The MRI therapists have emphasized that ordinary life regularly brings "difficulties" to everyone. Difficulties arise in the course of normal individual and family development, when shifts in roles and relationships are necessary. A difficulty may become a problem when an ordinary difficulty is, for some reason, defined as "problematic" by the client or the family, or, on the other hand, when the existence of a normal, stage-appropriate difficulty is denied (Watzlawick, Weakland, and Fisch, 1974).

As people go about their lives, doing their best to resolve difficulties and manage transitions, they do whatever makes sense to them. For example, if someone is depressed, family members attempt to cheer the person up. Sometimes that "works," but sometimes it does not; the depressed person may feel more misunderstood, more abnormal, and therefore more melancholy. At this point the well-intentioned family members will frequently apply "more of the same" attempted solution, and, in response, the depressed person's feelings are further intensified. Thus, the action intended to decrease something actually increases it. The continuation and exacerbation of a problem result from the creation of a positive feedback loop (Weakland et al., 1974). The people involved are usually unaware of this pattern.

It should be emphasized that no assumption is made about "secondary gain" or any deliberate attempt to maintain problems. Nor is there any assumption of a basic deficit in the structural organization of the family. Long-standing symptoms are not seen as "chronicity" (in terms of a basic deficit in biology, individual character structure, or an interpersonal system), but as evidence of a difficulty that has been mishandled for a longer period of time (Weakland et al., 1974). Problems, including long-standing and severe ones, are maintained inadvertently, and often with the best of intentions.

If well-intended solution behaviors maintain problems, then interrupting the problem-maintaining feedback loop should decrease the problem behavior. The MRI therapists assert that an initially small change can interrupt the cycle. Just "a little less" of the unsuccessful attempted solution should lead to "a little less" of the problem behavior, leading to increasingly less unsuccessful solution, increasingly less problem, and so on. The therapist is seen as an active agent of change, who deliberately initiates the change process. In order to do this, the therapist needs to: (1) evaluate the problem; (2) evaluate what is maintaining it; (3) consider what might interrupt the cycle; and (4) determine how that change might best be implemented. Therapy is practical, brief, and problem focused, aimed at getting people back "on track," so that they may confront the next developmentally appropriate "difficulty."

The word "strategic" refers to the therapist's task of developing a strategy, or a plan, to interrupt the unsuccessful attempted solution. (This is somewhat different from the strategic model as developed by Haley [1976] and Madanes [1981], where problems are seen as having a system-maintaining purpose. The strategic therapy referred to in this book is primarily the MRI strategic model.)

The purpose of MRI brief strategic therapy is to resolve the original complaint to the client's satisfaction. If change can be brought about by simple and direct intervention, so much the better (Fisch et al., 1982). However, sometimes common sense and direct suggestions fail to achieve the desired results. Thus, the MRI therapists sometimes use means of promoting beneficial change that may seem illogical. Sometimes they prescribe behaviors that appear to move away from the goal rather than toward it. In spite of limits on the number of sessions in the original Brief Therapy Center project, MRI therapists may stress "taking one's time" or "going slow." Similarly, therapists may recommend relapse or point out "the dangers of improvement," especially after some initial positive change (Fisch et al., 1982). These interventions may bring desired change when common-sense, direct admonition to change has failed or even exacerbated the problem.

Fisch et al. (1982, p. 128) described the following five types of common unsuccessful attempted solutions, each of which can be interrupted with specific interventions:

1. people frequently attempt to force something that can only occur spontaneously
2. people frequently attempt to master a feared event by postponing it
3. people frequently attempt to reach accord through opposition
4. people frequently attempt to obtain compliance through volunteerism
5. people frequently attempt to decrease an accuser's suspicions by attempting to defend themselves

Other common interventions include "the gentle art of reframing . . . (designed) to change the conceptual and/or emotional setting or viewpoint in which a situation is experienced and to place it in another frame which fits the 'facts' of the same concrete situation equally well or even better, and thereby changes its entire meaning" (Watzlawick et al., 1974, p. 95). Clients are also sometimes encouraged to act "as if" some critical variable were different.

MRI therapists believe that it is possible to influence an entire system through appropriate change in any member. Thus, they often concentrate their efforts and attention on whoever seems the most ready for change or on whoever has the greatest influence on the system. When the problem is a child's behavior, they may work primarily with the parents. When addressing couple problems, they may see the partners separately, or they may work with only one partner.

Once the brief strategic therapist has an idea about an intervention that, if performed, would interrupt an unsuccessful attempted solution, the next task is to motivate the client to implement it. Understandably, clients may be reluctant to follow suggestions that seem to move away from the goal rather than toward it. They may be hesitant about discontinuing the old behavior. People often cling to old, tried-and-true attempted solutions, almost in desperation, as if they are thinking, "I know this hasn't worked perfectly yet, but if I stopped, think how bad things would be!"

When the therapeutic plan involves the introduction of an idea likely to elicit this kind of reaction, it is particularly important to consider the client's "position." "Position" encompasses values, beliefs about the self and others, and the "language," literal and figurative, that is spoken. For example, if the client thinks in terms of sacrifice, he or she might be told that what the therapist is about to request may be a difficult sacrifice, but that it may be the client's duty as a parent (spouse, etc.) to consider this suggestion carefully.

⋆ Occasionally clients may protest that they are unwilling to "pretend" or "play games." Or they may voice concerns about intervention using "reverse psychology" or "manipulation." MRI brief strategic therapists have responded to such concerns by pointing out that influence is inherent in all interaction. Clients pursue psychotherapy precisely because they are seeking to change something. Whether deliberate or not, therapists influence clients, and this kind of therapy designs deliberate strategies for producing the desired results (Weakland et al., 1974).

Solution Focused Therapy: The BFTC Approach

Solution focused therapy began as a variant on the MRI approach. At the Brief Family Therapy Center (BFTC) in Milwaukee, Wisconsin, Steve de Shazer, Insoo Kim Berg, and their colleagues began to modify the brief strategic approach. The problem exploration phase became shorter, sometimes skipping the full description of the problem and clarification of the attempted solution. More emphasis was placed on those times that the complaint did *not* happen. The therapists began to vigorously initiate the search for such occasions, and they invited the client to consider what was different when the problem was absent (Molnar and de Shazer, 1987). The times when the problem was absent were called "exceptions."

If exceptions were identified, the therapist then attempted to use a systemic concept that Molnar and de Shazer called "deviation amplification." The goal was to expand and extend these "pockets" of problem absence. The assumption was that minimal change is sufficient to begin a "deviation-amplifying" cycle. Any change or difference in behavior, no matter how small, could be enough to make the client more satisfied. Moreover, any change could be expected to lead to progressively more change and more satisfaction. If "exceptions" to the problem were *not* identified by the client, the therapists frequently gave a task designed to encourage detection of "exceptions." They asked clients to "notice those things that are already happening that you would like to continue."

The BFTC therapists then noticed that positive change can begin even *before* the first session. The discovery of pretreatment change was made during an exploratory study, where Weiner-Davis, de Shazer, and Gingerich (1987) found that a high percentage of their clients had noticed some kind of change in the desired direction between the time they called for an appointment and the time of the appointment. Focus on the changes observed led to the recognition that these changes could be highlighted and further amplified by certain kinds of therapist input. If movement in the desired direction was already occurring, the therapist no longer needed to initiate change. Rather, the aim was *continuing* change. When the therapist's suggestion involved doing more of what was already happening, and what was already pleasing, many clients were quite ready to cooperate. This effect could be enhanced when the therapist complimented the client on having begun to move in the desired direction.

The BFTC therapists also noticed that complex problems did not necessarily call for complex solutions. Every complaint, no matter how complicated and severe, seemed to have some kind of exception, which could point the way toward a solution. In fact, sometimes it did not seem to matter *what* the details of the problem were. Traditionally, problems have come before solutions. However, de Shazer (1985) came to the conclusion that for an intervention to work, it was not necessary to have detailed information about the complaint. Departing from the MRI model, he further asserted that it was not necessary to recognize how the problem was maintained. Rather, "all that is necessary is that the person involved in a troublesome situation *does something different* [de Shazer's italics], even if that behavior is seemingly irrational, certainly irrelevant, obviously bizarre, or humorous" (de Shazer, 1988, p. 7). A single solution could be like a "skeleton key" that opens many doors.

The goal of solution focused therapy was not so much the elimination of symptoms as the achievement of a stated or inferred goal. Skipping the description of the problem and attempted solution, therapy moved to a vision of the future where the complaint was resolved. The therapists began to ask the "miracle question" (de Shazer, 1988).

Berg has said that the BFTC therapists came upon the miracle question by chance (Hayes, 1991). According to Hayes, Berg has described how the therapists heard clients saying "It would take a miracle to solve my problem" and thought: why not use that common saying ("it would take a miracle") and find out what the client meant by it? As de Shazer (1988) points out, the miracle question is an adaptation of Milton Erickson's crystal ball technique (Erickson, 1954, in de Shazer, 1988). Erickson had his client, while in trance, create a representation of the future with the problem solved. Erickson then had his client look backward from the future and identify how he or she had arrived at a solution. Solution focused therapists typically ask the miracle question without formal trance induction.

After the mid-1980s, the miracle question took on a more central role in solution focused therapy, and the therapists frequently asked the question earlier in the session, before the initiation of a search for exceptions (Miller, 1991). After the client described a "miracle scenario," the therapists often asked about exceptions by questioning whether any "pieces of the miracle" were already happening.

The BFTC therapists also increasingly used scaling questions (BFTC, 1991).

Scaling questions can have many functions. They can provide a baseline measure, indicate degree of client motivation for change, and assess variables such as degree of confidence that change will be maintained (BFTC, 1991). Of much importance, it seemed that even when the problem was unclear, clients could often make a numerical rating (e.g., on a scale of zero to ten) of "where I am now."

The "absolute value" of a numerical rating is not as important as the client's response to the questioning that follows it (BFTC, 1992). Questions such as "How did you get to a 'three'?" might clarify important solution behaviors. When a client's rating indicated that a problem was severe (e.g., a rating of "zero"), questioning might inquire about finding the "just noticeable difference." For example, the therapist might ask what will be different when the client has moved to a "one."

The solution focused therapist's questioning often aims at translating miracle question answers into "well-formed goals." de Shazer (1991, p. 112) outlines the following characteristics of well-formed goals:

1. they are small;
2. they are salient;
3. they are described in specific behavioral terms;
4. they are achievable in the practical context of clients' lives;
5. they are perceived by the client as involving "hard work";
6. they are described as the "start of something" and not as the "end of something"; and
7. they involve the initiation of new behaviors rather than the absence or cessation of existing behaviors.

De Shazer (1992) has described the process of "deconstruction." The elements already in a situation, in the client's life or in the miracle scenario are "broken down" and rearranged in a new way. The resulting configuration may become part of the solution.

Solution focused inquiry usually results in identification of "pieces of the solution" that can be amplified. Occasionally, however, no positive comments can be elicited. When this occurs, the BFTC therapists ask "coping questions" (Berg, 1992, personal communication; Miller, 1991). These questions encourage clients to identify how they have managed as well as they have, and they implicitly (or explicitly) compliment clients for their valiant coping endeavors. In these cases, the coping behaviors are what the therapist attempts to reinforce and amplify.

Combining Models

Within the field of systemic therapy, brief strategic therapy and solution focused therapy have each become separate, well-respected models, increasingly differentiated from each other. Should such therapy approaches be further differentiated, or should they be integrated? This question has been debated in the systemic therapy literature (Efron, 1994). Roberts (1986) has taken the position that combined models may be useful. Stanton (1981) proposed that a therapist might begin with a structural approach and then switch to a strategic technique if the first approach did not prove helpful. Gurman (1978) referred to the advantages gained by combining the strongest aspects of specific approaches. Liddle (1984) has advocated "creating integrative models at more than just the level of technique . . . [building on] the notion that they [the models] have complementary theories of change" (p. 153). Writing about solution focused therapy, Simon (1993) stressed that it is important not to "reify" a model, solution focused therapy included. She emphasized that there is no one "right way" to do treatment, implying that integration is possible and perhaps desirable.

Held (1984, in Duncan, Solovey, and Rusk, 1992) discussed combining the MRI approach with other models. Using the term "strategic eclecticism," she described ways of using MRI-type interventions to enhance compliance with directives suggested by other orientations. For example, the therapist might offer a psychoanalytic interpretation but suggest that the client be cautious about implementing it. Or the therapist might think in terms of the MRI problem-maintenance model (when conceptualizing the *process* by which problems are formed) but work with *content* different from that which is typically described by MRI therapists (Held, 1986).

More recently, Duncan and his colleagues have combined strategic and narrative approaches (Duncan et al., 1992). They describe an approach where the clients' stories about the problem and views about how the problem came to be will influence therapists' goals. Intervention is designed to interrupt problem cycles, to revise meaning, and to validate the client's experience. Duncan's evolving model stresses "revision of meaning." Eron and Lund (1993) also discuss adding a narrative perspective to the precision of a strategic approach. Their therapy attempts to enable clients to act in ways that are consistent with the "preferred view" of the self. Bischof (1992) has written about an approach that integrates solution focused therapy with experiential family treatment, while Efron, Clouthier, and Lefcoe (1994) describe combining solution focused therapy with Michael White's model (White and Epston, 1990) and other approaches.

Randolf (1994) has described an approach called integrated strategic systemic therapy. Influenced by thinkers including Erickson, Haley, Watzlawick, and White, this model emphasizes maintaining maneuverability. A key factor is recognizing when one position is no longer working, so that the therapist may switch to another position. Kuwabara and Tansley (1994) describe a solution focused strategic therapy, an evolving approach that uses both of the models described here.

Writing specifically about the MRI and BFTC models, some authors have cautioned that the models perhaps cannot (or should not) be combined (Eisenberg and Wahrman, 1991). Because one model focuses more on the problem and one more on the solution, these authors assert that the two models are fundamentally different.

Conversely, proponents of either parent model might argue that a combined model is not needed. A strategic therapist could claim that solution focused therapy is "just a variation" on strategic therapy, while a solution focused therapist could assert that solution focused therapy already includes the essential components of the strategic model.

This book takes the position that a *planned* combination of strategic and solution focused therapy is of value, going beyond what either model offers separately. Although in practice, highly skilled strategic *and* solution focused therapists may use methods emphasized by the other approach, the author believes that most presentations of the models, in the literature and in introductory workshops, have not stressed this fact. The current approach makes this combination explicit by labeling it. The strategic solution focused therapist is directly encouraged to consider certain procedures together. Using the blended model, the therapist can select the therapeutic tools most likely to be helpful in a particular situation. In addition, combining the models can solve some of the problems that may arise from the use of either model separately, an issue that is addressed more extensively in other chapters.

The Strategic Solution Focused Model

The current model integrates strategic therapy and solution focused therapy in two main ways. First, it combines strategic therapy's focus on precise clarification of the problem with solution focused therapy's emphasis on detailed exploration of the solution. Second, it blends the solution focused emphasis on amplification of what works with the strategic emphasis on interruption of what does not. In the combined model, problem clarification complements and enhances solution elaboration, while amplification of successful solutions complements and enhances interruption of unsuccessful solutions. Precise clarification of the problem and detailed amplification of the solution *both* lead to increased specificity and to "deconstruction" of global problems (e.g., "depression") and global goals (e.g., "self-esteem").[2]

Which component of the model is emphasized will shift, depending on the needs of the case and the position of the client at any particular point in treatment. Treatment is always tailored to fit the specifics of the situation. The therapist follows the model's central guidelines in deciding what to do next with a

[2]These concepts are discussed in more detail in later chapters.

client. When a technique or intervention appears to be "working," the therapist is likely to continue it, and when it is not working, the therapist probably should "do something different."

Both strategic therapy and solution focused therapy have been described as "minimalist" approaches (Budman, Hoyt, and Friedman, 1992), because the focus in each is on creating a small initial change that will lead to greater change. There is also a "minimalist" quality in the theoretical simplicity of each model. (However, it must be stressed that just because a model is theoretically simple, it does *not* necessarily follow that the application of that model is equally simple.) Like the parent models, the strategic solution focused model is considered to be a "minimalist" approach.

It should be emphasized here that strategic solution focused therapy is *not* intended to be a new "hybrid" approach, radically different from the parent models. The procedures and theory are not original. What is central to the current model is the *deliberate plan* to use the component parts together in an interactional, constructivist approach.

A summary presenting the steps of strategic solution focused therapy in outline form appears on the following two pages.

Strategic Solution Focused Therapy[3]

The Theory

> 1. What's the trouble? ("If it's not broken, don't fix it.")
> 2. If it works, do more of it.
> 3. If it doesn't work, stop doing it. Do something different.

1. **Problem clarification**

   a. *"What's the trouble* (you're here today about/you're hoping I can help you with)?"

   b. Definition of *highest-priority* problem. *In what way* is it a problem? Why now? What is your hope about *how* I will help?

2. **Solution amplification**

   a. *Miracle question*—You wake up tomorrow and the problem you're here about is solved. What will be different? What else? What will (name of person in your life) notice about you? How will he (she) be different? What else will be different as a result of these changes? What else? What else?

   b. *Exceptions*—Are there "pieces of the solution" that are already happening? How did you do that?!

   c. *Scaling questions*

0 ——————————— "Progress" ——————————— 10

"When the problem
was at its worst."

"The problem is solved
to your satisfaction.
You don't need to
come back."

(x = client's response)

How did you do that?!
How did you get to x?
First sign of change—How will you know you're at $x + 1$?

---

[3]An earlier version of this outline was described in *Journal of Systemic Therapies* (Quick, 1994a).

3. **Assessment of attempted solutions**
   a. What have you tried? How did you do that? Exactly what did you say?
   b. Did it work?

4. **Intervention**
   Would you like some feedback? (if yes):
   a. **Validate** chief complaint (e.g., "I don't blame you for feeling distressed . . .")
   b. **Compliment** (e.g., "I'm impressed that even in the face of . . . you've been able to . . . ")
   c. **Suggestion/homework**

If what you're doing works:	If what you're doing doesn't work:
Do more of it!	Stop doing it!
Pay attention to *how* you do it.	Do something different!
	Pay attention to how you "turn the problem up and down."
	Pay attention to how you cope with the problem.
	Therapist formulates alternate response that would, if performed, interrupt unsuccessful attempted solution.
	Therapist presents that alternative in language/context client is most likely to hear.

5. **Plan for additional service**
   a. "Where shall we go from here? Do you want to make another appointment with me?" If yes, "When?" (No predetermined number of appointments or standard interval between appointments assumed.) "Or should we leave it open-ended?" (Family practice/intermittent care model)
   b. Referral/plan for other service (medication consult, group, class, feedback to other provider, etc.) as indicated.

2

Clarifying the Problem
What's the Trouble?

T he first step in strategic solution focused therapy is clarification of the complaint. As Weakland, Fisch, Watzlawick, and Bodin (1974, p. 147) have pointed out, "the presenting symptom offers, in one package, what the patient is ready to work on, a concentrated manifestation of whatever is wrong, and a concrete index of any progress made." When treatment proceeds without adequate clarification of the problem, therapy is often more difficult. In a retrospective study of cases that did not go well, Fisch, Weakland, and Segal (1982) concluded that treatment was more likely to fail when the problem was insufficiently clear.

Strategic solution focused therapy is therapy with a "focus." It is *not* a therapy characterized by open-ended conversation, with a great deal of free association. The presence of a "focus" is not unique to strategic solution focused therapy. Budman, Hoyt, and Friedman (1992) have noted that a common factor among brief therapy models of many different orientations is that they all have a focus. Several short-term psychoanalytically oriented therapies emphasize rapid identification of the "triangle" that appears when one central issue emerges from the past, in the present, and in the transference. Cognitive therapy emphasizes the labeling of the client's core dysfunctional beliefs or schemas; crisis intervention focuses on the crisis and its meaning. Theme-centered classes, groups, and individual protocols emphasize a central topic, such as assertiveness or bulimia.

Problem clarification in strategic solution focused therapy means identifying the complaint that the client is "here about," that which he or she is hoping the therapy will help to resolve. Identifying the problem helps to guide any therapy, even when length and number of sessions are not critical issues. Clarifying the problem makes the therapy relevant. The author remembers several graduate school debates about the relative importance of "support versus confrontation" in therapy—and the input from mentors that the critical issue was not "support or confrontation," but *relevance*. Creating a problem focus is homing in on whatever is most relevant, where change will make the most difference.

Prioritizing Problems

Clients do not usually present one clear-cut problem. They come with complex, multifaceted life situations and symptoms. One client may say, "I'm overwhelmed—it's everything." Another may say, "I'm stressed at work, my girlfriend is using drugs again, and I think she's running around on me. I'm depressed, I've always been codependent, and I have an outbreak of herpes, so I'll never meet anyone else—Help!"

How does the therapist identify a focus in all of that? The first step is usually to ask, in a straightforward way, "Which of those things is bothering you most?" Or the therapist might say, "When you called, which of those things were you hoping that I might help you with?" When asked directly, a surprisingly large number of clients can answer directly. This is true even when multiple issues are involved, as the following example illustrates.

Sarah,[1] age forty, recently divorced, came to her first appointment describing distress about many recent changes in her life. Her husband had left her, and the divorce was final last month. Her brother-in-law in another state had been killed in a motorcycle crash two weeks ago. Sarah's thirteen-year-old daughter did not like the man Sarah was beginning to date. The retail clothing store for which Sarah worked as a manager was closing several branches, and she would be demoted if she stayed with the company. Sarah was having trouble sleeping and was acting "crabby" with everyone. As she talked about all of these issues, it was not at all obvious which distressed her the most. The therapist asked, "Sarah, which of these things is bothering you most?" Without hesitation, Sarah responded, "Mandy (the daughter) being rude to Rob (the man she was seeing)."

The therapist could not have predicted that this was the highest priority concern. However, as problem clarification continued, it became increasingly clear that an interaction involving Mandy, Rob, and Sarah had led Sarah to call, and this was the issue for which she "wanted therapy."

Not all clients, of course, narrow in on one problem so quickly. When simple, direct questioning about what is most distressing fails to elicit clarification, some

---

[1]To safeguard confidentiality, names and identifying details have been changed in all case material and dialogue included in this book.

additional explanation might be given about what the therapist is requesting, and why. The therapist might begin by acknowledging that the situation is complicated, saying, for example, "From what you've described, it sounds like there's a tremendous amount going on for you. And you're right: things *are* connected. But I'm concerned that if we try to look at everything simultaneously, we're going to get so diffused that we won't solve anything. So, in that spirit, which piece is bothering you most?" Another way of asking it is this: "To make the most difference, where should you and I start?"

In response to that, most people will select an issue. Once they do, the therapist may make it clear that other problems will *not* be taken up at this point. When the client says that "work" is the biggest problem, the therapist may say, "Okay, let's put the marriage and in-law parts aside for now, not because they're unimportant, but so that we don't distract ourselves with them. Now, tell me what the trouble is at work."

Sometimes clients respond to "What's the trouble?" with hesitation, saying that they "don't know where to start." This response provides an excellent opportunity for the therapist to clarify what is being requested. The therapist can explain that "What's the trouble?" means "What's the problem you're here to see me about?" Clients sometimes assume that the question is asking about etiology or deeper issues, and the therapist can quickly clarify that the question is about what happened that led the client to be concerned.

"Who, What, When, and Where?"

What the therapist wants to know is this: what happened that was distressing? Who did (or said) what, to whom, under what circumstances, that led to this person being here now (not two months ago, not six months in the future, but *now*)? The therapist wants the same kind of information that news reporters are trained to seek, the "who, what, where, and when" of what happened.

O'Hanlon and O'Hanlon (1991) use the term "videotalk" to describe the information that the therapist wants. "If I had a three-minute video segment of how it goes, what would I see and hear?" is one way of requesting the specifics. To encourage clients to operationalize complaints such as depression, O'Hanlon and Weiner-Davis (1989) use humor to describe the way in which many people "do" depression. They describe the following behaviors: one reduces external stimuli, one darkens the room, one does nothing that requires movement or breathing too much "because it is difficult to maintain a good depression that way" (p. 98), one refrains from talking very much, and if one must speak, one talks about personal misery. They note that by the time this "monologue" is completed, clients frequently smile or nod with recognition. They are then more likely to be able to describe how they personally "do depression."

Sometimes detailed questioning is needed to clarify which component of the situation is the problem. For example, a mother says, in one breath, that her son "doesn't obey and talks back." These may or may not be separate issues. Or a man says, "I don't like paying taxes." The therapist is unclear whether the problem is that taxes are overdue or that the man does not enjoy paying them.

As Coyne (1986) and Weakland (1992b) point out, therapists sometimes substitute conceptualization for inquiry and make unjustified inferential leaps. When clients are vague, it is tempting for therapists to want to seem astute or empathic, acting "as if" they understand more than is actually the case. Weakland observes that therapists may not devote the time or effort necessary to clarify just what is happening. Coyne suggests that the therapist "play dumb," taking what the MRI therapists have called a one-down position (Fisch, Weakland, and Segal, 1982). When the client says, "You know what I mean," and the therapist does *not* know, the strategic solution focused therapist will avoid agreeing too readily. Instead, the therapist may say something like, "No, I don't yet, and I really want to," attempting to communicate concern and attentiveness through precise clarification rather than through hasty assumptions about understanding.

When an interaction is the problem, precise inquiry can be immensely helpful. Some questions suggested by Fisch (1992, personal communication) include: "Is it what she *says* or what she *does?*"; "Is it *what* he says, or the way he puts it?" Clarifying when and where the interaction occurs is also of value. Clients typically relate primarily what the other person did (wrong), but in response to detailed questioning, they can frequently describe the context, as well as the behaviors and words that led up to the complaint. This increased specificity often makes the complaint far less global, and therefore more manageable.

For example, Fran complains of Andrew's "lack of commitment to the relationship." Is it what he says or what he does? What he says, she clarifies. What does he say? "I don't know why I stick around here." When does Andrew say this? After detailed questioning about the dyadic interaction, it becomes clear that he says this after Fran has cross-examined him about his routine in putting the children to bed. That is, Andrew does not just look up from his supper one evening and proclaim this "out of the blue," he does not scream it in a drunken rage, and he does not say it as the fifth sentence of a description of how he has been struggling with his increasing ambivalence about the marriage.

After an interaction has been described, the therapist might check with the client about whether this is a representative example of the context in which the problem occurs. For example, the therapist might ask Fran, "Is it typical that this happens when you two disagree about managing the kids?" If so, the therapist might do what Fisch (1994, personal communication) has called "confirming the parameters of the problem." In this case, that could mean saying, "Am I clear, then, that the main thing you're coming in about is this stuff Andrew says about leaving, and that the main time that this comes up is when you disagree about the kids?" Knowing the interactional context makes this complaint much more specific and much easier to approach.

Often a client's complaint is an affective or cognitive state, such as "I'm depressed (worried, too angry, etc.)." When the problem is a feeling, the therapist immediately asks what happened that led the client to feel that way. Just as in any other case, the therapist wants to clarify who did what to whom. The assumption is that the person is distressed because something happened; if that something were not happening, then the distress would diminish. The depressed person is asked what he is sad about; the angry person is asked what she is angry about or at whom she is aggravated; the anxious person is asked what he is worried about. Whenever possible, "clinical" language is translated into lay terms; anxiety becomes "worried" or "concerned," for example. The questioning subtly attempts to normalize the reaction, a process to be described in more detail later in this chapter.

Even when symptoms and reactions are unusual or severe, the starting assumption is that the client is an intelligent person who has some good reason for feeling as he or she does (Fisch, 1992, personal communication). For example, a man describes severe depression: "I'm at the end of my rope." The therapist responds, "You're feeling very bad, and that's why you're here. Tell me what happened that has you feeling so down."

In What Way Is This a Problem?

How something is problematic is a question that clients, and therapists, sometime fail to consider. They may assume that they know, and the meaning that may seem obvious can sometimes be misleading. Weakland (1992b) described a woman who complained that her husband was seeing another woman. The way in which this is problematic may seem evident, and some therapists might hesitate to inquire, lest they seem dense or unfeeling. The therapist nevertheless asked the woman how her husband's involvement with the other woman was a problem. She answered, "He's wasting time at her house, when he should be out making money for us."

Clarifying how something is a problem has direct implications for what happens in the therapy. Maria requested treatment for her "OCD." When asked for an example, she talked about "obsessive house cleaning." Therapist inquiry pursued how this was a problem, and Maria began to describe how frustrated she felt when her in-laws came, uninvited, for weekend visits, leaving messes behind them. Maria's husband, Carlos, was upset because he wanted his home to be open to his brother, and Maria was giving him a hard time when the brother came over. That information made a tremendous difference in what was addressed during treatment, as the therapist focused on how Maria spoke to Carlos about the visiting in-laws. If a "standard protocol for obsessive compulsive disorder" had been prematurely applied, significant time and effort could have been spent on issues tangential to what was truly distressing to Maria.

Therapist inquiry into how something is a problem is aimed at determining whether the complaint is a problem in some *tangible* way (Fisch, 1992, personal communication). Is this problem resulting in a behavioral excess of some kind? Examples of "excess" would be "Because of this I'm yelling at my kids all the time" or "I'm smoking too much." Is something troublesome because it is producing a behavioral deficit? Examples of "deficit" might include "I'm not paying my bills" or "I've stopped showering and shaving." If something is a problem in a tangible way, the therapist can ask, "If you *were* doing X (or if you were to *stop* doing Y), would that make a significant difference?" If so, those specific behaviors might become important targets for intervention.

Frequently, however, behavioral excess or deficit is not the main reason that a situation is problematic. Instead, the problem is that something—a situation, a state of affairs, an interaction—is unpleasant, uncomfortable, or ego-dystonic. Many people can clearly say, "No, this thing isn't interfering with my functioning; it's a problem because I don't like it. I don't want to feel this way." If that is the case, then the most relevant treatment may address modifying, or accepting, certain thoughts and feelings, as opposed to changing behaviors.

To Whom Is This a Problem?

Another critical variable in problem clarification involves identifying *who* is finding *what* troublesome. One way of looking at this concept involves asking, "Who is the 'customer,' and for what?" Some therapists find it useful to classify levels of motivation in the following way: "Customers" are people who complain and demonstrate motivation to change something, "complainants" are people who complain and do not demonstrate motivation for change, and "visitors" are people who do not have a complaint (Miller, 1991).

Identifying the customer is most obviously an issue for clients who are referred by someone else, such as school, work, or family practice. For example, a written referral says: "Anger problem—please treat." Jane's "angry outbursts" may be a problem for her supervisor and co-workers, but they may not particularly bother Jane. If there is anything she is a "customer" for, it may be the fact that "work is on my back again."

As Miller (1992a) points out, this is an especially important variable in substance abuse treatment. A focus on "drinking" as a problem will not be helpful for a client who is not distressed by drinking. That same client may be quite distressed about getting arrested, however. A client may be a "visitor" for the problem for which the referral was made, but with precise problem clarification, the therapist can frequently discover that the same client is a "customer" for something else. Thus the "customer," "complainant," and "visitor" categories are most useful when they are viewed as ever-shifting constructs rather than as fixed labels.

Clarifying who is most motivated for change is also important when working with clients who initially seem to be self-referred, but who are actually there at someone else's request. A parent, partner, AA sponsor, or friend may be more motivated than the person in the office. It is therefore useful to inquire how the referral came to be. If someone else suggested that the client call, it can be useful to ask how eager the client was to come. Fisch (1993, personal communication) points out that deliberate use of the word "eager" (rather than "willing") highlights the degree of motivation. The therapist may even say, "If Dr. Jones (or your girlfriend, or whoever) had called you yesterday and said, 'I know I told you that you ought to go see a therapist, but I changed my mind; I don't think you really need to go if you don't want to,' would you have kept this appointment today?" If the answer is "no," that is a signal to be alert to the possibility that if this client is a customer for anything, the complaint may involve that other person in some way. On the other hand, if the client says that he or she would have come anyway, the therapist can say, "Oh, how come?" and go on to clarify the complaint.

Sometimes the therapist has information about issues that the client has not mentioned or emphasized. In general, the strategic solution focused therapist respects the client's ability to focus on what is primary. Behavior that is psychiatrically "diagnosable" but not currently bothering anyone is typically ignored, in the spirit of "if it's not broke don't fix it" (Miller, 1991). However, there are important exceptions to this rule. If the client is doing something that violates principles of law or ethics, taking appropriate action takes precedence over "doing therapy." Certain clinician responses are required when child abuse, spousal abuse, or elder abuse is suspected, or when there is an immediate danger to self or others.

Another customer to consider is the therapist, who never works in a vacuum. Subtly or overtly, therapists are both rewarded and sanctioned for focusing on certain issues and gathering certain information. For example, if the therapist must write a detailed medical history in order to be reimbursed, medical information may need to be gathered, regardless of whether it is relevant to the complaint. Clients can usually understand and accept this, especially if the therapist clarifies which topics are discussed primarily for the purpose of meeting procedural or organizational needs.

Translating Vague Constructs to Clear Complaints

Sometimes inquiries about the problem elicit responses like "I need confidence" or "I want to build my self-esteem." Constructs that the client labels "confidence" or "self-esteem" may eventually be involved in the solution, and the therapist will certainly want to keep in mind that these words are part of the "language" that the client speaks. However, the fact remains that a response like "I need confidence" does not answer the "What's the trouble?" question.

This interaction parallels what happens when a patient consults an internist and, when asked about the complaint, answers, "I need an antibiotic." The patient may be right, and an antibiotic might be quite appropriate, but the internist will need to take the time to clarify the problem that the patient thinks an antibiotic will cure. The same is true for the psychotherapist. The nature of the problem frequently has important implications for development of the solution.

It is sometimes useful to share the internist analogy with the client, for the purpose of explaining the therapist's rationale for wanting to know more about the problem. Of course, a client who initially says, "I need confidence" may well answer "lack of confidence" when further encouraged to define the problem. That is still vague, but in some ways it is more workable, because now the therapist can say, "What happened that makes you feel you're lacking in confidence?," "Give me an example," or "In what situations?" It is often fairly easy to establish that "lack of confidence" is not global, occurring in every context. Most people will agree that they do not particularly lack confidence about knowing their phone number or how to take a shower. The therapist can ask, "So, this lack of confidence, you say it happens at work and in social situations. Which one concerns you more?" Further questioning attempts to operationalize the who, what, and where of the situation.

Sometimes questions about the problem bring answers that are adjectives. The client may say, "I'm codependent," "I'm passive aggressive," or even "I'm borderline." The adjectives typically describe "traits" rather than "states," so they are somewhat different from adjectives like "depressed" that frequently imply a temporary state of feeling sad about something. Rather, these adjectives tend to refer to enduring characteristics that the person claims he or she wants to change.

Again, the therapist attempts to translate these descriptions into specific behaviors by asking for examples. The goal is to turn adjectives into verbs. O'Hanlon and O'Hanlon (1991) talk about a woman who, during a couples session, complains that her husband is passive aggressive. The therapist slides his chair away from the man, saying, "Passive aggressive? I've heard that's nasty stuff, but I'm not sure what it means. Is he doing it now? . . . If he starts doing it during the session, will you let me know?" The authors claim that this kind of approach usually brings laughter—and increased willingness to translate "kvetching" to action language.

When clients use words like "passive aggressive" or "codependent," it can be extremely useful to find out where they acquired such labels, because the use of adjectives like these frequently signals the presence of a relationship issue. If the adjective was used by someone in the client's life (partner, parent, whoever), the therapist may want to determine what the client did that prompted use of that word. It may have been said in a pejorative manner; these adjectives are not usually intended to be compliments. Other common sources for the labels include self-help books and the media. If the client adopted the word from one of these, the therapist might want to know what led to reading that book. Sometimes the client encountered the phrase merely by chance (e.g., "They were talking about it on TV"). When that is the case, the therapist may want to know what led the client to apply the term to the self.

Some clients emphasize that the problem is a pattern, a repeated behavior, such as, "I keep getting into destructive relationships." Again, the problem is likely to be most workable if described in terms of the *current* destructive relationship, along with discussion of what happened that brought the client in *now*.

When the Problem Is the Past

A similar approach is used when the client defines the problem as an event (or series of events) from the past. Usually something has occurred that led the client to seek treatment now, and that something can generally be identified. Many clients verbalize wishes to "understand the past," for example, "I need to come to terms with my upbringing." As mentioned, "I need to . . . " statements are more treatable in strategic solution focused therapy when they are restated as problems. Most clients agree when the therapist says something like, "I hear you saying that you very much want to understand your past. Would it be accurate, then, to say that there is something about not understanding it that's a problem?" If the answer is "yes," the therapist can go on to ask *how* that lack of understanding is a problem.

For most people, the answer to that question has something to do with ways that interactions or feelings from the past are recurring in the present. After all, concerns about what happened in the past are not usually expressed by people who previously experienced discomfort but who, for whatever reason, believe that the past pain is not adversely affecting them now. The therapist can investigate how much current difficulties are really the issue by asking this: "If it were possible to be different in the present without fully understanding what happened before, would that be okay?" (Usually it would.) The reverse is usually not true:

clients generally do not feel they would be satisfied by understanding their past if altered feelings or behaviors did not follow.

An extremely powerful question that addresses the role of understanding is this: "Do you have to wait to understand the past in order to make things better for you, or are there things you can do to make it better even while you're still working on the understanding part?" (Berg, 1992, personal communication) Frequently, the answer is "No, I don't have to wait for understanding. I *can* do some things now." The lack of understanding now takes on less importance as a problem. On the other hand, if the answer is, "I really do need the understanding before I can make things better," the therapist must not minimize this. There will need to be further inquiry about how lack of understanding is a problem.

A Different Problem Every Time

Sometimes the therapist completes an appointment believing that there has been therapist–client consensus about the nature of the highest priority problem. At the next appointment, however, the client introduces a different topic. There are various ways to handle this situation. What the strategic solution focused therapist typically does *not* do is to proceed without comment. On the contrary, the therapist will frequently say, "My understanding from last time was that X was the biggest problem, and I notice that today you're talking about Y. What happened?"

One possible reason for the switch is that the first problem has been resolved to the client's satisfaction. Therefore, the therapist will want to specifically inquire about this. If there is any hesitancy about whether the initial complaint has been fully resolved, the therapist might respond in a manner similar to that suggested by Fisch (1989, personal communication). He has cautioned clients about "the inadvisability of moving on to 'Problem Number Two' before 'Problem Number One' is fully resolved, lest 'Problem Number One' rear its ugly head again."

The client may respond to that by reconsidering and returning to the initial complaint. On the other hand, the response may be an assertion that even in the absence of full resolution of the original problem, the second area is more important and relevant now. The client is making a choice, and the therapist will address the new complaint. At the same time, the therapist has "gone on record" as expressing some skepticism about the usefulness of focusing on too much simultaneously. If it does happen that the client "jumps" between so many topics (either during a session or between sessions) that little is accomplished, the therapist can gently refer back to his or her concern about addressing too much at once.

Sometimes, of course, clients *do* legitimately decide that they want to address a different issue before the initially identified complaint has been resolved. This can occur when events in one's life change what is most important. Change in the focus also happens after careful consideration of what is most distressing. Sometimes such reevaluation is the direct result of thought-provoking therapist inquiry about priorities. What is important for the strategic solution focused therapist is the clear acknowledgment that the focus has shifted, in contrast to the therapist and/or client acting "as if" the initial problem had been resolved.

Problem Clarification as Intervention

As noted above, inquiry about the problem can stimulate important thinking about what is most distressing. Thus, questions about the complaint often serve a dual function. On one level, they provide information about the problem and help to create a focus. At the same time, problem clarification questions can become interventions in themselves. Tomm (1987, in O'Hanlon and Weiner-Davis, 1989) describes "interventive interviewing" and reflexive questioning. O'Hanlon and Weiner-Davis use the term "presuppositional questioning" to describe inquiry designed both to elicit information and to influence the client's perceptions. For example, the therapist might say, "Are you aware how you do it when you don't let the voices interfere with your concentration?"

There are several ways in which problem clarification can be therapeutic. One way occurs when questioning operationalizes what has been vague. If a client has presented with a global complaint and the therapist asks for clarity, the clarification process can demystify the problem (Fisch, 1992a). That which is vague and amorphous seems overwhelming and impossible to grasp; what is specific is potentially more manageable.

Clients who are experiencing painful affect often feel that something is terribly wrong with them. Problem clarification can help them make sense of strong and puzzling emotions. When the client says, "I feel desperate; I don't see any light at the end of the tunnel," and the therapist asks what happened to elicit that feeling, the implicit message is: "You are not crazy. You seem like a reasonable person to me, so your reaction doesn't seem to be insanity or childish whim. I assume you have a good reason for feeling as you do. Tell me what happened." Labeling the problem is thus identified as a critical first step toward solving it. The therapist's inquiry about specific detail conveys interest and concern, and it communicates that the client's pain is being taken seriously.

Clarification questions can assist clients who are struggling with the sense they are not entitled to have certain feelings, or that certain things are too dangerous to say openly. Writing about couples, Wile (1981) points out that clarifying the situation can make a difference. He describes saying to a woman, "I get the idea that, to put it a little sharply, you are saying that you have lost all feeling for your husband and are thinking of ending the relationship. You haven't quite said this, but is this what you are saying?" "That *is* (italics Wile's) pretty sharp," the woman replied, "but I guess that is what I feel" (Wile, 1981, p. 114). Wile emphasizes that clarifying what has been vague and unspoken can give both partners a greater sense of clarity and control.

As mentioned earlier in this chapter, normalization of affect can occur during problem clarification. The therapist may ask, "Is the problem that you don't show up for your performance review, or that you show up, but you don't look forward to it?" If the client says, "I do it, but I don't like it," the therapist may respond by saying, "I know people who would say that a person who looks forward to performance reviews has problems!" In the same way, if the answer to the "in what way is this a problem?" questioning is that something is uncomfortable, the therapist can ask whether the client thinks that the degree of discomfort is appropriate to the magnitude of the stressor. Even if the answer is, "No, I think I'm more distressed than I 'should' be," the very asking of the question introduces the notion that *some* discomfort might be expected and is not necessarily a symptom of a diagnosable psychiatric condition.

Some of the inquiry during problem clarification is conducted for the purpose of establishing whether the problem varies in intensity. "This worry you are describing, have you noticed that sometimes it's more distracting and sometimes less so?" If the client has noticed variability, the process of deconstructing the global complaint "anxiety" has begun, as described above. In addition, the therapist can ask if the client is aware of how he or she has made the change happen. If the client says that he or she *is* aware, the therapist can elicit elaboration. If not, the therapist can say, "Okay, we're not yet aware of how you do it; we'll keep that in mind." In either case, the therapist has introduced the idea that intensity of discomfort varies predictably in response to something the client does (even if the client has not yet identified what that "something" is). Inclusion of the word "yet" implies that identification of the "something" will, in fact, occur.

Celeste: "My Mother Was Very Sick Mentally"

The following case example illustrates the problem clarification phase of strategic solution focused therapy. The client, Celeste, had contacted her employee assistance representative to ask for a referral for therapy. The referral information stated that Celeste was about to be laid off. In this excerpt, the therapist begins to inquire about the problem.

Therapist: Now, tell me what the trouble is that you're here about.

Celeste: Why I'm here?

Therapist:	Yes, what the problem is.
Celeste:	Um, um, because I feel that I want to—um—I want to come here before . . . you see, my mother was very sick mentally. And I always had this fear it might come about with me.

Celeste's initial response emphasizes a feeling—fear. The therapist wants to know what is happening that elicits this fear now.

Therapist:	And what is happening that is making you scared that this might be coming about with you?
Celeste:	Um—well, I, hmm. My mother—I'm . . . [becomes tearful] I don't know why I'm crying.
Therapist:	Well, I'm asking you some questions about some things that must be pretty painful.
Celeste:	I think my mother must have had some things happen in her life, and she didn't seek help, and she became really, really, sick. I mean, she was a confirmed mental case. I've told people around me that if they ever saw me act strangely or whatever, that they should tell me, because I don't want to become like my mother. And I always have the fear that it might run in the family. And, um, no one tells me that I'm . . . well, my father always used to tell me that I'm becoming just like my mother, and he's not here to tell me. And I feel that people are too nice and wouldn't tell me anyway.
Therapist:	Has anyone recently told you that you're showing behaviors that . . .
Celeste:	No.
Therapist:	. . . have them concerned?
Celeste:	No, no. I just feel I'm losing it.
Therapist:	And what's happening that's making you feel like you're losing it?
Celeste:	Well, I have problems making friends. And I'm in a department now where no one likes me. Right from the start they made it clear that I was unwelcome there. And it happened when I was in the other department, too, but there I kind of worked things out. I always seem to bring out things like that with people. Maybe it's not them; maybe it's me.

This interaction illustrates a common occurrence: the therapist asks a question about the complaint, and the client's response introduces a (seemingly) different problem. How (or if) "problems making friends" is connected with "fear of losing it" remains unclear. The therapist keeps trying to understand.

Therapist:	You've worked in the current department for how long?
Celeste:	This one, for six months.
Therapist:	You went to see Linda [the employee assistance representative] last week. Maybe the question I should ask is . . .
Celeste:	What is the relevance?
Therapist:	What I mean is . . .
Celeste:	[interrupting] Well, I guess the thing is . . . I suppose I'm questioning—Why was I laid off? Why weren't they? I guess I was the easiest one for them to get rid of. Um, I guess I'm getting suspicious of my boss. I don't understand why it's happening.
Therapist:	What have you been told about why you're being laid off?
Celeste:	Different things, actually. When I asked if I could go back to the other department, I was told there wasn't enough work there. But then I got told by some of the engineers that there is work, so I don't know what's going on.
Therapist:	Just to make sure I have this clear, you worked in your department for six months, and you were with the company in a different department before that. Right?
Celeste:	Yes, for three years. First I was a secretary and then I went to school for drafting, and I was in that department for two years. But even when I was a secretary, come to think of it, I had problems with people. People seem to think I'm arrogant, just because I seem to be sure of myself.
Therapist:	This may not be connected to the problem you're here about, but I'm wondering what you're going to do after you're laid off.
Celeste:	I don't know.
Therapist:	When does the layoff become effective?
Celeste:	In ten days. I have different feelings. When I found out I was going to be laid off, I went into my boss's office and asked him if he'd play along with me, if I told the people I work with, especial-

ly those guys, that I'm the one that asked to be laid off, that this was a voluntary thing. And he said, "Sure. But why?" I said, "So I can walk out of here with my head high and not give those guys the satisfaction of knowing the company did it to me." And he said, "No problem," as long as I'd write a memo that I wouldn't sue the company.

Therapist:	And did you do that?
Celeste:	Yes, after he assured me that it wouldn't affect my unemployment package. We get a week for every year we are there.
Therapist:	So, you get three and half weeks, right?
Celeste:	Uh-huh.
Therapist:	So, you're going to look for another job, or what?
Celeste:	Yes, I've begun to do that. I'm sending out resumes, and I went for one interview.

Celeste has not specifically said that the layoff is a problem economically. (It may not be; layoffs sometimes provide a welcome break, and unemployment payments are sufficient.) But since financial concerns are so common in similar situations, the therapist decides to specifically inquire about them. Another purpose of the next therapist statement is to communicate that "being worried about a layoff is normal. It does not mean that one is 'losing it.' "

Therapist:	What I don't hear you saying, and I just want to make sure this is *not* the problem you're here about—some people in your situation would be saying: Given that I'm about to be laid off, I'm depressed and scared, and I'm not sleeping so well. And I wonder if I'll find another job, and if I'll make it financially. So I want to check out with you . . .
Celeste:	[interrupting] I go up and down. Sometimes I get really worried about that, and I think, what if I don't find work, or whatever. And I think actually that being at work now, and having to answer in a positive manner to people coming up to me, that helps me. People come up to me, and instead of saying, "Oh, I hear you got laid off," or whatever, they say "Good for you, Celeste. You're taking control. Pretty gutsy of you to just take off. Wish I had the guts to do that. Do you have another job?" "No, I don't." "Well, aren't you afraid?" "Well, I came to a different country without a job, no car, no insurance, nothing, and I can do it again." This is

helping me, you know, kind of talking myself into it. But when I go home at night, it's another story. Yeah, I'm scared.

Therapist: So, you've described several problems. One is that, with the situation of being laid off, when you frankly don't think you deserve it, you're feeling somewhat scared about whether you'll get another job and how you'll be financially. Another problem is the fear that you might be getting sick, like your mother was. Another problem is your long-standing sense that you have trouble getting along with people. Which of those is the problem that you're hoping I can help you with, that you're here about right now?

Celeste: Um, when I feel out of control, when I'm scared, when I don't know what to do. And when I say I'm out of control, I don't know what I mean by that.

Therapist: Maybe it would be helpful if you could give me an example of a time when that happened. Like if we had a three-minute video segment, on an occasion when you feel out of control, and you played it for me.

Celeste: Well, usually, I can't breathe right. Like I can't take in air, like if I were to yawn, it would relieve it—but I can't get a full breath. But what I feel, I don't know.

Therapist: When that happens—when is the last time that happened, by the way?

Celeste: A few nights ago.

Therapist: Okay, so it happens at night.

Celeste: Yeah, like I'm sleeping, and I wake up. And I don't know what I'm thinking before that.

Therapist: So you woke up and you were unable to get some air. Is that what you mean when you say you feel out of control?

Celeste: Not because I'm out of control with my breathing, but because I get scared, and I don't know why.

Therapist: Scared of what? What are you scared is going to happen?

Celeste: I don't know.

Therapist: You said it's not because of the breathing. It's not because you're afraid you won't take in air.

Celeste:	No, because I've had that before. I feel panicky. I don't know. Maybe it's that I'm all alone. I'm not sure.
Therapist:	Well, I don't mean in a philosophical or psychological sense of what the issue is. I just mean: at that moment, you wake up, you're kind of gasping for air, and you're scared. What's the thought that flashes through your head?
Celeste:	I don't know.
Therapist:	And when that happened, a couple of nights ago, and you woke up feeling very frightened, what did you do?
Celeste:	I got up and actually tried to realize what was going on, and I talked to myself: It's all right. In a while, when it's daylight and I'm around people again, I'll be okay.
Therapist:	And what was the effect of saying that to yourself?
Celeste:	It was all right.
Therapist:	That helped you?
Celeste:	That's right.
Therapist:	And what did you do after you got up and said to yourself, "It'll be all right"?
Celeste:	I went back to sleep, and slept through the night.
Therapist:	[pause] If I'm looking puzzled, it's because I'm trying to understand how that episode is a problem.

This is an example of a therapist's attempt to clarify *in what way* the breathing is a problem. After all, Celeste has just said that she knows that she will eventually take in air (i.e., not suffocate), and she was able to get back to sleep. This time the inquiry is successful in eliciting *how* the complaint is problematic.

Celeste:	I don't like waking up like that. I guess I don't want to think and do what I did when I first came here, when I desperately had to see a therapist.
Therapist:	That was nine years ago, right?
Celeste:	Uh-huh. And I think I want to catch it before I get that way, or like my mom was.
Therapist:	So your answer to my question about the biggest problem is: that

feeling of being so out of control. And what's happening when you feel so out of control is that you wake up at night and you can't breathe, and you feel scared. Am I hearing you right?

Celeste: Yes.

Therapist: And what's scary about that is *not* the breathing part, that you're not going to get air, but that you'll get as you were nine years ago, or, worse yet, that you're becoming like your mother was.

Celeste: Yes. That's right.

As Celeste's case illustrates, problem clarification is not always straightforward or brief. Considerable time and inquiry were required in this example to clarify that the "waking up gasping" was the experience that stirred Celeste's concern that she would become like her mother. Without that clarification, therapy might have focused much more on social interaction, something that was a long-standing issue but *not* the precipitant for the immediate anxiety. The nature of the problem made a significant difference in how the rest of the interview was conducted.

3

Amplifying the Solution
Variations on the Miracle Question

After the problem has been identified, the next step is development of the solution. In this approach, the term "solution" means much more than "single solution to the initial statement of the problem." Solution development is a process, often used as a means to an end. However, it might be noted that goal setting is not unique to strategic solution focused therapy; most models of therapy emphasize the importance of goal setting of some kind. In some approaches, the desired end point is the same for everyone (e.g., to develop assertive communication skills); in others, the goals are individualized. But without a goal of some kind, the therapy lacks direction. The client who has no goal is like the customer who goes to the airline counter requesting a ticket but who has no particular destination in mind. The destination determines which ticket the passenger receives; in the same way, the goal influences what happens in treatment. Without a destination, neither the passenger nor the client is going anywhere.

Sometimes the goal is implicit in a well-identified problem. When a mother complains that her son is not going to school, it seems highly likely that his attendance at school is the desired end point. But cessation of something problematic may not be sufficient, as illustrated by this Wizard of Id comic strip vignette. In the first frame, the king asks the wizard if he can stop the rain. In a succeeding frame, it is snowing. In the final frame, the wizard asks, "What is it you really want?" (Parker and Hart, 1983).

Thus, clarity about the solution is just as important as clarity about the problem. Just as vague problems (e.g., "depression") need elaboration, vague goals and wishes (e.g., "feeling better") become significantly more achievable when translated into clear and specific solutions.

The Miracle Question

The therapist's task, then, is to inquire about the solution. There are a number of ways of doing this. Sometimes a simple question, such as, "What do you want from coming here?" elicits the desired information. More often, however, the answer continues to be vague, and additional inquiry is needed.

Interview techniques derived from "the miracle question" can be extremely useful in eliciting solution information. As de Shazer phrased it, the "basic miracle question" goes something like this:

> *"Suppose that one night, while you were asleep, there was a miracle and this problem was solved. How would you know? What would be different? How would (significant other) know without your saying a word to (him or her) about it?" (de Shazer, 1988, p. 5)*

Multiple messages and suggestions are implicit in this wording. First, the use of the word "suppose" encourages the acceptance of a suppositional frame. Synonyms (each with a slightly different connotation) include "imagine," "presume," "assume," and "pretend." All of these verbs indicate a temporary suspension of "reality thinking." Second, as Weakland has pointed out (Weakland, in de Shazer, 1988), the word "miracle" taps into the client's expectation (or hope) for therapy: clients come to therapy wanting a miracle. "Supposing there was a miracle" also sets the response apart from previous problem solving efforts. (It should be noted, however, that use of the word "miracle" is *not* a requirement of the approach. Sometimes the therapist will deliberately choose not to use that word. This will be discussed more fully when variations on the miracle question are addressed in another section.)

The phrase "while you were asleep" suggests that change may occur without conscious awareness or deliberate action. A message is also conveyed when the therapist specifies that the miracle is that "this problem is solved." The problem is not "gone"; it has not "disappeared"; rather, it has been solved. In addition, the inclusion of the words "this problem" communicates that this is not an invitation to imagine a "sweeping" miracle that removes every imperfection from the self, others, or the world. Rather, *this* problem, implicitly the one the client is here about, is solved.

The wording further conveys that one *will* recognize that change has occurred. "Something" (deliberately open ended) will be different. The use of the future tense is significant here. "How would (significant other) know without your saying a word about it?" communicates that something nonverbal will be noticeably different; mention of a significant other also introduces the notion that interpersonal relationships will be affected.

Miracle questions (both the original version and the variations) can be further set apart from earlier conversation when they are prefaced by the therapist's announcing that a shift in the dialogue is about to occur. The therapist may choose to say, "I'd like to shift gears now and ask you a different kind of question. It's sort of an unusual question." This kind of preface creates a "set" that something different is about to happen. Of course, whether or not to create such a set is a clinical decision. With some clients, or at some points in treatment, the therapist may not want to set presuppositional questioning apart from other parts of the interview. A smoother transition might be selected.

After the miracle question has been asked, the therapist's follow-up is of critical importance. Whatever the client says, the therapist will follow up with continued questioning, designed to invite the client to describe the solution in detail, as vividly as possible. The therapist follows the client's language; if there is visual imagery, the therapist will make sure to ask what will look different, and what others will see when they look at the client. As elaboration becomes more specific, the opportunities for amplifying pieces of the scenario increase.

If the therapist chooses to use a miracle question, it is usually important to pursue the inquiry. If it seems unclear how a response might usefully be amplified, the therapist may be tempted to discard the inquiry prematurely. Doing so can leave the client with a feeling of pessimism about the huge discrepancy that exists between the initial vision of the miracle and the current miserable situation. Even when the therapist attempts to specify that *the problem that you're here about* is what is solved, the initial client response may be a highly improbable event, such as inheriting ten million dollars or weighing a hundred pounds less overnight. The therapist can attempt to pursue the discussion, acting "as if" the response were quite reasonable, and asking questions that prompt a shift to a description of behavior. For example, the therapist can ask, "And what else will you be *doing* when . . . What else? What else will be different as a result of (behavior just described)?"

Miller (1991) described an extreme example of this phenomenon: A client responded to the miracle question with, "My parents would not have died when I was a child." The therapist calmly responded, "Okay, so what would you do then?" The client proceeded to describe some significant changes in the present, including returning to school. Later in the interview, the client spontaneously wondered aloud, "Why can't I start doing some of these things now?" The therapist responded, "Hmm. That's an interesting question. Which one would you like to do first?"

Most clients do not verbalize such clearly impossible miracles. (And when they do, the therapist may understandably feel a bit anxious!) But, as mentioned, clients frequently do begin with scenarios that seem unlikely. After all, the therapist has asked for a miracle! This is not necessarily a cause for concern, and it is certainly not an indication for abandoning miracle question interviewing. It is not at all unusual for the subsequent inquiry to elicit concrete, small, and achievable detail. Nor is it unusual for clients to spontaneously recognize that they may not need to wait for the full-blown miracle in order to implement some of these changes. When the client does not spontaneously mention this possibility, the idea is nonetheless implicit, and the therapist may choose to introduce the notion at an appropriate time. If it is later established that some of the change is already occurring, the therapist can observe that the client was able to implement this change even in the absence of the miracle. This kind of intervention will be described in more detail later.

Sometimes clients' initial descriptions of their "miracles" are highly discrepant with their life situations, and the therapist has reason to believe that elaboration of the initial miracle would be counterproductive. In these cases, the therapist will take a different approach. Instead of amplifying the initial response, the therapist can empathize with the wish and then attempt to elicit an alternative scenario. This is still solution development.

In an example of this, Lipchik (1994) describes using the miracle question with a poor and chronically ill client and receiving the response that he would be healthy and rich. Together, the client and therapist laughed. Lipchik told him that she wished she could make that come true, but that what she meant was this: given his physical and financial condition, what would make a significant difference in his future? The client went on to describe some concerns involving his wife and some things he could do to improve that relationship, thereby creating an alternate solution scenario.

Initial answers to miracle questions sometimes emphasize elimination of the problem (in spite of the therapist's wording "that the problem is *solved*, not eliminated"). For example, the client says, "I won't be obsessed with food." Here, therapist follow-up that emphasizes *behavior* is particularly important. "And, when you're not thinking about food so much, what will you be *doing*?" The same holds true when the response emphasizes altered feelings (e.g., "I'll be happy, content inside"). The therapist responds, "Of course. And as a result of that happiness, that inner feeling of contentment, what will you be doing?" In this case, the client whose miracle began with "I won't be obsessed with food" began to describe grooming and walking her dog.

As the previous examples illustrate, it is difficult to predict in advance what elaboration of the miracle question will elicit. Walking and grooming the dog are not obviously related to decreased obsessing about food; nor is returning to school obviously connected to the "My parents would not have died" miracle in Miller's example. Specific solution behaviors frequently appear unconnected both with the problem and with the initial description of the solution. Amplification of the miracle question introduces a range of possibilities that frequently surprise the therapist; some of them may surprise the client, as well. As de Shazer (1988, p. 10) put it, "The process of solution development can be summed up as helping an unrecognized difference become a difference that makes a difference."

David: "I Wouldn't Hate Going to Work"

The following case example illustrates the process of solution elaboration described above. David is a twenty-seven-year-old, married employee at a large retail store. He came for therapy because of anxiety and dissatisfaction with his job. David feels "stuck," unable to voice his concerns to his boss and fearful of seeking employment elsewhere. The following is David's response to the miracle question:

Therapist: Let me shift gears and ask you a different kind of question. It's kind of a strange question. Can I ask you a strange question?

David: Sure. Go for it.

Therapist: I want you to pretend, for a moment, that after you and I get done talking today, and you go back to work, and then you go home and go to bed, that tonight, while you're sleeping, a miracle happens. And the miracle is that this problem, that you're here about today, is solved. Because you're sleeping, you don't know that this happened, but it has. Tomorrow morning, what will be the very first thing that will be different, that will let you know that this problem has been solved?

David: Probably the first thing would be that I wouldn't hate going to work.

Therapist: You wouldn't hate going to work. And what you *would* be thinking and feeling, when you get up would be . . . ?

David: I'd look forward to going to work, to planning out my day.

David's initial response stresses that he will be *feeling* different (more positive) about work. The next questions ask what David will be *doing* differently as a result of feeling different.

Therapist: What would you be planning for tomorrow, as you plan out your day? And I'm being very concrete, tomorrow, Wednesday.

David:	I would be kind of planning out what I have to do.
Therapist:	Uh-huh.
David:	Like specific tasks.
Therapist:	Mm-hmm. And which task would you be planning to do first?
David:	Well, there's an inventory report I have to work on, that I would sit down and do, and then there's correspondence I have to respond to, and . . .
Therapist:	So the report you'd be doing first?
David:	Yes.
Therapist:	Now, when you get up tomorrow, is Angie (David's wife) still at home?
David:	No, she leaves at six.
Therapist:	Okay. When you are up and about in the morning, you're in the house alone, right?
David:	Yeah.
Therapist:	So if there were a fly on the wall, if flies could think and talk and stuff like that, what would that fly see you doing that would be different from what you were doing today or yesterday?
David:	Well, I'd probably get up a little earlier.
Therapist:	Uh-huh.
David:	And, um, maybe I'd take some time, eat some breakfast, and wake up before I go. The pattern right now is, I get up, get my clothes on, and I'm out of the house in fifteen minutes.
Therapist:	So how would that make a difference for you, that you take some time, and eat some breakfast?
David:	Well, I'd feel better about the starting of the day.
Therapist:	And, when you get to work tomorrow, after starting the day like that, who will be the first person to notice that you're different?
David:	Probably my boss. No, probably not. Probably a co-worker.
Therapist:	Whose first name is . . . ?
David:	Naomi.

Therapist:	What will Naomi notice about you?
David:	That I was awake, that I was with it.
Therapist:	Tell me more about how Naomi will know that you're with it.
David:	I probably would look awake. I wouldn't be kind of mumbling behind my coffee at my desk and just sitting there.
Therapist:	Instead of just sitting there, what you would be doing and saying would be . . . ?
David:	Oh, starting to work right away.
Therapist:	Not mumbling, not just sitting there, but starting to work right away. What else will be different?
David:	I have to think about that for a minute.
Therapist:	Take your time.
David:	I would probably be able to prioritize better what I need to do.
Therapist:	How will you do that?
David:	Well, I have a "to do" box, and there is a wholesaler problem that has been sitting there, and I'd probably just take that out and handle it.
Therapist:	How will you do that?
David:	Well, I probably would just make some phone calls and set up some meetings.
Therapist:	And how will that make a difference, that you've taken that wholesaler problem from the bottom of the "to do" box, made those calls, set up those meetings?
David:	I won't have to deal with it again. I won't have to be reminded of it.
Therapist:	Mm-hmm. And as the day goes on, who else besides Naomi will notice?
David:	No one. Well, maybe Megan.
Therapist:	What will Megan notice?
David:	I'd probably tell her, "I feel better today."
Therapist:	And how will she be different as a result of you telling her that you're feeling better?

David: She'd probably say that she felt like crap, or else that she felt better too.

Therapist: And your boss, what will your boss notice?

David: Nothing. He's totally distant, in his office, door closed, on the phone. One of the problems I have is, when I was hired for this job, my title was supposed to be inventory manager. Then when I came, they said that I had to fill in for this guy who was out on disability. Well, he's still out—he probably will be indefinitely—and I'm still doing his job, which is basically clerical. And no one is doing anything about it.

Therapist: How will you be dealing with that difficulty, that fact that you're supposed to be an inventory manager, and you're really more a clerk, when you're feeling more on track?

David: Well, I think I need to sit down and talk with my boss, and tell him, "Hey, when you hired me, this was for inventory manager. I know I needed to help out for a while, but it's gone on too long. It's just not okay."

Therapist: Wow.

David: Yeah, but I've gone through that with him.

Therapist: What will be different about how you'll be doing it now?

David: I could probably—first of all, I wouldn't be having a case of nerves about just having a meeting with him.

Therapist: So instead of having a case of nerves, you'd be—what?

David: Anticipating that he'd listen to me. [Pause] No, he probably won't listen any more this time either.

Therapist: So, being very realistic, your attitude when you go in this time will be . . . ?

David: I don't know. I suspect that talking to him is as good as useless.

Therapist: So you'd be real aware that this may not change anything.

David: Yes, but there's no harm in trying.

Therapist: He'll notice that about you, that you're bringing it up again.

David: Yes.

Therapist: And he'll respond?

David:	He'll probably say, "Look, David, we talked about this before. I'm sorry, but there's nothing I can do. I need to ask you to hang in there a little longer."
Therapist:	And you'll say?
David:	I'm not waiting. I can't do it. See, I have these fantasies of walking out at times, and maybe if I was feeling more in control I would. And that's not being very realistic.

David realizes that the work problems may not change much, that he sometimes wants to quit, *and* that quitting may be "unrealistic." The inquiry in the following section encourages elaboration of a "miracle" in which David will cope with this reality directly. The therapist's questions invite consideration of specific details in David's plan.

Therapist:	Okay, so how will you be dealing with the fact that sometimes you have these fantasies of quitting?
David:	Well, ideally, if I was feeling real in control, I'd go in and sit down with him, and say, "Listen. I was hired for that, not this, and unless you, or someone, can fix it, I'm giving you two weeks notice. I'm going to find something else."
Therapist:	And he'd say?
David:	Well, he'd probably start rationalizing and giving me this bullshit about the budget, and maybe in six months and so on.
Therapist:	And you'd say?
David:	You're not offering what I need here.
Therapist:	And then, what would be different, as a result of having said that?
David:	I'd probably go back to finish what I had to do, and then I'd go look for another job.
Therapist:	Tell me more about how you would do that.
David:	Well, I guess I'd update my resume and, um, do some phone networking, and send out some resumes.
Therapist:	How will you go about doing that?
David:	Like I did before. I used the newspaper, talked to people, called people, the whole job search bit.
Therapist:	And how will that make a difference for you?

David:	Well, you mean you're talking about in the miracle thing?
Therapist:	Yes.
David:	Well, I'd be okay with it. I wouldn't be panicking that I didn't have a job. I'd interview better, and I'd probably find something pretty quickly.
Therapist:	And if it was getting close to the end of the two weeks, and you were interviewing well, but the economy being what it is, if something hadn't come through yet, how would you . . .
David:	Well, keep looking.
Therapist:	What would you be doing financially, to take care of yourself and Angie?
David:	Well, we could get by for a little while.
Therapist:	What would your plan be in terms of benefits and health coverage and stuff like that?
David:	I'd probably plan it out so I had coverage until the end of the month, or until Angie can pick me up on her insurance. I think they have open enrollment pretty soon.
Therapist:	And Angie, what will she notice that's different about you?
David:	She'd notice that I was feeling better about myself.
Therapist:	How would she know?
David:	Well, I wouldn't come home from work exhausted, withdrawn, cranky. I'd come home, I'd be in a good mood, I'd be happy to see her. I'd give her a hug, we'd have dinner, and we'd laugh.
Therapist:	What would she hear you talking about?
David:	Our days, our plans. What to do on the weekend.
Therapist:	How would you be describing where you are with work, and the mess there?
David:	I'd tell her. Well, actually she'd probably freak out if I told her I gave two weeks notice. I mean, she's supportive, and she wants me to find a better job, but she's a realist, you know. We bought a condo, and she wants to get pregnant, and then she might want to quit her job. I just can't walk. So she'd probably be a little bit edgy.

Therapist:	What will you say when she gets a little edgy?
David:	Well, maybe I wouldn't actually give two weeks notice right away. Maybe I'd apply for other jobs first, and lay low with the giving notice part until one comes through.
Therapist:	And as a result of doing that, how will you be different at work while you're waiting for a job to come through?
David:	Not so dragged out, I guess. Seeing some light at the end of the tunnel.
Therapist:	Interesting.

By the end of solution elaboration, David was recognizing that he did not have to *either* "quit" *or* "like work" in order to start to make things better. His solution amplification raised multiple possibilities. These included: getting up earlier, having breakfast, getting the inventory report done, telling his boss that continuing this work assignment is not okay, giving two weeks notice, sending out resumes, networking, looking in the newspaper, job hunting in combination with waiting to give notice until a new job comes through, giving Angie a hug, talking to Angie about his plans, extending his health coverage, and enrolling on Angie's health plan. Implementation of any of these possibilities, alone or in combination, could make a significant difference in the long run. As this case illustrates, elaboration on the miracle question can deconstruct[1] the problem, increase options, and decrease a sense of hopelessness about a seemingly impossible situation.

Identifying and Amplifying Exceptions

After the miracle question has been developed, the therapist will want to determine if "pieces of the miracle," sometimes called "instances of the solution," are already happening. "This scenario you've described—are there any pieces of it that are already happening these days?" The deliberate placement of this inquiry immediately after miracle scenario development increases the likelihood that the client will recognize that some of the details he or she has described are already occurring—and that waiting for the "full miracle" is not necessary.

With most clients, it is useful for the therapist to specifically ask *if* exceptions have been observed (as opposed to assuming that they *have* been observed). If the client does *not* see pieces of the miracle happening yet, this is useful information

[1]As described by de Shazer (1992) and discussed in Chapter 1.

that will guide the therapist's response. The therapist may want to communicate respectful recognition of the fact that this is indeed a difficult situation, and that the change has not *yet* become apparent (the word "yet" implies that it *will* become apparent at some future time). The client might be encouraged to be curious about where change will emerge first. Or the therapist might want to proceed directly to scaling question inquiry, described more fully below.

With other clients, the therapist may want to select wording for the "exceptions inquiry" that presupposes that change is occurring. Instead of asking, "*Are* there times that pieces of this are happening?" the therapist may deliberately say, "Tell me about the times *when* pieces of this are happening these days." This approach might be used when the therapist has reason to believe that exceptions *are* in fact happening, but that the client will be likely to minimize or deny their presence.

Once it has been established that some components of the miracle scenario are occurring, the therapist will ask for the same kind of detail that is used when inquiring about the problem: who did or said what, where, when, and so on. "How did you do that?" is a common question, one which implies both that the *client* made the positive change happen, and that *how* he or she "did it" can be known and described. Therapist tone and nonverbal behaviors that convey surprise, respect, and/or enthusiasm are also used at this point, in a way congruent with the client's style.

"Exception talk" emerges periodically at other times during the therapy. Throughout every interview, the therapist will want to remain alert to spontaneous mention of times when the problem, for whatever reason, does not happen or is less problematic.[2] For example, Nancy intends to complain about her husband and is definitely not searching for exceptions when she says, "Sam never helps out unless his brother is there." The therapist guides the discussion to highlight the exception. "So, he does help when his brother is there? Tell me more about that."

Direct inquiry about exceptions can also be used without miracle questioning at any point that it might lead to useful clarification or reframing. Walter and Peller (1992a, p. 95) give an example of a man who heard voices telling him that people were after him and that he should be careful. The therapist asked how this was a problem (implying that the voices were *not* necessarily a problem in and of themselves), and the client clarified that they were a problem because neighbors were telling him that he was acting weird and suspicious. The therapist asked if there were times when the voices were not a problem. The man replied that the voices were there all the time. "So, do you listen to them all the time?" asked the therapist. The client said no, he did not. Sometimes he was too busy, and sometimes he trusted his own opinion. The therapist asked how he did that,

---

[2]These occasions are *not* necessarily the same as times that "instances of the solution" *are* present.

and the client answered, "I just ignore the voice, like a radio station I don't like." It also became clear that there were times when the client *wanted* to listen to the voices—because some of his former drug-dealing friends probably did want to get back at him.

Once exceptions have been identified, the therapist needs to confirm that they are relevant to the problem and the goal. As noted, the relationship between problem and solution is not always apparent, and seemingly unconnected solution behaviors can be extremely important and highly relevant. But it is also possible that a particular exception or instance of the solution is not related to the most important problem. This is important information, because amplification of that behavior may waste therapy time and effort that would be better spent on searching for or creating a more relevant exception or solution. To determine the importance of an exception or instance of the solution, the therapist can ask, "If this were happening more, how much difference would it make?"

If the client believes that continuation of a particular exception or instance of the solution would make a significant difference, the therapist may want to determine if continuation of the existing solution behavior would be sufficient. "If you kept doing . . . , would that be good enough?" is one way of finding this out. Maybe amplification is not really needed (in the sense of increasing the intensity of the solution in some way); increasing the duration or the frequency may be sufficient. If so, therapist inquiry will focus on how the client can keep this going.

Scaling Questions

One way to determine if exceptions are "differences that make a difference" is through the use of scaling questions (Berg and de Shazer, 1993). Although scaling questions can be used at any time that seems appropriate, most frequently they are introduced after some inquiry about exceptions. The therapist might say, "I'm going to ask you a scaling question now. On a zero to ten scale, where zero is when the problem was at its worst, and ten is when it's solved to your satisfaction, give me a number that best describes where you are now." As noted, even when the problem is unclear, clients can frequently make a subjective numerical rating.

Sometimes the number given is consistent with the response to the inquiry about exceptions; that is, clients who report many exceptions tend to give higher numbers than those who report few or none. However, sometimes the therapist will be surprised by the client's response. A client who describes various exceptions but gives a low number may be signaling that those are "differences that do *not* make a difference."

Some clients feel so soothed and encouraged by the therapy experience—particularly after describing a miracle scenario—that they respond to scaling questions at a nine or ten, but that number means "I'm feeling very comforted and positive right now, at this moment," not "The problem is almost solved." The therapist might suspect that this is happening when an extremely high number is given by a client who has just reported extreme symptomatology and/or a very difficult life situation, the miracle scenario is unlikely, and exceptions are minimal. To check out how lasting the client expects the positive feeling to be, the therapist might ask the following question: "How confident do you feel that you will maintain this number over the next twenty-four hours, where ten is 'I'm totally confident' and zero is 'I'm not confident at all—I could be back to square one in an hour'?" The answer to this question may keep the therapist—and the client—from underestimating the distance to the goal. On the other hand, it can also confirm that shifting how one looks at things can make a significant difference, even in a genuinely difficult situation.

Scaling questions can be used to assess variables involving relationships. After the client has made a rating, the therapist can ask, "Do you think your husband would agree with that number?" or "On that zero to ten scale, what number do you think your daughter would give you?" If the client's number is higher, the therapist might add, "Hmm. What do you know that she doesn't know?" or "What will it take for her to agree with your number?" As with much of the inquiry in strategic solution focused therapy, the questioning is designed to reframe as well as to gather information.

After the client makes a numerical rating of "where I am now," the therapist can use that information to inquire about the first (or next) sign of change. (The exception to this occurs when the number given is ten; then the questioning examines the degree of confidence that this level can be continued, ways of maintaining change, and relapse management.) Inquiry designed to operationalize the "next step" includes questions like this: "Okay, if you're at a two now, what will have to be different for you to be able to say 'I'm at a three'?" Questions about the next step can also be stated in relational terms; for example, "What will your partner notice that will let her know you've moved from five to six? Will she notice it first in what you say or in what you do?"

Clients sometimes respond to "next step" questions with answers that are "too big"; that is, the behavior, feeling, or interaction described is not significantly different from the desired goal or end point. When this happens, the therapist points this out gently, perhaps with humor, and encourages identification of a smaller step. Specificity of behavior at the "next step" is not as critical as "size"; even vague responses like "I'll feel *a little* better" may be meaningful to the client. At this point, the most important thing is that something about the step is "small"—and therefore potentially more achievable. Identification of a small goal leads naturally to inquiry about what (if anything) has been tried in attempts to reach that goal, which is often the next step in the therapy.

Variations on the Miracle Question

As mentioned, despite frequent use of the phrase "miracle question," inclusion of the word "miracle" is not an absolute requirement of a future scenario. In fact, for some clients there are good reasons for deliberately avoiding the use of the word. For example, when Vivian increasingly suspected that her son's school was being run by "religious fanatics, maybe even a cult," her therapist made a point of asking about a solution scenario without any reference to miracles. Some practical-minded, logical clients might best be approached with other language.

One alternate way of asking the question, suggested by Fisch (1993, personal communication), is: If you woke up tomorrow and, for some reason or other, this crying (or whatever) were no longer a problem, what would be different? This wording introduces two possibilities. First, the crying might not be there; second, it might be there but "for some reason or other" not a problem—that is, the person might not be bothered by it. Weiner-Davis (1992) expands on the latter possibility with this kind of question: What's different about the times when the problem occurs, but something productive results from it?

Walter and Peller (1992a) often encourage clients to notice how they will know that they are "on track." Using this phrase, the therapist might say, "Suppose you wake up tomorrow, and you haven't yet solved this thing, but you're on track. What will you be doing that's different?" To clarify what others will notice, the therapist might ask, "What will your husband notice that will let him know that you're moving in the right direction?"

Some kinds of inquiry highlight what will need to occur for the client to conclude that the therapy has been useful. "The therapy" can refer to either "this appointment" or a series of appointments, as appropriate. "What will have to happen for you to be able to say that it was worth the trip downtown today to talk to that counselor?" is an example of a question that implies that this session will have been helpful. The following refers to this course of therapy: "Pretend that it's our last appointment, and you're telling me that you don't need to come back anymore, because this has really been helpful, in exactly the way you hoped it would be. The problem that you came here about back on [today's date] isn't a problem for you anymore. What will you be doing differently that will make you able to say that?"

Regardless of the wording chosen by the therapist, some clients respond to inquiry about what will be different by saying, "I don't know." Walter and Peller (1992a) suggest this follow-up from the therapist: "Well, if you *did* know, what would you say?" At one level, this question is illogical and redundant; after all, the client has just said that he or she "didn't know." At another level, however, the question invites a further suspension of reality and the adoption of a hypothetical stance. In response, clients frequently laugh or smile, and then they proceed to answer.

An important miracle question variation suggests a "specific" miracle rather than a general one. The following example illustrates this variation. Andre has complained that he "can't say no" to his partner, Simon. The therapist says to him, "Andre, I'd like you to imagine, for a moment, that while you're sleeping tonight, a miracle happens. And the miracle is that this one piece is different: you have the ability to say 'no' to Simon. That's the *only* piece that's different. Simon is as he has always been—with his never-ending demands; your income is the same; time constraints are the same; those painful memories about being betrayed by your mother are as they've always been. The one thing that's different is your ability to say 'no.' You wake up. You open your eyes. What will be the first thing that will be different, as a result of that knowledge, inside, that you now can say 'no' to Simon if you choose to do so?"

Different changes can be highlighted with the same client. Andre's therapist could propose consideration of a different solution scenario, either instead of or in addition to the one described above. For example, the therapist could say, "Now let's imagine it a different way. Pretend, for a moment, that when you awaken tomorrow, the one thing that's different is this: the memory of what your mother did to you is, for some reason, not as painful, not so much of a problem. What will be the first thing that Simon will notice, that will let him know that you are different?"

How does the therapist decide which miracle question to use? Should the inquiry be general or specific, and if specific, which change should be highlighted? When should "multiple miracles" be proposed? There are no fixed formulas for making these decisions, and clinical judgment is always required. As a general guideline, however, the therapist can consider whether there was clear identification of a complaint during the problem clarification phase of interviewing. If so, it may be useful to focus the miracle on the resolution of that problem. If problem clarification never resulted in the specification of a clear complaint, a more general miracle question may be more useful.

When the client views the biggest problem as "lack of insight," the therapist may want to propose a miracle that emphasizes the "achievement of insight." The therapist might say, "Imagine that the miracle is that while you're sleeping, you've achieved that understanding, that insight. What will be the first thing that will be different, when you awake, as a result of that understanding?" If, as is frequently the case, it later appears that pieces of the "understanding miracle" are already happening, the therapist can highlight the client's "insight" in recognizing that he or she did not need to wait for complete understanding in order to begin important changes in the present.

"Multiple miracles" may be particularly useful when the client has equivocated about which of several complaints is most distressing. "Gosh, I don't know which one bugs me more, my mother-in-law or my kid. They're *both* pains in the butt," said Larry. Here, the therapist suggested that Larry pursue one miracle where the "mother-in-law situation" was resolved (but the "kid" problem was not) and another where the "kid problem" was the only part that was different.

Another common situation that may call for amplification of different scenarios is that where the client's spouse, partner, or primary loved one is either overtly rejecting the client or more subtly pulling away. One miracle scenario may be the one where "he's come back"; another may be the one where the client is "over him" and doing quite well; while another may be the one where the client is grieving but beginning the process of healing.

Miracle Questioning as Problem Clarification

Usually problem clarification precedes miracle questioning. However, there are instances where amplification of the solution creates a feedback loop that enhances clarification of which problem is most important to address. With Larry, who initially complained about both his mother-in-law and his "kid," elaboration of the two miracles clarified that if his son's behavior changed, the mother-in-law's interference might spontaneously diminish and no longer be a concern. The opposite was not at all the case; decreased mother-in-law interference would not, in and of itself, diminish his son's disturbing behavior in any way. Elaboration of both scenarios clarified for both Larry and the therapist that the initial focus should be on how he was responding to his son's misbehavior.

When the problem remains vague, a general miracle question can lead to a destructuring process that results in increased clarity. de Shazer (1991) described a man who had difficulty specifying what distressed him most. Sometimes he thought he was depressed; he also thought that he might be suffering a midlife crisis, be dissatisfied with his job, or be "increasingly unhappy with my marriage." He experienced vague dissatisfaction and feelings of emptiness. The more he thought about it, the more confused he became; he wondered which part was the real problem, whether the difficulty might be a combination of things, and whether all of the dissatisfaction could be the result of a still undiscovered problem. In this kind of case, further direct attempts at problem clarification may only exacerbate the confusion. Exploring what would be different if the problem (whatever its nature) were solved can guide both therapist and client toward the area where imagined change is most salient and will make the biggest difference.

The following example illustrates how elaboration of evolving solution scenarios can lead to definition of the problem that is more focused and relevant than the initial presentation. Lulu was depressed and angry about how Aaron, her husband, neglected her. He never approached her for sex, he played Nintendo rather than helping out, and he didn't talk about much of anything. The therapist asked Lulu to imagine a specific miracle, that the problem of "Aaron's neglect" has been solved.

Lulu:	He gets up, he's all laughing and smiling.
Therapist:	And you? How are you different as a result of Aaron's laughs and smiles?
Lulu:	I guess I'd be smiling too. [Pause. She looks sullen] No, I wouldn't be. I'd be pretty pissed, actually. Here he'd be acting like everything's okay, expecting me to act like nothing's happened, and it just don't work that way. It don't all go away overnight.
Therapist:	[Softly] This isn't sounding like much of a miracle.
Lulu:	No, it ain't, come to think of it. He can't just turn on the charm and expect everything to be okay.
Therapist:	You sound pretty angry at Aaron.
Lulu:	I am. I been angry at him for a long, long time.
Therapist:	Lulu, can you envision a picture where you're still pretty aggravated at Aaron, but, for some reason, he's just the tiniest bit less neglecting in some way?
Lulu:	I suppose if he . . . No, I really can't. I just feel so trapped. And I can't leave him because of the kids. He's their daddy. They love him. And boys need a daddy.
Therapist:	You really care about your boys. And you feel pretty stuck.
Lulu:	I sure do. And I don't see no way out of it.
Therapist:	Lulu, let's try this miracle picture a different way. Can you pretend that Aaron is still as he is, but the miracle is that you're not feeling so trapped? If that happened, what would be the first thing that would be different?
Lulu:	I'd be alone. I'd go out with the kids, and not have to listen to him yapping.
Therapist:	Where would you go?
Lulu:	Shopping probably. To get some pizza.
Therapist:	And your boys, which one would notice first that Mom's different?
Lulu:	The little one. Ollie.

Therapist:	What will Ollie notice?
Lulu:	That I'm not yelling. I'm joking with them. I'm having a good time.
Therapist:	And how will you be managing your concerns about Ollie and Abe needing their daddy?
Lulu:	I'll just tell them that they *will* see him, just not now.

Lulu's face was shining. This time it *was* "feeling like a miracle" to her. When the therapist asked if any pieces of this scenario were already happening, Lulu immediately said that they were. Of much importance, she had not needed to separate from Aaron in order to do some things that made a difference. Sometimes she just took the boys out somewhere. How did she do that? She "just pretended Aaron wasn't there." The therapist asked Lulu how much difference it would make if Aaron's neglect were to diminish a bit. Not much, she said. She wanted the therapist to help her to "think through" what she was going to do about her difficult situation.

If the definition of the problem had stayed at the "neglect" level, much time and energy could have been spent on efforts to change "Aaron's neglect," which at this point was not the main problem with which Lulu wanted assistance. Following miracle question elaboration, the problem became clear: Lulu was increasingly unhappy in her marriage, and she wanted to be sure that she did not leave impulsively, both because of her concern for her sons and because of financial realities. Lulu's dilemma was the problem that the therapy needed to address.

Miracle Questioning as Intervention

Just as problem clarification both provides information about the complaint and becomes an intervention in and of itself, solution amplification both gives information about the goal and functions as a clinical intervention. As indicated, miracle questioning is especially powerful when followed by identification of exceptions and the realization that the client did not need to wait for a full miracle to make positive change occur. This process is not limited to those occasions when the therapist conducts a full and elaborate inquiry about the solution. The same kind of questions that are used to amplify a miracle can be used as process intervention at any time that the therapist believes they might be useful. O'Hanlon and Weiner-Davis (1989) call these "little miracle questions" or "fast forward" questions. Using little miracle questions, the therapist can guide desired parts of the interview into the future. This style of interviewing is conducted in the future tense and asks about specifics of what will be different in a variety of specific situations.

The following example illustrates how little miracle questions can be used in a session where no full solution inquiry is conducted. Angelica, age nineteen, was becoming increasingly suspicious of everyone. She quit her job and began to "talk funny," according to her mother. She was sure that people were discriminating against her because of her Guatemalan background (in a community where most Hispanics were of Mexican background). One night, after an altercation with her brother, Angelica ran out into the street. Her mother called the police, who picked Angelica up and took her to the hospital emergency room. Angelica received a diagnosis of "incipient schizophrenia." Medication was prescribed, and an outpatient appointment was scheduled for Angelica and her mother with the therapist the next morning. Angelica very reluctantly agreed to take the medication; she did not think there was a problem, but she did wish to avoid hospitalization and being hauled down to the emergency room again.

Therapist:	If the three of us were meeting here again next week, and that medicine—or whatever—was making a difference, what would you ladies be telling me?
Mother:	She'd be playing Pictionary. She'd be beating me at Pictionary.
Therapist:	What else?
Mother:	She'd be making sense. She'd be talking to her friends.
Therapist:	[To Angelica] And what will you be noticing about your mom?
Angelica:	She'll be nicer to me. She won't be calling no police on me.

This interchange was part of the intervention. It implicitly suggested that Angelica might be playing Pictionary and talking to her friends, and that her mother might be "talking nicer." It also set the stage for inquiry in the follow-up session about how much of this scenario had actually happened over the last week, and what Angelica and her mother had done to make things better.

Sometimes interventions involving solution amplification are enhanced by deliberately shifting the discussion away from a particular subject. As mentioned in the previous chapter, addressing too many issues simultaneously diffuses the focus, and sometimes the therapist wants to deliberately narrow the field. This is the case especially when the therapist is attempting to highlight an exception that seems significant. For example, Wayne has had problems with his temper for years, and he has assumed that his difficulty has to do with "women—all bitches like my mother." However, in several recent arguments with his girlfriend, he has managed to leave the house without hitting her. This interchange shows how the therapist selectively ignores it when Wayne makes references to his mother.

Therapist:	It sounds like you've had every reason to be furious with her [girl-friend] lately. So how do you do it, when getting mad doesn't get you in trouble?
Wayne:	Beats me. I want to sock her lights out when she pulls that. It's the same crap my mother used to give me.
Therapist:	So how did you manage to get out the door last night?

Shifting the discussion away from Wayne's mother, in combination with high-lighting his recent success in de-escalating with his girlfriend, helped to accentuate an important difference. The therapist's goal was to introduce the notion that even if all women were like his mother (in some ways), there could be important differences between Wayne's past violent behavior with his mother and other women and his behavior with his girlfriend now. It should be emphasized that Wayne's comments about his mother and other women were *not* ignored in this way throughout his treatment. The choice here was deliberate, designed to enhance a particular therapeutic effect.

Sometimes the therapist will suggest a hypothetical miracle in order to introduce a new frame. This was done with Celeste, the woman described in Chapter 2 who feared becoming like her "mentally sick" mother.

Therapist:	Let me ask you this question. If we could somehow know that you will not sink as deep as when you first got here, that you will never get very sick mentally, like your mother, that it will actually continue to be as it is now; that you'll occasionally wake up, gasping for breath, you'll get out of bed, you'll reassure yourself, you'll go back to bed, you'll fall asleep, and it'll get better the next day, what difference would that make?
Celeste:	As far as . . . ?
Therapist:	How much of a problem it would be.
Celeste:	If I knew that, that it would just be a passing thing?
Therapist:	Yeah.
Celeste:	Then I'd be able to deal with it.
Therapist:	That would make a difference for you?
Celeste:	Yeah. It would.
Therapist:	And if we could know, and of course this is hypothetical, because we can't know, how would you be dealing with it when you woke up gasping in the middle of the night?

Celeste: I guess I'd kind of laugh at myself.

Therapist: And how would that make a difference?

Celeste: I guess I wouldn't be so scared.

It clearly is not possible to know in advance that Celeste (or anyone) will not be sick mentally, and that reality needs to be made explicit when this kind of hypothetical miracle is introduced. Nonetheless, the idea that being less fearful about the future can make an important difference in the present can become a powerful intervention.

Evaluating Attempted Solutions
If It Doesn't Work, Do Something Different

Following problem clarification and solution elaboration, the therapist and the client ideally will have specified the following: the nature of the primary problem, the vision of the solution, and a description of a first step in the right direction. The next step is inquiry about attempted solutions.

Of course, therapy does not always proceed according to plan. All three variables (problem, solution, first step) may not be fully clear at times. Fortunately, the evaluation of attempted solutions can occur even when some variable remains a little vague. The process may be more difficult and less precise, but like progress in the client's life, the therapy can proceed even in the absence of ideal conditions.

The therapist's task here is the assessment of what has already been tried in attempts to solve the problem or arrive at the goal. Clarity about attempted solutions and their outcome is critical, because the therapist will base central decisions on this information. The therapy can take two possible directions.

One possibility is that the attempted solution is "working." If this is the case, the primary intervention may involve encouraging the client to continue or expand it. It may also be important to assess whether there are obstacles to doing more of this behavior. After all, if "doing more of it" were that straightforward, the client might not have come to therapy in the first place.

The other possibility is that the attempted solution is not working, or not working well enough. If this is the case, the primary intervention may be to encourage the person to discontinue it and do something different.

Eliciting Attempted Solutions

The process of clarifying attempted solutions is frequently easier and more straightforward than either problem clarification or solution elaboration. People can often articulate fairly easily what they have done and what has been advised. Straightforward inquiry may be sufficient to elicit this information. The therapist might first confirm that he or she is clear on what has already been discussed.

Therapist: Let me see if I have this straight. You're saying that your mother's criticizing you about Wally [client's boyfriend] is what bothers you the most. You want her to accept and like him, or at least respect your right to be with him. You know that's not likely to happen right away, but you'll feel like things are moving in the right direction when the tirade is a little shorter. Have I got that right?

Deanna: Yeah, that about sums it up.

Therapist: Now let me ask you this. Before coming here, what have you tried in your best attempt to get your mother to stop criticizing you about Wally?

The strategic solution focused therapist will frequently add, at this point, that he or she is particularly interested in knowing what does *not* work. The rationale behind this interest can be made explicit: "I don't want us, you and I, to waste energy by doing things you already know don't work."

With clients who indicate at this point that this logic makes sense to them, the therapist may add the following: "I happen to believe that if something works, you do more of it, and if something doesn't work, you do something different." The therapist who chooses to say this has basically summarized the theory of strategic solution focused therapy! This is a perfectly legitimate thing to do, and it often speeds up the process. Because this is a collaborative approach, there is no reason to keep the theory "hidden." The therapist's openness about the theory guiding the work can enhance client participation in the problem solving efforts. The client who understands the rationale may collaborate more effectively with the therapist, as they search together for clues about what works and what does not.

When eliciting attempted solutions, the therapist seeks the same clarity of detail that is desired in other phases of strategic solution focused therapy. For example, when Deanna says, "I tried to talk to my mother," the therapist requests more detail. "Tell me how that goes," "What words did you use?" or "How did you put it?" are questions that can elicit increased specificity.

The therapist also wants to understand the client's rationale for using a particular approach. That is, how was this thing that was said or done supposed to help? Direct questions such as "What did you have in mind?" or "How did you hope that would help?" may be useful here. For example, Deanna has further clarified that she tells her mother, "Wally doesn't do drugs anymore. He's going to school now." In response to the therapist's inquiry about her rationale for saying this, Deanna says, "If I can convince her that he's not a loser, maybe she'll change her mind about him." This information will be useful later, when the therapist is planning an intervention to suggest to Deanna.

"What Else?"

"What else have you tried?" is an important follow-up question. The therapist wants to understand the full range of what has been attempted or suggested. Heath and Atkinson (1989) described four kinds of attempted solutions: (1) those that have failed; (2) those that have succeeded (although fleetingly); (3) those advised by others; and (4) those "outlandish" ideas that the client has previously, perhaps momentarily, considered and then discarded. It can be useful to specifically inquire about all of these.

When clients describe the various "different" things they have tried, they frequently assume that these things are in fact different. Close examination of supposedly different attempted solutions often reveals that they are actually variations on the same theme. As de Shazer (1985, p. 124) points out, "Punishment is still punishment, whether it be grounding, restricting, or yelling." It is therefore useful to recognize common themes, or the main thrust of attempted solutions, successful or unsuccessful.

For example, a person who has been depressed may have tried the following: exercise, going to the movies, and telling herself "Don't dwell on it." These attempted solutions may seem distinct, but they are all similar in an important way: all are "distraction" techniques. Here is another example. Ed's wife has threatened to leave him, and Ed does not want her to go. In his attempts to dissuade her from leaving, Ed has bought flowers and theater tickets. He has volunteered to take the garbage out; he has promised that he will "change"; he is even "seeking therapy." These behaviors are all variations on a theme of "I've eliminated (or am in the process of eliminating) what you have complained about." If this approach is successful, so much the better. But if it is not—and the likelihood is that it is not, since Ed is sitting in the therapist's office—the therapist will probably want to steer away from additional variations on the same theme.

Being Specific

When inquiring about attempted solutions, it is important to be clear about the problem that the attempted solution is supposed to be addressing. This may seem obvious, but in practice, it is all too easy to ask for a "generic" attempted solution. For example, Laurel has complained about her boss's pickiness and her own difficulty coping with that pickiness. In the attempted solution inquiry, the therapist will want to be clear, because "What have you done in an attempt to get him to not be so picky?" and "What have you done to cope with it after he is picky?" are two separate questions. Which to pursue could be determined by which of the two problems Laurel wants to address, as reviewed in the discussion of problem clarification. Unless Laurel is convinced that the boss's pickiness is unchangeable, it may be preferable to start with investigation of what she has tried to diminish the pickiness. After all, if the pickiness were decreased, "coping with it" would not be an issue.

Even when the therapist clearly asks, "What have you done in an attempt to prevent or decrease the occurrence of the problem?" some clients answer by describing something slightly different. They explain what they have done in response to discomfort that has occurred as the result of some failed attempted solution. These behaviors are "spin-offs" of an unsuccessful attempted solution (Emard, 1991). For example, Jared cannot urinate in public restrooms. He tells himself, "You shouldn't be nervous. Just go." This self-talk is unsuccessful; his anxiety increases, his sphincter muscles tighten, and he cannot go. In response to this discomfort, Jared is careful to restrict his fluid intake whenever he will be going out. He does this not to facilitate urination in public, but to decrease the discomfort that results from the unsuccessful attempts "to go." If investigation of attempted solutions (for urination) elicits "fluid restriction," the therapist may want to clarify further. This may involve asking, "What did you do before you did that?" In this instance, the "don't be nervous; just go" self-talk is the primary attempted solution.

When "Nothing" Has Been Tried

Sometimes clients respond to questions about attempted solutions by saying that they "have not tried anything." Sometimes the client has assumed that the therapist is asking only about attempts that have succeeded (Fisch, 1994, personal communication). The therapist can check this out, especially since he or she may be particularly interested in what does not work well enough. If the client still insists that nothing has been tried, the therapist might inquire about whether the client has tried a common sense approach. For example, the therapist might say, "People who get depressed frequently tell themselves to cheer up. I'm curious if you've told yourself that, or if anyone has suggested that to you." This kind of input sometimes clarifies attempted solutions. Occasionally, however, a client really has not tried anything. In this case, the attempted solution might best be described as "doing nothing."

Did It Work?

Once attempted solutions have been identified, the therapist wants to know if they have been successful. The best way to find that out is usually to inquire about what happened after the attempt was made. Specific behaviors and words are again requested. "Okay, when you said that, what did she say?" Sometimes identification of these specifics immediately answers the question of "whether it worked." If it is unclear, the therapist can ask if the results were satisfactory.

The therapist sometimes discovers that the client has done something that worked in the past, but that he or she has stopped doing it. It may appear that if that solution were applied again, it would work again. However, as O'Hanlon and Weiner-Davis (1989) point out, people sometimes erroneously assume that if a problem was eliminated, but later the same or similar problem reappeared, then the original solution was therefore ineffective. This is not always the case. What frequently happens is that once a problem is solved, people tend to relax their efforts, and they return to previous, less effective behaviors. Maybe it is "too much trouble" to apply the solution, or the client simply forgets, or something else is a higher priority. Predictably, the problem reappears. Solutions, like sunscreen, may "work" when applied, but the sunscreen used yesterday does no good after today's shower. Reapplication is needed. When this is the case, the therapist's inquiry may need to focus on whether there is any obstacle to reapplying the solution.

Interrupting Unsuccessful Attempted Solutions

Once the effectiveness of the attempted solution has been evaluated, the therapist has an idea about whether the treatment should attempt to amplify or interrupt an existing behavior. More detailed indications about which intervention to select, and when to present the intervention, will be discussed later. The emphasis in this chapter is on those situations where the attempted solution has been unsuccessful. When this is the case, the therapist's task is to conceptualize alternate responses that, if applied, would be likely to interrupt the unsuccessful attempted solution.

When it is clear that a particular approach has failed to produce the desired results, the therapist at least knows not to suggest "more of the same." However, simply discontinuing the unsuccessful attempted solution may not be sufficient. "Silence" from a wife who has previously complained can be construed by the husband as "just a temporary pause." "She's not saying it out loud at this moment, but she's thinking it. She'll say it again pretty soon," the husband may be thinking. Thus, the wife who has previously "complained" in her (heretofore unsuccessful) attempts to get her husband to plan outings may need to do more than simply discontinue the complaining. She may need to replace "complaining" with very different words or behavior.

Disrupting Solutions

To "do something different," the client might alter the pattern or context of a complaint. Milton Erickson frequently planned approaches that shifted the timing or performance of a behavior in some small, seemingly insignificant way. O'Hanlon and Weiner-Davis (1989) describe the following things that can be altered in order to disrupt an unsuccessful pattern:

1. increase or decrease the frequency of a behavior
2. change the time of day a behavior occurs
3. lengthen or shorten the duration of a behavior
4. alter the location of a behavior (e.g., room of the house, outdoors versus indoors, etc.)
5. add a new behavior or element to the complaint
6. change the sequence of behaviors or events
7. break the behavior down into smaller parts
8. link the performance of one behavior to the performance of some burdensome activity

O'Hanlon and Weiner-Davis use the following example to illustrate how behaviors that typically occur together can be separated. A woman frequently binges on food, and on those days that she binges, she typically does not go out with her friends. To disrupt the connection between binging and "not going out," she might be instructed to deliberately go out with friends after a binge. Such instruction would *not* be saying, "You must not binge," (which may be a significant component of advice already given by the self and/or by others). Rather, the assumption is that she *will* binge, and that when she does so, she should go out with her friends.

The introduction of chance elements into a situation can produce a positive change. Watzlawick (1991) described a couple who complained of decreased sexual intimacy. Figure 1 shows how they slept at home.

Each partner got into bed on his or her "own side." While on vacation, they

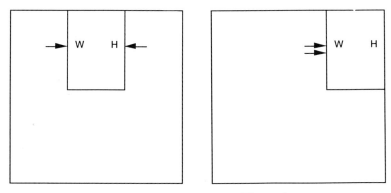

Figure 1 Bed at home.   ***Figure 2*** Bed on vacation.

slept in a room where the bed was in a different position; during the vacation, the problem diminished. What changed? In the new setting, the bed was in the position shown in Figure 2.

The man got out of bed in the middle of the night to use the bathroom. When he returned, his usual route to the right side of the bed was blocked. He had to climb in from the left instead, and en route to "his" side, he found "something of interest." Watzlawick used this example to illustrate how the therapist can deliberately introduce events similar to such chance events, thereby interrupting a pattern.

Reversing Solutions

Simply discontinuing what is not working can interrupt an unsuccessful attempted solution, but, as mentioned, this kind of interruption can sometimes come across as "just a pause before more of the same." Replacing the unsuccessful attempted solution with a variation that changes the context can reduce the likelihood of this difficulty to some extent. An even more powerful interruption occurs if the alternate response does more than simply stop or alter the previous response. An alternative that points in the opposite direction from the previous response can reverse the thrust of an unsuccessful attempted solution (Fisch, Weakland, and Segal, 1982). Conceptualizing this kind of shift involves determining what would be the "180 degree opposite" from the current behavior.

The alternative most likely to be effective in a particular case always needs to be individually tailored to the specifics of the situation. Nonetheless, some clusters of unsuccessful attempted solutions occur so commonly that it is possible to categorize them. In response to certain problems, very different people frequently make remarkably similar responses. Therefore, consideration of the most common attempted solution and the alternative most likely to reverse it can be extremely useful to the strategic solution focused therapist.

Change Slowly

A general message is implicit in much therapy, as well as in nontherapy situations where someone is trying to overcome a problem. That message is one of encouragement and optimism. When initial signs of change occur, the spontaneous response is often praise and/or encouragement of additional movement. The theory of operant conditioning supports this approach: behaviors that are reinforced should increase in frequency. When this approach succeeds, it clearly can be applied. Sometimes, however, optimism, encouragement, and reinforcement are not followed by continued change. When this occurs in therapy, a different response needs to be considered.

The "go slow" messages extensively described in the MRI literature (Watzlawick, Weakland, and Fisch, 1974) can be considered when straightforward encouragement to change, or to change more, is not successful. Caution not to change too quickly, to consider the disadvantages of improvement, and to take all the time one needs can reverse the pressure frequently perceived (accurately or not) from others, as well as diminish self-talk that imposes pressure for rapid accomplishment.

There is another way in which optimistic messages sometimes become counterproductive. People seeking therapy often receive strong messages, from other people, the media, or the self, about the general helpfulness of therapy. When a client has had (or knows of others who have had) previous treatment experiences that have not proven helpful, a too-positive message does not resonate with personal experience, and a position of greater pessimism is sometimes more useful. This is also the case when a person is requesting therapy for a complex life dilemma that may not have simple answers.

The general position of restraint from change, the reverse of "you should or must change," can be expressed in many different ways. It appears in various forms in the general alternatives to many unsuccessful attempted solutions. The reader will find this position implicit in much of what is described throughout this book.

Depression: When "Cheer Up" Doesn't Work

Depression is one of the most frequent complaints described by psychotherapy clients. Many people consult therapists following bereavement, relationship breakup, financial setbacks, health problems, and many other losses. Other people seek therapy when they just feel bad but cannot say why. With or without a clear-cut precipitant, depression often receives a message that is a variation of "cheer up." When there is a definable loss, well-meaning people frequently encourage the depressed person to "get on with life," often by investing energy in alternate objects and endeavors. People who are blue "for no reason" tell themselves, and are told by others, to "snap out of it," because "there is nothing to be depressed about." Advice to focus on the positive is logical, and sometimes it is quite helpful. However, when depression persists in spite of such messages, alternative therapeutic approaches may warrant consideration.

Depression after a Loss

One extremely common precipitant of depression is the anticipated or actual loss of a relationship. For example, Maureen's boyfriend of three years, Ray, has "dumped" her for another woman. The apartment they shared is too expensive for Maureen's income alone, so she has to move. Maureen is devastated. Several friends, who never thought much of Ray in the first place, tell her that she should say "good riddance." "A new love is the best cure for a broken heart," her sister advises. She urges Maureen to go out dancing and to forget about "that turd."

Maureen cannot understand what is wrong with her. Even when she was with Ray, she considered herself basically a feminist. She should be using this time "between relationships" to pursue independent activities, she tells herself. She used to love to sketch, but sketching does not interest her at all now. Maureen remembers the poster in her college dorm years ago that read: "A woman needs a man like a fish needs a bicycle." "Am I so codependent and weak that I really need a man, this man, to feel whole?" she wonders.

Both the "find someone new" messages from others and the "you shouldn't need a man" self-talk are variations of "Cheer up. Don't be sad." Neither variation is helping Maureen to feel better. Therefore, the therapist may want to consider ways of reversing the "cheer up" message. There are a number of ways of doing this. One is to emphasize the normalcy and appropriateness of mourning for any meaningful loss. The opposite of "Get on with your life" is "Be sure to give your healing all the time it needs." Maureen might be cautioned not to rush precipitously into a new relationship. Of course she will be hesitant to trust her judgment about men for a while, so she may not feel like going dancing. And if she does go dancing, it may be mostly to pacify her sister; she certainly should not expect to enjoy it too much.

Maureen might be reminded that the loss is not just of Ray, but also of her living situation. Not only is she reeling from the loss; she also is facing the many tasks involved in apartment hunting and moving. Who has the luxury of time for or interest in sketching when so many tasks need to be done? To interrupt "You shouldn't need a man," the therapist might point out that most feminists value the capacity for interpersonal connectedness. A person who can forget a significant relationship of three years overnight might be viewed as superficial. Maureen's feelings for Ray may bring pain, but they are evidence of her capacity to care deeply.

Depression "Without Reason"

In depression without a clear-cut precipitant, the "cheer up" solution attempted by oneself and others typically emphasizes the fact that nothing drastically bad has occurred. Glen has felt out of sorts for weeks. Nothing seems to interest him these days. Nothing in his life has changed. "So why am I depressed?" he asks himself. Glen has a stable job at the post office, a devoted wife of four years, one little girl, and another baby on the way. This is exactly the kind of life his dad never had when he was Glen's age, as his dad always used to tell him. "You brood too much," Glen's wife tells him. When the feelings of sadness emerge, Glen tries to push them away, but he is not having much success.

The opposite of "Don't brood. Don't think about it" is "*Do* pay attention to the feelings. In fact, pay *closer* attention to them. Notice when and where they emerge, and how you do it when you make them bigger and smaller." Designed to interrupt the "distract yourself" cognition, this therapist statement simultaneously can lead to problem clarification, as Glen notices what elicits sadness, and to solution amplification, as Glen recognizes what is different when the sadness is not so intense.

In Glen's case, paying attention to what he was sad about led to recognition of feelings of boredom. As his life became more "stable," Glen was missing some of the excitement and independence of his single years. Acknowledging this to himself and discussing it with his wife led to Glen's planning some rafting trips, something he had once enjoyed but had not initiated for some time.

Anxiety: When "Don't Worry" Doesn't Work

When the complaint is anxiety, the most common attempted solution is a variation on "Don't worry." Well-meaning friends logically explain to the freeway-phobic driver that freeways are safer than surface streets. The person who lives in dread of earthquakes is reminded that anxiety does not deter them: "Your worrying won't keep one from happening, so just don't think about it." Panic attack sufferers are taught that panic attacks pass and that the sensations do not invariably lead to heart attacks or insanity. This kind of input can be extremely helpful to many people, but it is not universally successful. When anxiety persists, this approach becomes the unsuccessful attempted solution.

The opposite of "Don't worry" is "*Do* worry." Worry is reframed as legitimate, appropriate, perhaps desirable. The earthquake phobic might be told that perhaps most California residents do not worry enough. If earthquake anxiety prompts a person to fasten heavy bookcases to the wall, that anxiety could save a life. To guard against becoming too casual or nonchalant, the anxious person might be instructed to take a full five minutes to give the danger the thought and attention it deserves. Watzlawick (1992) describes the following way of reversing "reassurance" that is not alleviating anxiety. He asks the client to deliberately try to be irrational and to create the worst fantasy imaginable. Whatever the client says, Watzlawick says that he tells the client, "But I told you to be irrational—and what you just said could happen!" Madanes (1981) reverses "I'm afraid I'll have an anxiety attack" by encouraging the client to "have it now and get it over with." The relative of the anxious client whose reassurances fall on deaf ears can be encouraged to say, "I realize after talking to the therapist that maybe I've been too casual about this. I'm more worried than I let on or even admit to myself."

Interrupting Avoidance

People frequently avoid what frightens them. "If I don't drive on the freeway, then I won't get nervous," Anne reasons. Avoidance is thus part of her attempted solution for the anxiety. It is an unsuccessful attempted solution, however, because Anne is anxious anyway. Now she has these thoughts: "What if my son gets sick and I have to drive him to the emergency room? What if my boss asks me to fill in at the store across town?"

The other part of Anne's unsuccessful attempted solution is a variation on a "Don't be scared" message that emphasizes decreasing the anxiety first, before attempting the behavior. Anne tells herself, "Once I finally get rid of the anxiety, then I'll try the freeway again." Until then, she carefully avoids all practice and exposure to freeway driving.

Interruption of this unsuccessful attempted solution involves reversing both the avoidance part and the "Wait to feel better" part. Just as is done in exposure and *in vivo* desensitization approaches, the therapist typically reverses avoidance by suggesting gradual exposure to what is frightening. To reverse "Wait till you're calm," the therapist may encourage Anne to fully experience her fear and not push it away. "You need to learn that you can be afraid and do it anyway" is the message, designed to reverse "Wait until your fear is gone to do it." This alternate message is especially powerful when the behavior practiced is extremely small, such as "experience fear fully while you're sitting in the car—without the car key."

Reversing "Concealing"

Anxious clients frequently go to great lengths to hide their anxiety. People who fear that they will embarrass themselves during public speaking try to contain that anxiety by concealing it. The harder they try, the more tense they become. This phenomenon commonly occurs with fears of blushing, stuttering, or having nothing to say. What is the opposite of concealing something? Watzlawick et al. (1974) use the term "advertising" to describe the opposite. Announcing or acknowledging in advance that the problem is likely to occur disrupts the fearful waiting for the unpleasant surprise.

Interrupting "Perfectionism"

A similar phenomenon occurs when the anxiety centers around making mistakes. Often described as obsessive or perfectionistic, the person who dreads mistakes uses this self-talk: "You must not make mistakes." Often the person procrastinates on tasks because he or she feels that the work will be imperfect. With sufficient procrastination, the task is never begun; the attempted solution is unsuccessful.

The opposite of striving for perfection is deliberately creating imperfection. Zeig (1987) has told "perfectionists" that "every work should have one perfectly good mistake." He adds that the person should insist on imperfection and obsess about where and how to create it. A variation on this alternative suggested by Madanes (1981) emphasizes the deliberate insertion of two errors, one noticeable and one so minute that only its creator can find it.

Interrupting Unsuccessful Attempted Solutions in Relationships

Many people consult therapists because of distress about interpersonal relationships. In addition, the problem clarification and solution amplification conducted in strategic solution focused therapy frequently reveal that many people who initially complain of general depression or dissatisfaction are depressed because of relationship difficulties. Therefore, evaluating attempted solutions in significant relationships is extremely important. Clarification of exactly what is said or done is particularly important here, and the therapist may often need to request specific dialogue. When the client says, " I tell him I don't like it," it is not clear if she is saying, "I'd appreciate it if you could let me know when you're running late," "God damn it, if you pull this shit one more time you're gonna get clobbered," or "You know me, I'm kind of rigid about time—I'll probably be on your back for a while tonight—bear with me." The effect of each may well be very different.

How much one talks about problems—whether a lot or a little—is part of the attempted solution at times. Some people constantly express and elaborate their feelings. When this does not work, talking less, or not at all, or saying, "The therapist thinks I talk too much about this" can interrupt the typical pattern. Other people speak little, feeling that "the less said, the better." For them, increased expression, to another person and/or to the therapist, represents a departure from usual behavior.

Reframing

Sometimes therapist reframing of the other person's behavior produces a shift that interrupts an unsuccessful attempted solution. Watzlawick (1992) describes a boss who thinks his subordinates dislike him. Behavior based on this assumption probably exacerbates the words and behaviors that come across as dislike. Watzlawick tells the man, "When you think this is happening, behave *as if* your subordinates were fearful and in need of reassurance."

Interrupting Ineffective Communication

How something is said makes a great deal of difference in its efficacy. As answers to the question "Is it what he says or how he puts it?" frequently reveal, the "how" is often what is most troublesome. The same content may fail to bring desired results when delivered one way but succeed when phrased and/or delivered differently.

This concept is by no means unique to strategic solution focused therapy. Communication, assertiveness, and social skills training classes all provide similar input: "You-messages," verbal attacks, and vague requests are not as effective as low-key, specific "I-messages." What may be emphasized more in strategic solution focused therapy (and in some cognitive behavior therapy) is the interruption of certain attitudes about interpersonal change.

"You Don't Have To Like It"

"He (or she) should *want* to do it" is a frequent complaint. Erica's complaint is not just that Fiona does not do her share of the housework; she should "*want* to." "If she were really committed to this relationship, she would think of it herself." Predictably, Erica's exhortations to Fiona that she "should want to" only bring counteraccusations: "You're always telling me what to do and how I should feel." To interrupt the "You should want to" statements, the therapist might encourage Erica to request that Fiona "just do" the tasks in question. "You don't have to like it, but I'd appreciate it if you did it anyway." Putting it this way may increase the likelihood of the tasks getting accomplished.

Sometimes a belief or assumption about what the client (not the other person) should or should not have to do is associated with the unsuccessful attempted solution. "I shouldn't have to give her a week's notice if I'm going to play golf on Sunday," Rich complains. However, when he announces his golf plans to his wife the day before, an argument follows, and usually the golf plans are cancelled. As Weiner-Davis (1992) has advised, "You don't have to like it; you just have to do it." (The reader will notice that this is essentially the same suggestion given to Erica to say to Fiona in the last example.) The case of Rich illustrates how an attempted solution can "work" on one level—that is, giving a week's notice results in Rich's wife's acceptance of his golf plans without a major conflict—but it may not be seen as a solution because of the client's belief that he or she "should not have to" do it.

Interrupting Promises of Change

When someone has repeatedly done something that a significant other is requesting that he or she change, the person who is being asked to change frequently promises to do so. This response makes sense; it demonstrates a wish to oblige, and the person who has made the request will probably express satisfaction—and stop complaining. Unfortunately, promises to change long-standing habits are notoriously hard to keep, even when those promises are made in all sincerity. All too often the well-intentioned person slips back into the old behavior, the other party seizes the opportunity to say, "See, you did it again," and the cycle of promise, relapse, criticism, and renewed promise continues.

An alternative to "I promise I'll change" is "I probably *won't* change." A very different effect is created when the client tells his or her significant other, "I know what I do is counterproductive. I wish I could tell you I'll stop it all together. But, to be brutally honest with you—and maybe most of all, with myself—I'm probably going to slip from time to time." Fisch (1992, personal communication) has suggested that the client add, "When I do, let me know, and take me with a grain of salt and ignore me."

In the following example, the therapist employed this alternative. Duane's complaint was that his friend Lisa "gets so upset" about how messy her mother keeps their house. To cheer her up, Duane says to her, "Why do you let it get to you? You know you can't control your mother." (Implication: "Don't be upset.") Duane readily acknowledged that this did not cheer Lisa up. She just softly said, "I know," turned her eyes down and away from him, and looked like she was about to cry.

Duane claimed that he was very interested in ideas about how to approach Lisa differently. The therapist and Duane talked about different things he might say to Lisa to reverse the "Don't get upset" message. The therapist roleplayed what Duane might say to Lisa: "You must get furious when your mom does that—I think I've underestimated how bad it must feel." Painstakingly Duane took notes and tried to rehearse how he would say this to Lisa. But Duane had great difficulty with that message. No matter how he tried to phrase it, he always ended his statement with a variation of "But you really shouldn't let it bother you."

Then the therapist suggested this variation: "Lisa, I know it doesn't help when I tell you not to get upset, but I think because of some of my stuff, I probably *will*. So, when I do, will you poke me in the ribs, and then ignore me?" Duane visibly relaxed. *That* he could say.

It might be noted here that promises made to oneself about eradicating bad habits are just as difficult to keep as promises made to others. Unsuccessful "You must change" messages to the self are interrupted in the same way: the client is encouraged to expect the self to slip, as well as to "warn" significant others that the slips will probably happen.

Interrupting "Please Stay"

When someone fears that a significant relationship is in jeopardy, he or she often feels desperate. The attempted solution often is a form of pleading with the partner. "I'll do *anything* so you won't leave" and "Please, please don't go" are the two main messages communicated. When these fail, as they frequently do, the more casual alternative described by Fisch (1989, personal communication) might be substituted: "I obviously don't want this to happen, but I can't say that I blame you. I'm a difficult person to live with."

As Weiner-Davis (1987) points out, people who desperately want to "save the relationship" typically chase their partners, ask a multitude of questions, and go out of their way to please the partner. The more the pursuer pursues, the more the pursued retreats. When the chaser stops chasing, the reluctant partner is more likely to take notice.

Weiner-Davis gives the following example of a woman who complained that her husband was staying out late with his buddies. The therapist asked the woman how she thought her husband would say she was handling the problem. She responded that he would say that she was constantly questioning and nagging him. The therapist asked whether the questioning seemed to be bringing him home earlier. The client acknowledged that it seemed to be having the opposite effect.

Then the therapist asked if the client might be willing to try something different, even if she felt strange about it at first. The client was interested. The therapist asked what she might do that would really surprise her husband and make him wonder what was going on with her. Her response included: going out on weekend nights with her own friends, getting some new, fashionable clothes, and not questioning his activities. Even being vague about what had happened in the therapy session would surprise him, the client predicted, because she typically told her husband everything she did. (Weiner-Davis reported that this client actually did some of these things, and that in response, her husband began to show more interest in her.)

Interrupting "You Must Decide"

Feelings of ambivalence lead many people to consult therapists. In relationships, one or both partners frequently will arrive at an impasse when struggling to decide to commit (or separate). The typical attempted solution here is: "Decide! Don't straddle the fence." When this works, this is useful advice. When it does not, a valuable alternative can be a message to remain indecisive. The therapist might point out that there is merit to making slow and careful choices rather than hasty ones (Todd, 1984). This alternative can be particularly useful for people who are dealing with difficult life situations, as will be discussed more fully in another chapter.

Parents and Children: Reversing What Doesn't Work

Problems with Children

Most parents care deeply about their children, and they experience significant distress when well-intentioned parenting efforts fail to bring the desired results. Parents frequently bend over backward to convince their children, especially older children and adolescents, that they are being "reasonable." When this does not work, an opposite response is to be unreasonable, or arbitrary. The same kind of "You don't have to like it; just do it because I said so" response mentioned in the last section can be useful in parent–child interactions.

Sometimes parents send a message that emphasizes "I'm doing this for your own good." When this does not bring the desired results, variations on an alternative suggested by Weakland (1978) might be used: "If I were a better mother, I'd probably do that—sometimes I'm not such a good mother."

Most parents endeavor to present a "united front" to their children. However, consensus about standards is sometimes difficult to achieve, and the disagreement between the parents becomes problematic, sometimes more so than the child's behavior. To reverse unsuccessful attempts at consensus, the therapist might propose that the parents "agree to disagree." Fisch (1992b) gives the following example of such an arrangement. When the child asks, "Can I?" of the parent who tends to acquiesce, that parent says, "You won't get in trouble with me, but if I were you, I'd check with your dad (mom)." When the child turns to the other parent with, "Mom (Dad) says I can," that parent says, "Well, it's not okay with me."

In such arrangements, part of the parents' agreement might be that the parent who disapproves sets and enforces the consequences. The other parent need not pretend that he or she agrees, but he or she will support the consequence in the spirit of "Well, you know your mother's (father's) rule." This kind of approach is consistent with some recent research that suggests that disagreement between parents is *not* necessarily harmful to children, especially when there is acceptance of differences (Cummings and Davies, 1994).

As parents of adolescents know all too well, statements that "you must" and "you must not" are increasingly difficult to enforce as adolescents acquire more autonomy. Certain limits may warrant enforcement at any cost, but enforcing every rule consistently would require constant surveillance, which is neither possible nor desirable. Parents sometimes wonder what alternative exists. After all, Roberta would certainly not want to interrupt "You must be home by eleven" by requiring that her son Warren stay out *past* eleven. To interrupt this kind of unsuccessful attempted solution, Roberta might say to Warren, "I'd like you to, but, to be honest, I can't make you."

Problems with Parents

Similar situations arise at times between adult children and aging parents. Again, there are times when the adult child simply must set arbitrary limits. There are also many "gray areas." For example, Martin is increasingly concerned about his father's ability to drive safely, even though his dad is not yet at the point where a doctor would prohibit all driving. When Martin tells his dad, "You really shouldn't drive anymore," his dad protests that this is "nonsense." An alternate approach might be for Martin to tell his dad, "You probably do just fine. But to help me with *my* anxiety, I'd sure appreciate it if you'd let me pick you up on Saturday."

Adult or adolescent children who are trying unsuccessfully to change their parents' minds about something can use similar approaches. Deanna, described earlier in this chapter, was trying to convince her mother that Wally was no longer a "loser." Her list of Wally's accomplishments and changes fell on deaf ears. Deanna might be encouraged to use this alternative: "You may be right—I may be making a huge mistake in trusting that Wally's changes will last. I guess only the test of time will show for sure."

Attempted Solutions to Eating Problems

When clients are concerned that they are overweight, their commonsense attempted solutions frequently involve dietary restriction. Unfortunately, many "diets" fail, and, for some people, dieting leads to anorexia or bulimia. To interrupt attempts at dietary restriction that are ineffective, the therapist may want to introduce the notion of some planned indulgence. Messages such as "Savor what you eat" and "Be sure to select something you really enjoy every day" can often interrupt messages given to oneself such as "Don't eat anything fattening" that are so hard to follow.

For clients who restrict so much that they become dangerously thin, the commonsense advice given by others is "Eat!" As in any emergency, safety comes first, and if there is truly a danger, the therapist may need to support weight maintenance, through intravenous feeding if need be. But in less severe situations, there are opportunities for alternatives to the "You must eat!" message that is met with resistance. The therapist (and/or significant others) can frequently teach the client ways of staying slender, and maintaining control, that do not result in others interfering in his or her life so much.

When purging occurs, messages such as "Don't purge" (from others) or "I must not purge" (from the self) sometimes lead to power struggles and become the unsuccessful attempted solution. Again, if there is a real medical danger, medical intervention may be needed. For many bulimics, preventing the binge (through planned indulgence, as described above) removes the need for the purge. But when purging is already regularly taking place, in spite of direct attempts to stop it, and when there does not seem to be a medical danger, an alternative to "You must not purge" might be used. This alternative involves planning the purge, as opposed to telling oneself "You must not do it." Perhaps the person could alter some small detail, or he or she could change the timing of the purge. Waiting even thirty additional seconds before throwing up can challenge the notion that "once I start, it's a pattern totally outside my control."

Sexual Solutions: Interrupting "Forced Arousal"

When sexual dysfunction is the problem, the attempted solution often involves "willing" sensations and responses to occur. Predictably, this is often ineffective; "trying too hard" and excessive self-monitoring often interfere with the relaxation and arousal that are desired. As Watzlawick et al. (1974) have pointed out, when inordinate attention to something begins to maintain a problem, deliberate inattention might be considered. Of course, it is hard to stop attending to sexual arousal when sexual arousal is what is desired. To interrupt self-talk such as "You must get and keep your erection" or "You must have an orgasm—is it happening yet?" the client can be instructed to pay attention in a different way.

As is well documented in the sex therapy literature (Kaplan, 1975; Zilbergeld, 1981), men can be instructed to deliberately lose erections, or to lose and regain them several times. Women can be encouraged to explore their genitals without creating orgasm (Barbach, 1980). In sensate focus exercises, partners can be asked to touch each other's bodies, while there is a "prohibition on intercourse" imposed by the therapist. The man who has been pressuring his wife "to enjoy sex more" can be encouraged to tell her, "The therapist thinks I'm making too big a deal out of this sex thing" (Fisch, 1990, personal communication). All of these suggestions disrupt the "trying too hard" unsuccessful attempted solution.

Recognizing Individualized Attempted Solutions

As described, certain clinical problems and life situations frequently lead to predictable attempts at resolution; therefore, it can be useful for the therapist to remain alert to the possibility that the most common responses have been tried. However, it must be emphasized that every person's response is unique, and the same response that fails for many people may succeed for this client, and vice versa. It is therefore critical to evaluate each client's attempted solutions, and their success or failure, on an individual basis. The fact that a certain response could, theoretically, be interrupted or reversed does not imply that the therapist will always or immediately choose to suggest that alternative. How to select and communicate an intervention is the subject of the following chapter.

Designing the Intervention
Validation, Compliment,
and Suggestion

The strategic solution focused therapist who is conducting therapy according to the guidelines outlined so far will ideally have information about the following things:

1. the highest priority problem, including the specifics of "how it goes," and in what way it is a problem
2. the solution, including what will be different in a variety of ways in the client's relationships and daily life
3. what "pieces of the solution," if any, are already present, and how the client created those
4. attempted solutions, including whether they have worked well enough

Now it is time to provide feedback to the client, in what is typically called the "intervention" phase of the session. The word "intervention" does not imply that there is necessarily anything forceful or intrusive (like a "surgical intervention"). Sometimes diverse words such as "input," "summary," "interpretation," "response," "homework," "feedback," or "observation" seem to be more appropriate descriptions. Lipchik (1992) suggests the term "summation"; she emphasizes the maintenance of a conversational, collaborative stance.

Whatever word is used, some input is given. Usually this occurs at the conclusion of a session, but this is a flexible guideline. As indicated, therapist input throughout the interview can create reframing. Thus intervention is not a formal, separate phase; feedback can be provided throughout the session, as part of the ongoing conversation. When input has been provided all along, what is said at the end may primarily summarize or reemphasize messages already given.

Whenever and however it is provided, input of some kind ends most sessions in strategic solution focused therapy. An intervention may be more formal and elaborated at the conclusion of a first session or during a planned termination, but even at the end of a session "in the middle" of a course of therapy, there is typically a message of some kind. That is, sessions do not usually end with "Our time is up. I'll see you next week." The implication is *not* that an open-ended conversation, cut short by the clock, will simply resume on another occasion, with input given only after extensive information is gathered. Even when the input includes the message "We need to talk about this further," there is implicit or explicit homework to notice or do something, along with some kind of observation about what has transpired.

Strategic solution focused interventions frequently include an element of surprise. Sometimes there is an unexpected "twist" to the way a client's statement is reframed; sometimes it is the homework or suggestion that may be "different," perhaps in a subtle way, from what was expected. The client ideally leaves feeling that he or she has received something. The therapist has deliberately designed that "something" to be maximally useful.

Watzlawick (1987) has made these general suggestions for intervention design. Interventions should be small, seemingly peripheral. When possible, homework should involve action (rather than words). Any suggestions should be "nondangerous" and minimal in "cost" (figuratively as well as literally) to the client. And input should be consistent with the client's principles.

The Three-Part Intervention

Interventions in strategic solution focused therapy are usually given in a three-part format that includes a *validation*, a *compliment*, and a *suggestion*. Each component is defined briefly here and will then be described in more detail.

1. *The Validation.* This section provides feedback that the therapist has heard the client's concerns and recognizes the legitimacy of the feelings and behaviors that have been described.

2. *The Compliment.* This section attempts to communicate respect and admiration for something that the client has said or done, especially in view of the situation that led the client to be in the therapist's office.

3. *The Suggestion.* This section provides some kind of "advice" or "homework." Sometimes the suggestion involves "doing"; sometimes it involves "notic-

ing." The suggestion may be specific or generic. It may involve expanding something that is working and/or changing something that is not working.

An image suggested by the BFTC staff (BFTC, 1992) captures the essence of the intervention. During the session, information is collected; in designing the intervention, the therapist "deconstructs" it, rearranging the component parts in a different way (hence the element of surprise). After doing this, the therapist "repackages it" (with "wrapping paper and a bow"—the compliment) and returns the original information to the client. The original information is returned in a different form, one which the therapist hopes will make a difference.

The "Break"

Interventions are not usually "ad-libbed," or made up just as they are spoken. This is especially true for the input given at the initial session. Near the end of the appointment time, the therapist typically asks if the client would like some feedback. The answer is almost always affirmative; after all, the client probably made the appointment for the very purpose of receiving input of some kind (unless he or she is there involuntarily, and even then the client is usually curious about the therapist's observations).

Planning what to say requires some thinking, and frequently the therapist takes a short break in order to do that thinking. At MRI and BFTC, therapists often work in teams. If colleagues are observing behind a one-way mirror, the break provides an opportunity to consult with them. Together the therapists can brainstorm and prepare the feedback that will be given.

Most therapists, of course, do not have the luxury of consulting with colleagues during the break. Some therapists choose to leave the office anyway, just as they would if consulting with colleagues. Briefly in another space, the therapist gathers his or her thoughts and usually makes some notes to guide what he or she will say.

Other therapists prefer to take the break without leaving the room. The therapist may say, "Okay, you want some feedback. I'm going to take a minute to think and (if notes have been taken) to look over my notes. You may see me writing; I think while I write. And I'll see if I can come up with something."

The break can be useful for both therapist and client. For the therapist, it provides an opportunity to detach a bit from the immediacy of the interaction. Even a short period of silence with the client still in the room provides an opportunity to prepare each of the three intervention components. The therapist tries to include a validation of some kind, asking him or herself, "What do I want to be sure to let the client know that I heard?" To create a compliment, the therapist searches for that which can be highlighted or complimented. And to design the suggestion, the therapist thinks, "In view of what I know, what 'suggestion'—or advice, or observation—seems to follow?"

For the client, the think break communicates the message that the therapist is taking the client seriously and doing some careful thinking about the situation. The pause can also create a sense of anticipation about whatever will follow. Ideas shared after a pause may be considered more thoroughly precisely because the therapist has taken the time to formulate the intervention.

In one way, a break creates a boundary between the information-gathering phase and the intervention phase of the interview. However, this does not have to be a rigid boundary, after which no further interaction is allowed. A previously conversational, collegial therapist does not become a prognosticating "expert" pronouncing words of wisdom from above. The therapist can be reflective and gentle, or crisp and precise, in accordance with the therapist's style and with the message to be conveyed.

Validating

The three-part intervention delivered after the break almost always begins with validation of the client's experience. The goal is to convey that the therapist has heard the client. "This is what I heard you say. Given those experiences you've described, your feelings and reactions make sense," are the messages the therapist hopes to communicate.

For years therapists have been taught about the importance of empathy, genuineness, and unconditional positive regard. Rogers (1961) called these variables "core conditions" for effective psychotherapy. When the client perceives that these conditions are present, a bond is established between therapist and client. This bond is often called the therapeutic alliance.

Recent research provides substantial evidence that the therapeutic alliance, as rated by client, therapist, and third party perspectives, is the best predictor of outcome (Alexander and Luborsky, 1986). *Client* perceptions of therapeutic alliance seem to be the most important factor (Miller, Hubble, and Duncan, 1995). At the same time, as Duncan (1992) points out, some of the literature on systemic approaches has de-emphasized relationship factors. Historically, as problem resolution received more attention, some systemic therapists may have in fact paid insufficient attention to the therapeutic alliance.

The therapeutic alliance may not be addressed explicitly in some descriptions of strategic and solution focused therapy, but a focus on joining with the client has always been present. Kleckner, Frank, Bland, and Amendt (1992) write:

> *We would like to suggest that one of strategic therapy's best kept secrets is its utilization of client feelings in the treatment process. It's not that strategic therapists don't deal with feelings—it's just*

that they don't talk about it with each other, write about it in the literature, or teach it to trainees.
. . . Strategic therapists use feelings to help clients reach their goals, rather than focus on them as the
main component of therapy. (p. 49)

Regardless of whether or not therapeutic alliance or relationship factors were addressed sufficiently in the earlier systemic therapy literature, the messages that the therapist is listening and that he or she believes that the client is entitled to the feelings expressed are explicit, not simply implicit, in strategic solution focused therapy. This is the essence of what the therapist wants to say: "I hear your words. I am trying to understand their unique meaning to you. I believe you. I want you to know that even though there is something you want to change about your feelings or your behavior—that is why you are here—I don't blame you for having those reactions, in light of your experiences."

How this message is presented will be tailored to fit the individual client's position and language. But however the message is given, the goal is validation of the client's experience. As Miller et al. (1995, p. 58) point out:

in contrast to what most therapists learned in graduate school, the research indicates that the major-
ity of clients do not experience empathy from the therapist as a nurturing, warm-and-fuzzy focus
on their feelings, but as discerning and thoughtful appreciation of their situation.

The validation of the intervention can interrupt the invalidation that clients so frequently receive both from the self and from others. The therapist's message "I don't blame you for feeling as you do" can reverse the "Boy-are-you-stupid" message in an extremely powerful way. Often clients relax visibly in response to this input.

For many people one important component of validation involves normalizing reactions that the client fears are dangerously pathological. Frequently clients do not realize (or they forget) that pain, anger, and confusion are normal and expectable responses in many life situations. "What you described is not abnormal or unusual. Most people react as you do," can be of great comfort to many people.

Like most other aspects of the therapy, normalization must be tailored to the individual. Some people are strongly invested in perceiving themselves as *unusual*, or out of the ordinary in some way. This view of the self may be linked to some significant past event or some exceptional characteristic. People who pride themselves on being unusual in some important way would feel insulted, not relieved, if a therapist were to imply that their reactions were "just like everyone else's." These people are likely to feel more validated by feedback that emphasizes their uniqueness: "Given the trauma you experienced, I'm not surprised that your reaction was so different from what the rest of your family described. It makes sense that you're experiencing it so much more intensely."

Complimenting

The second part of the intervention usually includes a compliment of some kind. *What* to compliment is one of the things the therapist considers during the break. Compliments may be easiest to construct when the client has indicated that pieces of the solution are already happening. The therapist may say, "I'm impressed by how much of your 'miracle' you've already created," and then continue by describing specific components of the solution that the client has just mentioned.

This kind of feedback may be particularly important when positive change has begun in the presence of significant symptomotology or external stress. Here are examples of therapist statements in this kind of situation: "I'm struck by the fact that even with the anxiety you've described, you managed to finish your report and turn it in," and "What strikes me as so remarkable is that in the midst of all that upheaval, you were able to respond to your son as you did." These statements are designed to convey the fact that change has occurred without full problem resolution, and they communicate an expectation that such change can continue.

When the client is struggling to do something that a significant other is trying to block, the compliment may emphasize the therapist's recognition of the effort required to create or maintain a change. Liz and Al both drank episodically, and not always at the same time. Both tried to participate in Alcoholics Anonymous, but they had difficulty maintaining their programs. Each had called the police on the other, and each had been in the emergency room because of alleged "spouse abuse." At different times, each moved out—and came back. On this occasion Liz had neither drunk nor hit Al during his most recent binge, and she came for an individual session. The therapist told Liz, "I'm absolutely amazed at your capacity to keep working your own program throughout all of this. It's darn tough doing that while Al is having so much trouble with his."

The compliment can focus on something that the client has mentioned in passing, when the therapist wants to highlight its importance. O'Hanlon and Weiner-Davis (1989) describe a mother who mentioned that she knew that she needed to give her daughter more freedom, but that it was difficult for her to do so. The therapist complimented the woman for her recognition that the daughter could benefit from increased independence, adding that many mothers fail to recognize their children's needs so clearly. When the client has mentioned this feature in passing, it may be particularly important to emphasize how difficult it can be for a parent to recognize and allow a child to separate. The therapist's message was, "I hear you. You see all too clearly that it is going to be hard and painful, and yet you're saying that you care enough about her that you are going to find ways to do what needs to be done." This message combined a validation and a compliment.

Similar compliments can be designed for clients who have not yet changed behaviorally but have verbalized a plan for change. "Your plan sounds realistic and well thought out." Caution and not moving too quickly can be complimented: "Many people would have rushed into action without such thorough consideration of all the variables. It takes careful planning to think things through so completely." Client elaboration of a miracle question frequently produces recognition of changes that, if implemented, would make a difference. The therapist's compliment may address that recognition: "It seems remarkable that you realize how much of a difference it will make when you talk to him as you've described today."

Sometimes the client has relapsed, and the therapist's task is to design a compliment for someone who has just said that he or she "failed," made a mistake, is feeling disappointed and angry at the self, or some combination of these things. Here, one goal is to normalize the ups and downs of the change process and to reinforce the client's capacity to tolerate and ride through relapse. "You're seeing that two steps forward, one step back is how it goes." "It really took some strength to come in here today and tell me all that."

Another goal is to enhance recognition of what created the relapse. Labeling what did not work, in a practical, matter-of-fact way, provides valuable information for problem solving and grasping control of the situation. The therapist may say, "It sounds like you know what you forgot to do," or "Well, we may not know yet what *is* going to solve this, but we do have something that's very, very important. I'm struck by how much you already know about what doesn't work for you. That information is so valuable, and I think it's going to speed up our work together, because now you and I know not to waste time on what you've already discovered doesn't work."

Some clients initially seem difficult to compliment. The person who has neither begun to implement a solution nor verbalized recognition of potential change-producing behaviors, nor acknowledged recognition of his or her role in relapse or problem maintenance obviously cannot be complimented on those particular things. Some clients seem to spend most of the session "complaining" or "blaming," even when the therapist attempts to redirect the interview. Here, the detailed description of the problem is what might be complimented. "Many people are not as observant of the details as you have been. You clearly care a lot about this situation, and you've devoted a lot of thought to describing it to me today."

Sometimes clients describe behaviors that the therapist cannot compliment, because they are so clearly destructive in some way. If the client displays *any* recognition that something he or she did was counterproductive, that recognition clearly warrants a compliment. "I'm impressed that you recognized that what you did last night got you in trouble. It takes real courage and ability to look at oneself to see that as you've been able to do."

Some clients, of course, fail to acknowledge any responsibility or recognition that their behavior was counterproductive. But if that behavior produced consequences that the client did not like, the therapist can use the relationship between behavior and consequence in feedback that is part validation and part compliment of the implicit intelligence sufficient to see the connection. "It sounds like it was a real bummer to get dragged off to jail after that stuff last week."

When there seems to be absolutely nothing to compliment, there is always one last piece to consider: the client's presence at the appointment. Unless he or she was literally dragged in, this person has kept an appointment, even one suggested or scheduled by someone else, and usually the person has participated in some manner. The therapist can always say, "I'm impressed by your willingness to be here today. I know it wasn't your idea to do this, and I'm impressed with your putting up with all my questions (or listening so thoughtfully, or whatever)."

Designing Suggestions for Customers, Complainants, and Visitors

The third component of the three-part intervention in strategic solution focused therapy is a suggestion (advice, input, feedback) of some kind. The validation and compliment components set the stage for this third and critical part. If the empathy is accurate and the compliment resonates with the client's experience, there is frequently increased receptivity to this third component. In deciding what to suggest, the therapist faces many possibilities and considers multiple variables. One important variable is the client's stance toward the therapy.

As mentioned, the "customer, complainant, visitor" categories can be useful ways of conceptualizing the client's stance. De Shazer (1988) and Miller (1991) have described some general guidelines for intervention design, guidelines that provide suggestions both about *what* to say and *how* to phrase the input.

"Customer" is the name given to the client who has gone farther than identifying a problem and complaining about it. This person has expressed a willingness to personally *do* something to effect change. Customers are candidates for behavioral "homework." If the client has described a miracle scenario, with pieces of the miracle already happening, the "customer" might be asked to continue or extend these behaviors. If the miracle has been described, but no pieces are happening yet, homework could involve occasionally "pretending" or "acting as if" pieces were beginning to occur. If a "customer" has acknowledged that an attempted solution is not working well enough, he or she might receive directions for behavior that would interrupt or reverse it.

The reader may notice that many of the interventions most frequently associated with strategic solution focused therapy and with both parent models (in this book and elsewhere) may be most appropriate for "customers." If similar suggestions are given to clients who have *not* indicated a readiness for behavioral action (or if the therapist's assessment is inaccurate, overestimating client motivation), an otherwise accurate and well-designed suggestion may not be implemented.

"Complainants" recognize and describe problems, but they typically fail to verbalize or demonstrate interest in personally doing anything to change the situation. The "complainant" stage is similar to the "contemplation" stage in the readiness to change model described by Prochaska and DiClemente (1992). Suggesting action to someone who has not expressed interest in taking action is unlikely to result in action; therefore it generally should be avoided. Since "complainants" tend to display interest in observation and description, homework is most likely to be effective when it involves those activities. "Noticing" homework, that which involves observing and recognizing instances when a problem is absent (or present, or different in some way) is well suited to "complainants."

"Visitors" are those people who have come to the appointment primarily at the request of someone else. They do not verbalize any particular problem or complaint for which they are seeking assistance. Using Prochaska and DiClemente's terminology, they are in the "precontemplation" phase of the change process. With "visitors," the therapist's task is to treat the client as one would treat a visitor in one's home. The therapist takes the role of a cordial host, who may compliment the visitor, thank him or her for paying a visit, and issue an invitation that welcomes the person to return again, if desired, in the future.

People who come to therapy appointments at the urging of someone else frequently expect to be given unsolicited advice or feedback. Frequently they have some idea about what that advice will be: a variation on the message given by the person who recommended or arranged the appointment. They are frequently less than enthusiastic about hearing more feedback of this kind. When that advice is not forthcoming, it can be a welcome surprise, producing feelings of relief, and perhaps more openness to the possibility of a future visit than the person would have anticipated.

During the course of therapy, client stances shift; visitors become complainants or customers (often for something different from the problem for which they were referred). Customers lose motivation and become complainants, and so on. How a client responded to previous therapeutic input may provide information about his or her current stance. For example, a client who verbalized motivation for behavior change but did not do the homework from the last session probably should be treated more as a complainant when the next intervention is designed.

Presenting the Suggestion: Using the Client's "Position"

As de Shazer (1985) points out, clients are always cooperating with their therapists. Client language, behavior, and style communicate how the person views both the problem and the process of change. When the therapist recognizes the client's unique way of "cooperating" (de Shazer, 1985) and paces the response accordingly, client cooperation is likely to be enhanced. The concept of "resistance" is not particularly important in strategic solution focused therapy or in either of the parent models. The task is not to manage resistance; rather, it is to discover and follow the client's idiosyncratic way of cooperating.

The therapist wants to understand how the client hopes that the therapy will be of help. Sometimes clients spontaneously volunteer this information; when they do not, a question such as "What is your hope of *how* I (this appointment, the therapy, etc.) might help?" will clarify the client's expectations. If the answer is, "Well, my friend is taking Prozac, and I hoped I could have some, too," or "I need your signature on this disability form," the therapist clearly wants to know that up front. The client who says, "I'm looking for some advice, some guidance" and the client who says, "I want you to help me understand my past" have very different belief systems about how change occurs. The therapist will want to take these views into consideration when presenting any suggestion.

Sometimes the strategic solution focused therapist faces the following situation. The suggestion he or she is considering involves changing something in the present. In the therapist's judgment, the origin of the problem is not the main thing that requires elaboration. However, the client believes strongly that understanding the origin of the problem is critical. In this situation, the therapist's attention to the client's concerns about etiology may be not only helpful but essential. If the therapist does not join with the client sufficiently in addressing his or her concern about the past, the client may never "hear" the therapist's suggestion (Duncan, 1992). With the feelings about the past validated, the client may be receptive to suggestions, including suggestions about changes in the present.

During intervention design, the therapist may believe that a certain intervention would be helpful, but he or she may not yet be sure how best to persuade the client to "try it." After all, most clients do not come to therapy expecting to be told to notice or perform some small, seemingly insignificant behavior, a frequent suggestion when pieces of the solution are present but need amplification. Nor do clients expect to be advised to discontinue or reverse commonsense measures. On the contrary, most people cling to the current attempted solution. It is as if they are thinking, "Granted, this isn't working perfectly. But if it weren't for these efforts, matters would be even worse."

To determine how to best phrase an intervention, client "position" variables can be considered. The term "position" was originally used by the MRI therapists (Fisch, Weakland, and Segal, 1982) to describe the language, literal and figurative, that the client speaks and hears. There are at least two types of "position" variables. First, there are those things that the client values culturally or occupationally (e.g., "values self-control"; "uses the scientific method"). Second, in interpersonal situations, there are client beliefs about what is "really" going on with the other person. Beliefs that the other is, at a deeper level, basically fragile, selfish, and so on will be of value in the presentation of the intervention (Quick, 1990b).

On the basis of position information, the therapist develops a plan for phrasing input in a way that is most likely to make sense to the client. The therapist will certainly want to avoid "arguing" with the client or countering cherished beliefs. On the contrary, the therapist will attempt to speak the client's language and use the client's own rationale. As Watzlawick (1987) has said, "If you want to convince someone, use their own arguments."

For example, Weakland and Fisch (1984) describe working with a man who has suffered a myocardial infarction. Because the client views himself as a "strong person," his providers are unlikely to gain his cooperation by reiterating that he has a serious medical condition and ought to take it easy. Rather, input to him might emphasize changes that "require special strength of character and self discipline." Similarly, a parent who is concerned about a child's sensitive nature might be reluctant to impose limits. However, if the therapist says, "At a deeper level, your daughter may be starved for leadership from you" (Watzlawick, 1987), the parent may be more likely to implement the therapist's suggestion.

Suggestions that appear to move away from the goal rather than toward it are frequently the most difficult for the therapist to present convincingly. When suggesting something that may seem unusual, the most straightforward rationale involves pointing out that the current, commonsense attempted solution simply is not working. For example, Rochelle wanted her husband, Darrell, to "talk to her," but when she pointed out to him that he was not using "good communication techniques," Darrell snarled and spoke even less. The therapist said to her, "Rochelle, it seems like what you're doing isn't working—otherwise you wouldn't be here, right? [Yes.] Well, from what you've described about Darrell, it seems like as long as you keep doing what you're doing, you're going to keep getting what you're getting. Are you willing to experiment with something different?"

When the suggestion involves deliberate continuation of the unwanted behavior, the therapist might present it in terms of gathering baseline data. "All the things that everyone has suggested are 'muddying the water,' so to speak, so that we don't really have a good idea of how Robbie's tantrums would go if you just left them alone. So, before we try anything new, maybe you should just watch the tantrums for a week, not doing anything in particular, so you can get a real clear picture of them."

Sometimes the therapist may want to recommend deliberate magnification (not just continuation) of certain unwanted behaviors. As noted, the intent of this suggestion would be to interrupt "trying too hard" to eliminate the behavior. A rationale for this kind of task can involve increasing one's sense of control over the behavior (Fisch, 1989, personal communication). "Do you think you can begin to grasp control of your anxiety by prolonging the sensations by ten seconds?"

In many "anger" or relationship problems, the goal is to interrupt the client's physical or verbal attacks. How can the therapist motivate an angry, vengeful person to cool down? Encouragement to "express your feelings in words" is too easily "shined on." Pointing out consequences, however, may grab the client's attention. If the therapist says, "I think you're missing an awfully good opportunity to tell him where to get off," the client may be quite interested.

Wilbur put his fist through a wall after his girlfriend taunted him for his poor grammar.

Therapist:	I'm afraid you let her win that one, Wilbur.
Wilbur:	What do you mean, let her win?
Therapist:	Well, sounds to me like she needs to be told in no uncertain terms to cut it out when she pulls that stuff.
Wilbur:	Damn right.
Therapist:	Problem is, when you messed up the wall, suddenly she's off on a tangent about your "anger problem." She's the poor little victim, looks lily white; you're the ogre, the bad guy. And the point you wanted to make in the first place—that she's got no business talking to you like that, *ever*, is totally gone.

After that interchange, Wilbur may be much more interested in the therapist's ideas about some different ways of responding to his girlfriend's taunts.

Some clients emphasize to the therapist that they "know about therapy," either in general, or about this therapeutic approach in particular. Watzlawick (1991) described a client who challenged, "I know all the tricks—can you still help me?" Watzlawick's response was, "That's marvelous; then I won't need to explain why I'm suggesting this."

Suggestions, Specific and "Generic"

Specific Suggestions

The suggestion component of the three-part intervention can be either specific or generic. A specific suggestion is usually preferable, if the therapist is clear about what behavior might be expanded or interrupted. Ideas for specific suggestions sometimes emerge quite clearly and naturally from the discussion.

For example, during scaling question inquiry, Janice said that she was at a "three." How had she arrived at a "three"? By telling her roommate to turn the TV off while she was doing her homework (instead of suffering and fuming silently), she said. How would Janice know that she was at a "four"? When she did that again tonight, she said. Constructing a suggestion for Janice was straight-forward: she could be encouraged to do exactly what she herself had described. In addition, the compliment leading up to the suggestion could highlight both Janice's discovery of something that made a difference and her recognition that continuing that behavior would continue the process.

The therapist said, "Janice, I'm impressed by your figuring out on your own that asking your roommate to turn down the TV would make a difference. And you were obviously able to say it in a way that she did it. And I'm further im-pressed that you realize that asking her to do it isn't just a one-time thing, and when it happens again, you can do more of what you did last night. So, my sug-gestion to you is that when the TV is on tonight and you're trying to do your math, that you do more of what you already know works for you, and notice how that makes a difference."

Specific suggestions that interrupt unsuccessful attempted solutions some-times are easy to design. For example, Carlos, who had been rejected by his girl-friend, Darlene, was telling himself, "Don't think about her." As one might ex-pect, this suggestion to himself was not working. The opposite of "Don't think about her" is fairly easy to articulate: "*Do* think about her." In presenting this suggestion, the therapist validated and normalized Carlos's feelings, compliment-ed Carlos on his capacity for caring, and presented the suggestion with a ratio-nale emphasizing the fact that since "Don't think about her" was not working, Carlos might want to try something else. "I don't blame you for feeling sadness. Darlene's leaving you is a shock, and it's a tremendous loss. Obviously you're a person who has the capacity to care very deeply, and I'm not surprised that you can't just push the feelings away. It's like if I say, '*Don't* think about Mickey Mouse. *Don't* see the shape of his ears. *Don't* think of the name of the theme park where he lives. And, whatever you do, *don't* think of the name of his girlfriend.' It all pops right into your head.[1] So, when the thought of Darlene comes into your head, I'm going to suggest that you look at your watch, and take a full three min-utes to think about her, as deeply as you can, and to give the thoughts all the time and respect they deserve."

Generic Suggestions

By the end of the session, when the therapist would like to provide feedback of some kind, it is not always clear what specific suggestion would be most rele-

[1]The Mickey Mouse analogy was originally described by Miller (1991).

vant. And some clients stay so vague that the specifics are *never* fully elaborated. In this situation, general or "generic" suggestions can be extremely useful. As mentioned, the generic suggestion is like the skeleton key that can open many doors. It is so powerful because it fits individual situations and at the same time is so general that it can be used when the problem and/or goal are unclear (de Shazer, 1985).

Amplifying solutions Sometimes the client has acknowledged that the intensity of the problem shifts over time. Here, the therapist can assign homework that involves "tracking times that the problem is absent (or less intense)." For clients who are facing difficult life situations, Molnar and de Shazer (1987) suggest this variation: "The situation is complicated and troublesome. Identify how you keep it from getting worse."

Another useful generic suggestion is what de Shazer (1985, p. 137) has described as the "first session formula task": "Between now and next time, observe, so you can describe to me, what happens in your life (family, relationship, etc.) that you want to continue to have happen." O'Hanlon and Weiner-Davis (1989) point out that clients frequently respond to this task by making precisely the changes needed to solve the problem. This occurs despite the fact that the task does not ask the client to change anything.

When there is a goal or a vision of a solution, even a vaguely defined one, the client can be asked to attend to those times when pieces of the solution are present. O'Hanlon and Weiner-Davis (1989) describe a man who wants "peace of mind." The therapist suggests that the man keep track of what he does that brings peace of mind. As O'Hanlon and Weiner-Davis point out, this suggestion implies three important things: (1) that there *will* be times when "peace of mind" is present; (2) that things the client does will contribute to the feeling; and (3) that the client can notice and describe those things.

Sometimes the client can describe a miracle scenario or desired end point, but he or she has not yet noticed any times when the desired state is present, even in a small way. In this situation, the client can be asked to "pretend" (Miller, 1991) or act "as if" (Watzlawick, 1987) some parts of the solution are already happening. As Watzlawick has pointed out, as long ago as the time of Blaise Pascal it has been recognized that change could occur through this process. Pascal examined the question of how a "nonbeliever" could attain faith. He suggested that nonbelievers act as if they already believed (by praying, etc.). The German philosopher Hans Vaihinger discussed similar ideas much later, in *The Philosophy of "As If"* (Vaihinger, 1924). It is interesting that these thinkers may have presented the suggestion much as present day strategic solution focused therapists do. Reportedly Pascal presented his suggestion to the nonbeliever in the spirit of "What do you have to lose?"

Do something different   Sometimes it is clear that the current attempted solution is not working, but it is far less obvious what alternative might be more successful. This situation arises when there has not been sufficient time to fully explore the situation; it also arises when the client's style is vague. Just as precise, clearly defined problems often call for equally precise suggestions, vague problems, vague goals, and vague attempted solutions fit quite nicely with generic suggestions.

When something different but still undefined is needed, the "skeleton key" suggestion is to "Do something different." The therapist does not tell the client *what* the "something different" should be; rather, he or she trusts that the client will recognize where and how the change should occur. As de Shazer (1985, p. 136) writes:

> *These interventions are minimally intrusive, and yet their impact seems inordinately large. The ripple effect . . . gives us some notions about how a small difference can become a big enough difference.*

The "Do something different" suggestion can be introduced through a metaphor or story. The following is a variation of a story described by de Shazer (1985) and elaborated by Pinter (1991, personal communication): "Once there were some parents whose son was having temper tantrums. They came to see a therapist, and the therapist told the parents, 'The next time your son has a temper tantrum, I want each of you to do something different. I won't tell you *what* it is—that's up to you.' So the next time the boy had a temper tantrum around Mom, she wasn't sure what to do, but she sang a little song. The next time the boy had a temper tantrum around Dad, he gave his son a dime. And, you know, the boy stopped having temper tantrums. The moral of the story is: it may not matter a whole lot *what* you do, as long as you do something different."

A generic suggestion that O'Hanlon and Weiner-Davis (1989) call "the surprise task" is a variation on the "Do something different" theme. Especially useful for relationship problems, this task suggests that the client do something that will surprise his or her partner (parents, child, etc.). When both members of a dyad are present in the session, both can be encouraged to do something surprising, unpredictable, or out of character. In addition, each can be asked to do the "something different" "secretly," without announcing to the other what behavior has been chosen. As part of the homework, or in a follow-up session, each person might be encouraged to "guess" what the other person has chosen. This variation on "Do something different" has a light, playful quality.

Deliberate performance of the problem   Suggestions that encourage the client to deliberately perform the complaint have been mentioned previously. These suggestions simultaneously facilitate the collection of baseline data and interrupt unsuccessful attempts to discontinue something. Such suggestions are "generic" when the therapist knows that the problem-solving behavior is ineffective, but the nature of the ineffective behavior is not yet clear. Requesting that the client observe and label what is *not* working can bring those behaviors into sharper focus. O'Hanlon (O'Hanlon and Weiner-Davis, 1989) describes asking a client who complained of a weight problem to teach him how to gain weight, because he had been so skinny all his life. Even if the client cannot immediately articulate a "weight gain plan," homework to notice how "not to stick to a diet" often reveals that severe restriction early in the day followed by hunger pangs and bingeing will reliably lead to overeating. In the same way, the therapist can suggest that the client search for information about how to "create a relapse" in any area. The therapist might emphasize that this is *not* a suggestion to *actually* relapse. Rather, the aim is to gain information about what will make things worse, since knowing that often provides invaluable information on how to create the opposite effect.

The "split team" approach   Sometimes a client is experiencing a dilemma or seeking "advice" (e.g., "Should I let my son live with me or make him stay with his mother?"), and the therapist wants to communicate the message that there is no single "right" answer. On the contrary, any of a variety of paths might lead to a solution. Here, the therapist might want to use an approach derived from work behind the one-way mirror.

Any clinician who has heard the interchange among therapists behind an actual one-way mirror (or during any discussion of clinical material, for that matter) knows that disagreement among therapists is common. That disagreement can be utilized in the intervention. The therapist might say something like, "Your situation certainly generated a lot of discussion among my colleagues. Several of them suggested that I encourage you to vigorously pursue what you have already begun. A few others had some reservations—they thought you were moving a bit too fast. They said that you ought to think about your alternatives a little more before taking any irreversible action. One person even wondered if it made any difference which path you chose! As for me, I'm frankly not sure, so I decided to just give you the input from all of them."

There is a variation on this approach that can be used when no team of colleagues is observing the session, (as is the case for most therapists most of the time). The therapist can tell the client, "If this window (wall, etc.) were a one-way mirror, and a team of my colleagues were behind it and observing us today, I suspect that one would say X, and another Y . . . ." This message conveys the legitimacy of multiple points of view, and it normalizes ambivalence (on the part of both therapist and client). In doing so, the message provides an important kind of "permission" for the client to select the suggestion that best fits with his or her world view.

Frequently clients present dilemmas involving continuing versus ending personal relationships. When there is uncertainty about the status of a relationship, the dilemma may involve "waiting" versus "moving on." A variation of the split team approach for this situation suggested by Miller (1992a) goes like this: "One part of me (or one of my colleagues) thinks you should wait for him to come back. At the same time, another part thinks you should get on with your life. And another little part thinks there might be some third alternative that neither of us has thought of yet."

Sometimes the therapist has a tentative idea about an intervention but is unsure how it would be received and/or how it would work. In that case, the therapist may want to maintain maneuverability by presenting it with some reservations. The therapist may also want to distance himself or herself from a particular idea, in order to better present a different position at another time. In this case, the therapist might say, "I have a thought about what one of my colleagues (teachers, the author of a book I'm reading, etc.) would say to you about this. Frankly, it doesn't totally make sense to me, but I'll tell you anyway. My colleague would say you'll understand."

Ethics and Humility in Intervention Design

As Cade and O'Hanlon (1993) have pointed out, interventions that have been deliberately designed and delivered sometimes are criticized for being inappropriately manipulative. "Paradoxical interventions" that appear to move the client away from the goal rather than toward it have been the targets of additional criticism. This author agrees with Weeks and L'Abate (1982, in Cade and O'Hanlon, 1993) that the therapist has an ethical responsibility *not* to use a technique, paradoxical or otherwise, as a gimmick or out of frustration when the therapist feels stuck or the client seems uncooperative. Weeks and L'Abate have also pointed out that, at the time they were writing, they knew of no evidence that paradoxical techniques had caused client deterioration. The worst result they knew of was that the desired change had not occurred.

Cade and O'Hanlon write about "paradox reconsidered: empathy, not trickery." As they point out,

> *Ambivalence can be seen as the concurrent existence of opposing arguments and constructs. . . . When the therapist becomes too clearly identified with the arguments in favor of change, it is as though . . . [the therapist] leaves available to the client . . . only the counter arguments (or the "yes, buts") to that change.*
>
> *Conversely, when the therapist identifies with and validates the arguments in favor of caution or against change . . . [clients] are then left with the ownership of the counter arguments (or the "yes, buts") to those cautions [i.e., in favor of change].*
>
> *It is our view that what have previously been termed paradoxical strategies have the effect of empowering clients through the process of acknowledging their perfectly valid cautious, more fearful concerns about change and leaving them to operate out of their own arguments as to why change should be attempted. (Cade and O'Hanlon, 1993, pp. 155–157)*

All guidelines for intervention design notwithstanding, therapists can benefit from remaining respectful of clients' ability to soundly reject interventions when, for whatever reason, they do not fit the person or the situation. Papp (1984, p. 25, in O'Hanlon and Weiner-Davis, 1989) reminds therapists that "sometimes clients turn our most mundane interventions into transcendental experiences . . . while at other times, they remain totally impervious to our strokes of genius." Remembering this can help therapists to stay appropriately humble.

Therapist Decisions
Clarifying, Amplifying, or Interrupting

Clarifying the problem, amplifying what works, and interrupting what does not are all important parts of strategic solution focused therapy. However, the therapist cannot do all three (or any two of the three) simultaneously, and throughout every session, the therapist usually has some awareness of which component he or she is emphasizing. Along with that awareness, there is often a kind of self-monitoring, as the therapist assesses whether this component seems to be the "right" one to be stressing at this moment. This chapter discusses how the therapist decides which piece of the model to emphasize and when to shift the focus.

One way of looking at this issue involves considering which component will bring the optimal amount of "novelty" into the therapy for this person at this time. As Budman, Hoyt, and Friedman (1992) point out, the introduction of novelty seems to be an important variable in therapy, especially brief therapy. The aim is to introduce something new, something different from the typical pattern, but not so discrepant from the client's world view that it will be rejected. As described, clarification of the problem, amplification of the solution, and interruption of the unsuccessful attempted solution all involve reframing, and all can introduce a novel and useful perspective. Deciding which kind of novelty to pursue becomes easier when the therapist considers some guidelines.

Within the structure of the model, a certain order is implicit: first comes problem clarification; then there is solution amplification, followed by assessment of attempted solutions; finally, there is intervention design. What is highly variable between clients is when to shift to the next phase. For example, the therapist could spend most of the session clarifying the problem—and with certain clients, he or she might do just that. With other clients, the same therapist might shift to solution elaboration after just a few minutes of problem clarification. The question is how the therapist determines when the complaint (or the miracle scenario, or the attempted solution) has been elaborated sufficiently.

Perhaps an even more important question involves the decision making in intervention design. The principles "If it works, do more of it; if it doesn't work, do something different" have been repeated many times. But exactly how does the strategic solution focused therapist decide when to amplify behavior and when to interrupt it? In most situations, there are both pieces that are "working" and pieces that are not. The *solution focused* therapist would probably reason that expanding existing solutions should take priority, while the *strategic* therapist would tend to see interrupting unsuccessful solutions as more important. The strategic solution focused therapist, in contrast, typically sees both components as equally important. Which to emphasize in a particular case depends on the specifics of the situation.

General Guidelines

Speak So the Client Will Hear

As emphasized in the discussion of client position in the previous chapter, one central guideline involves recognizing and resonating with the client's language, style, and beliefs about how change occurs. Friedman (1993) writes, "We must be ready to connect with clients at their points of readiness and to flexibly shift gears as the conversational process requires." As Friedman points out, therapy does not always proceed as planned. He makes a plea for therapy models that integrate approaches and articulate clearly what works with whom.

While it is often impossible to specify exactly what will work with clients, it is much easier to articulate what is likely to fail. Ignoring or violating position variables and proceeding with *any* invariant sequence increases the likelihood that the therapy will be ineffective. That means that all guidelines, *including those presented throughout this book*, must be applied flexibly. In a larger sense, flexible application of guidelines is a principle in itself.

Do What Works

The principle "If it works, do more of it; if it doesn't work, do something different" clearly applies to the strategic solution focused therapist as he or she proceeds with the work. If an approach is "working," the therapist will probably want to continue it; if it is not, he or she will want to shift to something different. This principle, or "rule," can point toward answers to the questions sometimes posed by the beginning strategic solution focused therapist, who may see the different stages of the model as potentially contradictory. The therapist new to the model may ask, "When do I compliment my client and encourage continuing solutions that have begun, and when do I caution against moving too quickly?" "When do I elicit precise definition of the complaint and how it is a problem, as opposed to de-emphasizing problem talk and creating a vision of the solution?"

The answer is: the therapist's choice is based on "what works." For example, if there have been unsuccessful attempts at encouragement, a "go slow" approach may be most appropriate. If, on the other hand, there has not been much encouragement given, or if there has been encouragement, and the client seems to have responded positively to it, a more positive message might be given. Shifting approaches will be addressed in more detail later in this chapter.

Other "Rules"

The reader might appropriately ask whether "rules" above and beyond "doing what works and changing what does not" can be articulated. The answer is "yes." As Gingerich and de Shazer (1991) have pointed out, therapists do seem to follow rules in their clinical decision making, and those rules can be articulated. It is neither necessary nor efficient to "make it up from scratch" in every clinical interaction.

De Shazer (1988) considers the question of how the therapist selects a task from "the set of all known tasks." This is where "rules" come into play. That is, guidelines that fit one situation frequently apply in other situations that are similar in some way. Some maps or algorithms have been constructed; for example, "If the client does X, consider Y." Like a musical theme with many variations, the idea may be articulated in different ways. It will need to be tailored to fit, but the theme can be selected on the basis of a set of rules (de Shazer, 1988).

One set of rules proposed by de Shazer considers the following variables: (1) what *is* working; (2) what *has* worked; (3) what *might* work; and (4) of these, prescribe the easiest (de Shazer, 1988). This way of thinking leads to the next guideline.

Straightforward Approaches First

There is a saying that one should not "use a sledgehammer to kill a fly when a fly swatter will do the job." This principle clearly applies to strategic solution focused therapy, becoming one of its "rules." All other things being equal, the most straightforward approach should be used first. As Zimmerman and Protinsky

(1990) point out in a discussion of "strategic parenting," a person typically first treats a headache with a nap or some aspirin. One goes to the doctor for a headache only if the first approaches have proven ineffective. Similarly, the therapist will determine whether straightforward, commonsense remedies (such as directly requesting what one wants) have been tried. The straightforward approach usually should be applied before anything more elaborate is suggested.

Another way of "doing the most straightforward thing first" involves conducting therapy in accordance with the steps in the model. That is, the therapist begins with the working assumption that a highest priority problem will be clarified, that a solution scenario will be elaborated, and so forth. At times, one or more of the elements will not proceed as planned, and the therapist will be prepared to shift to another mode, but creative modification of the model will seldom be the initial approach. Rather, the therapist invests some effort in eliciting the desired information, in the order described by the model.

If It Doesn't Work, Do Something Different

Straightforward approaches to problem resolution are often insufficient. As mentioned previously, if the commonsense approach to solving the client's problem usually worked well enough, and if there were no obstacles to applying it, most people would have no reason to consult psychotherapists. And if any single, fixed approach to the *therapist's* task (i.e., facilitating client problem resolution) were consistently effective, there would be no need for this chapter (or for much of the psychotherapy literature, for that matter).

It is precisely because matters do not always proceed as planned that the therapist needs to maintain maneuverability, a construct emphasized by Fisch, Weakland, and Segal (1982, p. 22): "A therapist needs to keep . . . options open as therapy progresses, shifting as needed during the course of treatment." These authors discuss the importance of recognizing small but definite indicators that something is not working. That is, the therapist shift does not need to wait for strong, obvious evidence of client displeasure or lack of progress. In what Fisch et al. call a "U-turn," the therapist may adopt a stance that is very different from that previously taken or implied. Sometimes a U-turn is introduced by the therapist's acknowledgment, from what the authors call a "one-down position," that he or she has missed something important.

The therapist may also state the obvious (and the theory): "It looks like what we're doing so far isn't working. I think we'd better do something different." In a description of a client who reports at a second session that things have not improved, de Shazer points out that the therapist needs to do something different from what was done in the first session, "because continuing to approach things in the same way is just more of the same of something that is not working, which is the exact definition of a problem" (de Shazer, 1994, p. 189).

There are a number of variables the therapist can shift. Some are superficially unrelated to the substance of the therapy (e.g., which office or what seating arrangement is used, time of day of the appointment, whether or not the session is recorded). Changing these variables sometimes makes a difference, perhaps simply because it metaphorically communicates the message "We must do something different," and perhaps for some other reason.

Tomm (1984) points out that the therapist can expand the field of observation by evaluating other members of the client's system. If this is an individual problem, the therapist might meet with the partner alone or conjointly with the client. Conversely, with a case that begins as "family therapy," the therapist might meet with individuals or subsets of the system as well. The "therapist team" can also be expanded or changed. This occurs when a case is discussed with colleagues, when a consultant gives an opinion, or when a different therapist is called in. All of these changes represent doing something different, something which may or may not appear to be related to the problem or the solution.

When "nothing is happening" in a session, Lipchik (1992) recommends that the therapist ask not only him- or herself but also the client what might be more useful. Lipchik describes saying to a client, "What we are doing here does not seem to be helpful to you. What would be helpful to you at this time?" She also shares a question suggested by Kubicki: "What is the question you would most like me to ask, or would be most helpful for me to ask you at this point?" (Lipchik, 1992, p. 70).

Storm (1991) discusses "change and stability signals" that clients communicate, and she recommends matching the intervention with the client's apparent need for one or the other. The parts of this model that involve directives, reframes, creating solution scenarios, and acting "as if" the solution were already occurring will emphasize change, while therapist input that highlights the risks of improving or prescribes continuation of the complaint will contribute to the maintenance of the status quo, or stability.

As Lipchik (1992) points out, the therapist needs to recognize and balance change and stability needs. Most people want to change; at the same time, they want things to stay the same. It is not as if one client is a "changer" and another a "nonchanger"; people are ambivalent, experiencing both wishes, simultaneously or one after the other. In fact, the urge for increased stability often follows a change spurt, and vice versa. Remaining sensitive to where the client is in his or her individual "change–stability cycle" can help the therapist to determine which component of the model to emphasize at a particular point in treatment.

Breaking the Rules

To emphasize the critical importance of therapist flexibility, an additional guideline is postulated: "All rules can be broken, at the therapist's discretion." As de Shazer (1988) has pointed out, psychotherapy can be seen as part science and part art; it may be best described as a "craft." Miller (1994) writes that many therapy approaches are initially described (by the originators and/or enthusiastic followers) as *the* model, as if its rules and results were superior to all those that came before. Over time, the similarities of apparently different approaches have become increasingly evident. Distinguished, pathfinding therapists including Freud and Erickson broke the rules (de Shazer, 1988). The craft of psychotherapy frequently involves combining approaches and selecting components tailored to fit the situation, breaking the rules when necessary.

When Problem Clarification Doesn't Clarify

In the spirit of doing the most straightforward thing first and starting at the beginning, most strategic solution focused therapy begins with problem clarification. As described extensively in Chapter 2, the therapist wants to know the nature of the highest priority complaint, the details of the problem, in interactional terms if possible, and how this situation is a problem. With careful inquiry, many initially complex situations can be clarified.

It is often apparent when problem clarification inquiry is working. The client breathes a sigh of relief and understanding when encouraged to "leave other problems on a back burner." He or she nods and smiles, joining with the therapist and collaborating in the elucidation of detailed description and dialogue. When the therapist asks, "What are you sad about?", the client answers specifically. In response to therapist prompting, initially vague uneasiness is transformed into understandable sadness about something that occurred. Or inquiry about how this is a problem elicits an important realization (or insight). Here, problem clarification and the associated reframing are making a difference, and the therapist will want to allow and encourage all the time and elaboration that the client can effectively use.

Some clients have much more difficulty with problem clarification. Unable to specify just what they are distressed about, they remain vague, even in the face of the therapist's inquiry. Here is an example of an interchange where attempts at problem clarification are neither providing much information nor leading to significant reframing.

Therapist:	What's the trouble?
Roger:	Depression. A very deep and dark depression.
Therapist:	What are you sad about?
Roger:	I don't know. I'm just depressed.

Therapist:	This depression you describe, have you noticed that it varies in intensity, that sometimes it's deeper and sometimes it's less deep?
Roger:	No, not really. It's there all the time.
Therapist:	You said "all the time." That means, since when?
Roger:	All my life, I think. I feel like I've been depressed forever.
Therapist:	You called for this appointment yesterday, and I'm thinking, there's always a reason you pick up the phone the day you do. So, you called yesterday for an appointment for a depression you've been experiencing for a very long time. What changed yesterday, that you decided to call?
Roger:	Nothing, really. I just decided to call.
Therapist:	This might seem like a strange question, but I want to understand your depression more deeply, and I'm wondering how this depression is a problem to you.
Roger:	I just don't like it. It's like a gray cloud, hanging over me all the time.
Therapist:	Your depression, like a gray cloud, does it interfere in your functioning, the stuff you have to do every day, in any way?
Roger:	No, not really. I just don't like it being there, my feeling so heavy, so down.
Therapist:	What's your hope about how I might be able to help you with this depression?
Roger:	Maybe you can help me figure out what I'm depressed about.

In response to statements similar to Roger's last comment, Fisch (1993, personal communication) has suggested the following response: "I appreciate your faith in my omniscience, but I'm afraid I've never been terribly good at figuring out what someone else is depressed about." But regardless of just how the therapist responds, it is apparent by this point in the interview that standard attempts at problem clarification are unlikely to work with Roger.

Other clients have difficulty narrowing in on a single complaint that distresses them most. Even when the therapist encourages prioritizing, the client cannot or will not do so. The issues are just too intertwined, the client claims; the many facets of the problem cannot be separated from one another. Here, if the therapist persists too long in encouraging the labeling of a single problem to address first, he or she may be doing more of something that does not work.

In these situations, a shift away from the problem clarification phase of inquiry is indicated. The nature of the complaint is not yet clear, but continuing to pursue it in the same way is unlikely to make it any clearer, and it may irritate the client and diminish his or her capacity to join with the therapist and to participate in other phases of the therapy later on.

In general, when attempts at problem clarification fail to clarify the problem, the strategic solution focused therapist will shift the focus to elaboration of the solution. The therapist may ask the miracle question or one of its many variations. As described in detail in Chapter 3, this inquiry is designed to elicit description of a scenario where the complaint is resolved, where the problem is less distressing, for whatever reason, or where the client is "on track" to a solution. Some clients who have struggled to articulate a complaint now relax and allow themselves to "spin a fantasy." As miracle questioning pursues what will be different in daily interactions and behaviors, and as the description becomes more concrete, the therapist may find an opportunity to identify "pieces of the miracle that are already happening" or that are within reach.

When the client has difficulty specifying which of several complaints is most central, the construction of multiple solution scenarios sometimes helps to clarify this. The "feedback loop" from miracle question elaboration back to problem clarification has been previously mentioned in Chapter 3. For example, John was concerned both about his work and about his girlfriend. Therapist inquiry about which concern was most distressing was not particularly helpful; John emphasized that he really was seeking therapy for both problems. He said that he understood the therapist's concern that they could not solve both problems simultaneously, but he really could not decide which they should address first.

In order to look at this from a different perspective, the therapist suggested that John elaborate two scenarios: one where the work problem was resolving but the relationship issue was unchanged, and one where the relationship problem was resolving but the work issue was unchanged. This John could do, and after describing both, he said that he now knew that he wanted to address the relationship problem first. While elaborating the solutions, he realized that the work issue was actually a long-standing dilemma, but that an incident with his girlfriend had prompted his calling for the appointment. John had not remembered this fact during the earlier discussion of the problem, even in response to a question about what led to his coming in now.

Another variation in procedure that can be used when the client has difficulty clarifying the complaint involves scaling question inquiry. Scaling questions, such as "On a zero to ten scale, where zero is when the problem was at its worst and ten is where it's solved to your satisfaction, where are you now?" are typically used later in the sequence, after a solution has been elaborated and the client has been asked if any pieces of that solution are already happening. That placement is generally used because it highlights any emerging sense of confidence; by that point in the interview, many clients realize that they have already begun the process of change. However, as de Shazer (1994) has pointed out, scaling questions can also be used much earlier in a session. This earlier placement can be particularly useful when the client is vague. Even if the problem is no more specific than "uneasiness," "anxiety about everything," or "low self-esteem," many clients can "give it a number."

This procedure might be used with Roger, the client described earlier in this section who was depressed but could not specify what he was sad about. The therapist might say, "Roger, I'm going to ask you to give your depression a number on this scale, where zero is when the depression was at its very deepest and darkest (the therapist is using Roger's words here) and ten is when it's solved and not a problem for you." Even if Roger's number is "zero," his acceptance of the task introduces the idea of a continuum, where a "one" is the next step for him. And if his number is higher than zero, there is an opportunity for inquiry about how Roger arrived at that level.

When Solution Amplification Doesn't Create Solutions

Client Variables

Sometimes shifting to solution amplification before the problem is fully clarified is extremely useful. On other occasions, however, the therapist's attempts at solution elaboration (with or without having clarified the problem) are unsuccessful, and at times they can become counterproductive. Some clients simply cannot fill in the details of the solution picture. Sometimes these are the same people who cannot describe the problem either.

For example, Rosemary's problem was "depression," never well clarified. Her response to the miracle question was "I'll be happy." Carefully the therapist attempted to identify how that happiness would show in her behavior and appearance. There was inquiry about who in Rosemary's life would notice that she was different. Rosemary could not say. "I'll just feel better," she said.

If a problem can be referred to as "being at a one" without the therapist knowing exactly to what "one" refers, then the beginnings of a solution can be described as "being at a two." Rather than persisting with inquiry about the details of the solution, the therapist may want to speak the client's more global language. When the therapist encourages "noticing how you do it when you move to a two," the implication is that even if the therapist cannot describe what the emerging solution will be like, the client will somehow know that he or she is moving in the right direction.

Other clients can describe the problem in great detail, but when asked about the solution, the response is markedly different. These people say that they simply cannot imagine problem resolution. Even when the inquiry shifts to encouraging visualization of a time when "things are just a little better" or "this therapy is beginning to help in the smallest way," these clients draw a blank. Sometimes this occurs when the client holds certain beliefs about therapy.

The therapist may believe that the problem has been described in sufficient detail and that it is now time to move to solution talk, but the client may not be equally ready. He or she may have come to talk and reflect about the problem, including its antecedents in the past, in thorough detail. There may be an expectation that this kind of elaboration will proceed slowly and continue during a number of sessions, and only after that will solutions begin to be considered. The therapist's introduction of the miracle question or other inquiry about the solution is experienced as jarring and premature.

A client who responded negatively to the therapist's attempts at solution elaboration is described by Nylund and Corsiglia (1994). This woman had been molested and believed that the anxiety and depression she was experiencing were related to the sexual abuse. When the therapist began asking future-oriented questions, the client found it difficult to answer. She left the appointment abruptly, and several days later she called to request an appointment with a different therapist. She said that she felt that the therapist had minimized her pain and had not allowed her to talk about what she found important. Subsequently she saw another therapist, who gave her time to talk more extensively about the details of her abuse before introducing possible solutions. The therapist complimented the client for knowing what she wanted, and eventually the woman was able to con-sider exceptions to the problem.

Clients such as the woman described above are not necessarily in crisis; their expectations about what one discusses in therapy are the primary obstacle to participating in solution elaboration when it is first introduced. Other clients have difficulty envisioning a solution because they are feeling overwhelmed in response to some immediate life situation. Lipchik (1994) describes a situation involving a woman whose boyfriend had left her. The client was tearful and wanted the boyfriend to return. When the therapist asked the miracle question, the only miracle the client would consider involved her boyfriend coming back. The therapist asked if there were any times now that she did not feel grief. "Never," the client answered. Next the therapist asked the client to imagine what would be different when she began to feel better. The client looked at the therapist uncomprehendingly and began to cry even harder. She never returned to the therapist. As Lipchik points out, out of zeal to apply the technique, the therapist had overlooked a basic requirement of any therapy: to join with the client.

This problem may occur somewhat more frequently in solution focused therapy than in strategic solution focused therapy, because in the former, solution elaboration frequently begins even earlier in the sequence, with minimal discussion of the problem. As Nylund and Corsiglia (1994) and Lipchik (1994) point out, some beginning solution focused therapists become so "problem phobic" that they erroneously believe that solution focused therapy should not address the problem at all. This is somewhat less of an issue in strategic solution focused therapy, where problem clarification is an important phase that has usually preceded any attempt at solution elaboration. However, it arises here as well, especially if the therapist overemphasizes procedure and fails to tailor the therapy to the needs of the individual client.

When the Miracle Is the Unsuccessful Attempted Solution

When a solution scenario has been well elaborated, sometimes the strategic solution focused therapist will consider a suggestion to act "as if" pieces of the miracle were already happening. However, sometimes the following occurs. The scenario developed during solution amplification is detailed, and it is described with enthusiasm. However, its content is essentially identical to something that the client has already been encouraging the self to do. This fact may or may not emerge overtly during inquiry about attempted solutions. For example, the anxious person describes a "miracle" where the anxiety has been eliminated. Or the person experiencing ambivalence describes a time where the choice is crystal clear. In such cases, "pieces of the miracle" are usually not present.

In this kind of situation, the client's message to the self to "eliminate anxiety" or to "make your decision" is the attempted solution, and it is basically an unsuccessful one. To encourage the client to pretend that "pieces of the miracle were already happening" would be to continue the application of something that is ineffective. Therefore the therapist will generally want to avoid "assigning the solution." Instead, it will probably be more helpful to develop an intervention that will encourage behavior different from that described in the miracle scenario. Interrupting the unsuccessful attempted solution may involve doing the opposite of what solution elaboration would suggest.

Sheila was self-conscious about being "shy." She felt this most intensely around her boyfriend's large extended family. She felt that everyone else could tell jokes and banter, while she could never think of much to say. In response to the miracle question, Sheila described in great detail a scenario where she was witty and outgoing. When asked if any parts of her miracle were already happening, Sheila sighed and said, "No." She spontaneously volunteered her attempted solution: "Every time I go out, I tell myself: 'Tonight you'll be funny.' I think of all these great things I'm going to say." This was not working; Sheila never succeeded in doing what she had planned.

If the intervention presented to Sheila were to emphasize speaking as she described in her miracle scenario, Sheila would be unlikely to experience success. The therapist would essentially be assigning the unsuccessful attempted solution.

Therefore an intervention designed to *reverse* "You must be outgoing and funny" was selected. Sheila was complimented on her ability to recognize that her promises to herself to "be different" were not working. She was encouraged to anticipate that she probably *would* become somewhat quiet in large groups, especially around her boyfriend's family. In addition, the therapist suggested that Sheila announce to her boyfriend that she probably would continue to be somewhat quiet, and to reassure him that this did not mean that she was "stuck up" or that she did not like his family.

Shifting from Amplifying to Interrupting

"When something works, do more of it" is a central tenet of strategic solution focused therapy. Often there is no indication whatsoever that a suggestion to amplify an emerging solution would repeat an unsuccessful attempted solution. On the contrary, there may be strong evidence that something is "working," and the therapist's intervention appropriately encourages the continuation or amplification of desired behaviors. Such suggestions are often extremely helpful. On other occasions, however, suggestions to "do more of what works" unexpectedly bring neither compliance nor increased satisfaction. Instead, the client may report at subsequent sessions that he or she just did not do the homework. Even more striking, the client may report actually doing the homework but then go on to belittle that homework, emphasizing that it has not made a difference (Lipchik, 1992). When this occurs, it is time for the therapist to "do something different."

One approach may be to take seriously the client's reservations about what had appeared to be a solution. The therapist might say, "You must have some reasons for not wanting to pursue what seemed, on the surface, to be a good idea. I'm interested in knowing more about them." Lipchik (1992) asks clients to consider whether having the problem has certain advantages, a question similar to the previously described MRI interventions that discourage too-rapid change. Lipchik encourages clients to recognize what she calls "both/and" options as opposed to an "either/or" stance. For example, she tells the client to notice a time that he is simultaneously competent and depressed.

To phrase this in a slightly different way, the client does not need to wait to totally eliminate "depression" in order to experience "competence." In fact, here the emphasis in the homework might shift from amplification of the "solution part" (confidence, social interaction, etc.) to a prescription of some aspect of the complaint experience. For example, the therapist might say, "Be sure you experience the twinge of sadness inside even as you show up for work with a smile on your face."

Simon (1994) describes a case where shifting the approach in this way made a difference. The client in Simon's case was a man who experienced conflict about his sexual identity. The therapist used an approach that emphasized searching for strengths and "exceptions to the problem" in a variety of creative ways, but the man's distress did not decrease. After consultation with another therapist (de Shazer), the therapist took a very different approach, one that involved apologizing for the therapist's failure to understand the magnitude of the man's predicament. Now the emphasis was on the complexity and difficulty of the situation, which, the therapist cautioned, might never be completely resolved. In response to this approach, the man told the therapist that he felt understood, and his symptoms diminished. When optimism fails, pessimism may succeed.

Simon, a solution focused therapist, appropriately cautions therapists against misinterpretation of solution focused therapy, as a model that simply says "be positive." As she points out, the focus has always been on detecting and amplifying differences that make a difference. In strategic solution focused therapy too, it is important to emphasize that reification of solution amplification—or problem clarification, or interruption of attempted solutions—can lead to oversimplification and misuse.

When Doing Something Different Doesn't Help

Just as "do more of what works" sometimes does not bring the desired results, "do something different" sometimes fails, as well. Although it is uncommon, some people respond to the generic suggestion to "do something different" by doing something that turns out to worsen the situation. Some clients are simply uncomfortable from the start with any suggestion to deliberately perform the complaint behavior, even when they recognize that "trying too hard" to eliminate that behavior has not been working. Other clients may not initially express, or even fully recognize, discomfort with suggestions that reverse straightforward attempted solutions, but later they realize that such suggestions just do not feel right.

It should be noted at this point that the presence of noncompliance with a "do something different" intervention is not sufficient for a conclusion that the approach was ineffective. On the contrary, the following sequence is extremely common: the therapist suggests that the client experience the complaint more fully, and the client returns saying that he or she did not actually do that homework, but that the problem is, for some reason, less troublesome. Clients typically do not complain when this occurs.

Two things occur that signal that "doing something different" is not helping. First, the problem may be experienced as greater in intensity—not just briefly, for "data collection purposes," but in a more extensive way. Second, the client may feel uncomfortable with the suggestion. The presence of either of these responses suggests that the intervention that elicited the discomfort has become an unsuccessful attempted solution.

When this occurs, the therapist needs to "do something different" as soon as possible. What is "different" from "doing something different"? Three approaches can be considered. First, the therapist might check to verify whether straightforward suggestions have been fully tried. Second, a shift to solution amplification might be warranted. Finally, the therapist might further clarify the problem and how the client hopes that therapy will help. Each of these possibilities will be described in more detail.

Straightforward Advice

A recommendation for deliberate continuation or extension of the problem usually will be made only after it has been determined that straightforward, commonsense solutions are not working. When a suggestion to "have the problem" is not helpful, the therapist may need to reassess whether "first-line" approaches have truly been given a sufficient trial. For example, Dana complained of anxiety. During the initial discussion of her attempted solutions, it appeared that both she and her husband were telling her "Don't worry." Because this advice was not helping, the therapist recommended that Dana deliberately extend the period of worry by one minute and notice what she discovered. Dana returned for a follow-up appointment saying that she had felt uncomfortable with that recommendation and had not tried it. Her anxiety had not diminished in any way; it had actually increased slightly in response to the thought that "therapy was not going to be of any help."

The therapist complimented Dana on her willingness to keep the follow-up appointment and to be honest with the therapist about her concerns. "I don't know either if therapy is going to help," said the therapist, "but I guess we know one more thing than we knew last time. And that is that a suggestion to extend the anxiety doesn't feel like the right thing right now. So, whatever you and I do, it will need to be something very different from that."

To guard against repeating the error, the therapist asked Dana to carefully review everything she had tried, all ideas that had been suggested, and what the results had been. Had they overlooked something that might be different both from "don't worry" and from "extending the symptom"? The therapist realized that Dana had not been offered a short written handout on anxiety management procedures that was available at the clinic. Had Dana seen this handout, or any similar literature? She had not. The therapist located the paper and gave Dana a copy.

Dana read the handout, and the therapist guided her through the breathing and relaxation exercises that were suggested there. Together they discussed the concepts in the handout (e.g., "panic attacks pass," and the frequency of anxiety in the population). Dana asked whether anxiety was a "genetic" or learned behavior, and the therapist answered as completely as possible.

This time Dana found the appointment useful. She returned two weeks later saying that her anxiety was still there, but that it seemed to be less of a problem. She mentioned that she had particularly liked one breathing exercise, and she had copied it onto a note card that she kept in her purse.

This therapist knew about the anxiety management handout and relaxation techniques, and, although not an expert on anxiety, the therapist had some familiarity with the anxiety management literature. Nonetheless the therapist had overlooked this information as a resource. Out of enthusiasm about applying strategic solution focused therapy, the therapist had erroneously assumed that when Dana said that "don't worry" messages did not work, she was referring to all anxiety management suggestions. Fortunately for Dana, the therapist recognized the error and did something different, which, in this case, involved returning to straightforward suggestion.

Back to the Solution

Just as a double negative produces a positive grammatically (as in the sentence "The therapist cannot not influence the client"), reversing "something different" suggests a return to the original behavior. For the strategic solution focused therapist, this involves refocusing on current interactions and searching for parts that contain a piece of the solution. Perhaps there are solution behaviors that the therapist missed; maybe there are variables that can be reframed in a way that will create a positive connotation. If not previously assigned, the therapist might give the simultaneously simple and powerful suggestion to "notice times when you're feeling on track to the solution, and how you do it."

Sometimes the therapist has assigned "Do something different" rather than "Do more of what works" precisely because the initial miracle question inquiry did not produce much meaningful material. Or perhaps solution inquiry was not conducted or completed, for whatever reason. It may be useful to conduct additional inquiry about the solution now, perhaps in a slightly different way. If a "generic" miracle question was used previously, perhaps a specific one would be more useful now. The nature and wording of the specific miracle question can emerge from the clinical material, as the following case illustrates.

Marshall's complaint was that he had been transferred to second shift. When asked to describe a solution scenario, being back on first shift was all Marshall could describe. When the therapist tried to elicit elaboration of a time when second shift would, for some reason, feel like less of a problem, Marshall insisted that such a picture was impossible to imagine. Marshall's attempted solution was requesting reassignment back to first shift, both verbally and in writing. His requests appeared reasonable, but, because of downsizing, his company was unable to accommodate him.

The therapist told Marshall that it sounded like he had every right to be distressed about the situation, and that when feelings of indignation emerged, he might begin to grasp control of them by experiencing them fully. Marshall did not like this idea. He said that he had consulted a therapist in order to do something about the problem of being on second shift, not to "wallow in self-pity." Using Marshall's language, the therapist suggested that Marshall imagine what would be different when he was taking action and "not just wallowing." This time Marshall responded with some creative ideas about transferring to another division of his company, plans that he eventually pursued.

Marshall's case is presented as an example of one where a therapist suggestion was rejected by the client and therefore interrupted. However, one could also assert that the suggestion to extend and experience the feelings of indignation did not actually "fail." It could be argued that the suggestion actually "moved the therapy along" by contributing to Marshall's statement that "wallowing" was unacceptable to him. But whether that suggestion is construed as a positive step in the therapy or as an "error" to be reversed, the movement occurred when the therapist built on Marshall's statement, shifting immediately to the solution scenario. Therapy can be like a dance, with the rhythm of one step toward change, a next step toward stability, another step toward change, and so on; the therapist follows and also leads.

Return to Clarification of Problems and Expectations

When the therapist needs to shift from a "doing something different" stance, another option involves a return to clarifying the problem and/or the client's expectations of how therapy is supposed to help. Taking a one-down position, the therapist might say, "It sounds like I missed the mark with that suggestion. Maybe I'd better make sure I'm clear on what's bothering you most. Tell me again what the trouble is." Sometimes the client's response describes the problem from a different perspective, or it sheds light on how the complaint is a problem.

For example, Bill had several complaints, but he claimed that his biggest concern was his relationship with his parents. He repeatedly spoke about wanting to "talk to them differently." The therapist made several suggestions about ways of interacting with the parents in a different manner, but these had not proved especially helpful. The therapist said, "Bill, I'm missing something here. Help me understand exactly what the trouble is that you're hoping that will be solved when you talk to your parents differently." Bill answered, "I just don't want to treat my wife and son the way my folks treated me." Gradually it became clear that Bill believed that he had to "settle things" with his parents in order to respond differently to his current family. Further inquiry clarified that Bill's primary complaint really involved his wife; once that problem was identified, effective intervention could be designed.

Clarifying the client's expectations about how the therapy is supposed to help can also be useful. As Dana's example in this chapter illustrates, sometimes a client wants straightforward suggestions. Other clients hope that they will receive off-work slips, medication, or a particular kind of intervention ("support," insight, etc.). Ideally these expectations have already been made explicit prior to the delivery of an intervention, but if an intervention has been unsuccessful, it may be useful to verify just how the client hoped that the therapy was going to help. If the client expected something that the therapist does not have the ability or expertise to provide, that is particularly important to clarify. Unrealistic expectations for therapy will be addressed in more detail in a later chapter.

Shifting Stances as Therapy Progresses

Shifting stances is not exclusively reserved for those times when something in the therapy is not working. On the contrary, when a "do something different" message has led to useful change, the therapist needs to recognize this and shift to "doing more of the same." Kral and Kowalski (1989) point this out, emphasizing that the therapist needs to monitor when change is sufficient and when additional change (in the same direction or in the opposite direction) would be useful.

Again, the balance between stability and change is critical. The therapist almost always wants to leave open the possibility of continued evolution and development of the solution. By definition, evolution assumes change; recommendations to "continue more of what works" are virtually never intended to block new growth. Amplifying solutions and doing something different are *both* encouraged when the therapist suggests that the client "do more of what works for you, and notice how that makes a difference."

Amplifying What Works *and* Interrupting What Doesn't

As the therapy progresses, the therapist continually adjusts the focus, moving back and forth between the different components as appropriate. This process is most evident when one examines a whole course of therapy. For example, an initial session might devote a fair amount of time to problem clarification and miracle question inquiry, ending with an intervention that emphasizes amplification of pieces of the miracle that are already happening. The next session might begin with elaboration of additional positive change that has occurred since the first appointment and how the client created that change. The therapist might then shift to a message cautioning against too much additional change.

The client might begin the next session by saying that the initial problem is no longer a concern, but that there is another issue to address. After some clarification of that complaint, there might be extensive discussion of attempted solutions, and perhaps the therapist might comment that the approach that seemed to be quite effective with the original complaint appears to be less helpful, perhaps even counterproductive, in the current situation. This might lead to a suggestion to reverse that behavior. And so the process continues. When the therapy ends, the therapist's concluding message encourages doing what works; at the same time, it may anticipate the development of relapses, perhaps even outlining how the client could deliberately create one.

Shifts in focus can occur between sessions; they also develop within the session. And sometimes an intervention emphasizes both amplification of one response *and* interruption of another. The following case illustrates this situation.

It has been eighteen years since Sharon and Don divorced, mostly at Sharon's initiative, but she feels a long-standing sense of regret about having left Don. The sadness and wish that things were different have intensified in the last few months, since Sharon has learned that Don has developed some serious medical problems, which could be life threatening. After becoming tearful at work on several occasions, Sharon spoke with her friend and co-worker, Rita, who suggested that Sharon seek therapy. When she did so, Sharon's principal complaint involved the intrusive thoughts about Don and her inability to "put Don behind me."

The therapist asked Sharon to visualize a scenario where the sadness was "not so much of a problem." Sharon was able to do so. She described being happy. She would begin her day by going for breakfast "for blueberry blintzes." She would have the desire to do more things, like going to the zoo, seeing a movie, and calling her brother in Houston. What would Rita notice about her? "Me smiling," Sharon said. She would be less preoccupied with Don. She would be more relaxed and have more fun. What would Don notice? (Sharon was already talking to him from time to time.) He would notice her "caring, but with more distance," Sharon said.

Were parts of this scenario already happening? Sharon said that there were. She had gone to the zoo last week. She was planning a weekend trip to a hygienists' meeting with some friends. She and Don had talked about their children in a way that felt "okay." She had not needed to "put Don behind me" in order to do those things. On a zero to ten scale, Sharon felt that she was at a "four." How had she moved to a "four"? "I realize I *have* gone on with my life," Sharon said. "I have to keep doing it, and it's hard work, especially now that Don's having a hard time."

What had Sharon tried in her best attempts to "put Don behind her"? She had made a list of all the reasons she had left him in the first place. "Maybe I'll stop regretting my decision," she said. When she woke at 2:00 A.M. feeling sad and wishing that she were the one nursing Don through his illness, not his new girlfriend, Sharon berated herself. As Rita had advised her to do, Sharon told herself to "let go already. It's been eighteen years already, girl. How long are you going to hold on?" None of this was working very well. Sharon still felt sad and wistful.

The therapist told Sharon, "I don't blame you for feeling sad and wishing that things were different. And I also hear that you don't like to feel that way. I'm tremendously impressed that you haven't allowed your sadness to stop you from becoming a hygienist, from enjoying your friends. And you realize that you didn't have to wait to put Don behind you to do that.

"I also have a thought about a piece in all this that maybe isn't working so well. It's the 'I have to put Don behind me' part—because maybe you're entitled to some wistful wondering about the road not taken, especially now, when Don's not doing so good, and you can't help thinking that he may not be around forever. And when Rita gives you a hard time about it, I wonder how it would change things if you told her that your therapist thinks that your sadness is legitimate, and that she's just going to have to bear with you."

Sharon told the therapist that this perspective seemed extremely helpful. She responded positively to this intervention, one that contained both solution amplification and solution interruption components. On one hand, the therapist encouraged continuation and expansion of the "pieces of the miracle" that were already present. At the same time, the therapist attempted to reverse the unsuccessful attempted solution given both by Sharon herself and by Rita. Would either component alone have been equally useful? Perhaps. But together, complementing one another, they provided a powerful and balanced message encouraging continuation of what worked and discontinuation of what did not.

Couples
Problems and Solutions

S ome therapists may say that they do not work with couples. But to not work with couples—or with couple (or relationship) problems, at least— seems to be exceedingly difficult, if not impossible, for a therapist to do. From a systemic perspective, any time a client comes in complaining about a partner in a significant intimate relationship, the therapist is addressing a "couple's problem," regardless of whether or not that partner is in the room. How strategic solution focused therapy approaches couples is the subject of this chapter.

In the long run, it makes little difference whether the treatment of a relationship problem begins in an individual or a conjoint session of strategic solution focused therapy. The therapy that begins with both partners present may rapidly become individual therapy with one or both people; conversely, when individual therapy addresses a relationship problem, the partner may soon be involved, in a conjoint appointment and/or an individual session. To "do what works," the therapist remains flexible, adapting the plan about who is seen when to the specifics of the situation.

Starting with the Couple Together

Some clients are very clear about wanting to come in with their partners. One or both partners will request "marriage counseling" (or relationship therapy—whatever term they use), and this is what they want. When this occurs, it generally makes sense to begin by offering a conjoint appointment. Just as the therapist wants to "speak the client's language" in other ways, here he or she will begin in a manner consistent with the client's position.

Clarifying the Problem(s)

As in any case, the first task is problem clarification. But whose problem is to be clarified when two people are in the room? There are different ways to conceptualize the problem definition issue. One possibility is to assume the existence of a shared "couple's problem," presuming that "the couple" (marriage, system, dyad, etc.) is the client. The assumption here is that the partners will achieve consensus about a common complaint. Another possibility is to assume that each partner will have his or her separate definition of the problem. The second approach is the starting assumption in strategic solution focused therapy.

From the beginning, the therapist wants to convey interest in understanding the problem as each partner sees it (Fisch, 1993, personal communication). The choice of the word "each" is deliberate. The therapist says, "I want to hear from each of you" in order to convey a particular attitude. The unstated implication is: "I will not assume that you two necessarily have a shared view of the problem just because you are in a relationship together. In fact, I *expect* that you will each have your own view of things, because you are two separate individuals."

If one partner begins to describe the problem as a shared one (e.g., "We don't communicate"), the therapist may make the expectation about individual views more explicit. "Let's see if I'm hearing you accurately, Lenore. You're saying that you and Karl don't communicate, and you don't like that." Of course, it is possible that Karl may verbalize a similar concern. If so, the therapist will certainly want to use that fact in the therapy, and it might be pointed out later that "you each have similar complaints." But a problem will be defined as a shared concern only after each partner has individually mentioned it.

During the problem clarification stage, the therapist will want to identify which partner is the primary customer for the therapy. Rarely is the motivation for treatment equal between partners. Usually the partner who called is the one most interested in treatment. The partner who did not make the request may well be a customer too, but it is still useful to know who initiated the process. If this is unclear, the therapist can easily ask, "Whose idea was it to come here?" following up, if needed, with additional information about the interaction and dialogue that preceded the decision to call.

As indicated, the therapist wants to hear a statement of the complaint from each partner separately. It is often useful to start with the primary customer, the one who wanted the appointment. Turning to that partner, the therapist asks what the trouble is as he or she sees it. The inquiry is similar to that used in an individual session, encouraging description of specific behaviors and words. The therapist might ask, "Is it what she *says* or what she *does?*" or "Is it *what* he says or *how* he puts it?"

In most couples' problems, the complaint clearly concerns the partner: he or she did this (bad thing) and/or failed to do that (desirable thing). If the initial statement does not include a recognizable complaint about the partner (as when the problem is defined as something that appears to be outside the dyad), the therapist may directly inquire. "Often when people come in as a couple, they have some gripe about the other person," the therapist might say. "I notice you're talking about [outside issue], and I'm wondering if there's something [partner] is or isn't doing about that that's bugging you?" Sometimes the problem genuinely *is* something other than the partner's behavior, and the couple has come in for the purpose of working together toward a solution. But before assuming that this is the case, the therapist wants to make very sure that there is not a "hidden" or implied complaint about the partner embedded in the statement of the problem.

As the therapist talks with the first partner, it is highly desirable to keep the second partner silent and listening. Frequently the therapist's initial explanation about wanting to hear from each partner separately is sufficient to establish a climate where the second partner "waits for a turn." Sometimes, however, the second partner repeatedly chimes in, unable or unwilling to wait. The therapist will make some attempts to complete the conversation with the first partner, after thanking the other for his or her patience. The therapist may also reassure the second partner that he or she will have a turn, and that the therapist will definitely not interpret silence as agreement with the person who is speaking.

Even if the second partner is not interrupting, the therapist does not want to keep him or her waiting too long. Therefore, elaboration of one partner's complaint might need to be cut short before the problem has been fully clarified. An interruption may occur at an earlier point in a cojoint session than in an individual appointment. The therapist attempts to summarize and reflect the problem as the first partner sees it. If the problem has not been adequately clarified, the summary acknowledges that fact: it is time to move on, even if the complaint is not yet fully clear.

In shifting the focus to the second partner, it is often useful to assess how eager that person was to come to the appointment. To evaluate that, Fisch (1993, personal communication) has suggested that the therapist might say something like this: "I'm not sure if you're here today primarily at the request of your partner, or if you have reasons of your own for wanting to be here." If the person has his or her own reasons, asking about these starts the problem clarification process. Just as was done with the first member of the couple, the therapist wants to identify specifics, and *how* behaviors and words are a problem. When someone is a reluctant participant, the therapist might be alert for the possibility that his or her main complaint is that "my partner is on my case about something—so much that he (she) dragged me to therapy."

If someone is here primarily at the other person's request, the therapist wants to acknowledge that openly. One purpose of this is to prevent the eager partner from assuming that the other is more of a customer than is actually the case. Another purpose is to communicate to the more reluctant partner that he or she is not "required" to identify a problem. There is also an opportunity to do some complimenting here, because the reluctant partner cared enough about the "customer" partner's concerns to come anyway.

Elaborating the Solution(s)

After both partners' perceptions of the problem have been identified, the therapist will shift the focus to elaboration of the solution. This usually involves asking the miracle question, twice, once for each partner. Again, it is emphasized that this is a separate question for each partner: "The 'miracle' is that the problem that you (as an individual) just described is solved (or not so much a problem, etc.)." Elaboration continues, as described in Chapter 3. "What will be the first thing that will be different . . . what will [partner] notice about you? . . . How will he (she) say you're different? . . . What else? . . . And how will [partner] be different as a result of these changes? . . . "

Again, the therapist attempts to keep the other person silent while the speaking partner is amplifying his or her solution scenario. The therapist's hope is that the silent partner is listening as detail is elaborated, because there are multiple opportunities for the silent partner to hear what the speaking partner thinks will make a positive difference. The silent partner is not required to respond, to make a commitment to attempt the behavior described, or even to acknowledge that a message was conveyed. But much information is conveyed, usually by both partners.

After both miracles have been elaborated, the therapist will ask about exceptions. "These miracles you have described—are there any pieces of them that are already happening?" If so, the therapist elicits descriptions of these. "How did you do that?" and "How did you figure out that saying that would make a difference?" are questions that will highlight both partners' roles in producing change. Scaling questions may be used here, as well.

At this point the therapist would ideally like to obtain some information about attempted solutions, but there is often a problem: the therapist is probably running out of time. With two complaints to clarify and two miracle questions to pursue, an initial appointment with a couple often needs to end before a full inquiry about attempted solutions can be conducted. Of course, the therapist can simply acknowledge that time is running out and schedule another conjoint appointment to continue the interview. Sometimes that may be the best plan. However, the therapist may already have enough information to plan the next step and to provide some feedback to the couple.

Three-Part Interventions for Couples

The same kind of three-part intervention that is used with individuals can be designed at the conclusion of a couple's appointment. The intervention will contain validation, compliment, and suggestion messages, frequently separate ones for each partner. As described in Chapter 5, the therapist will frequently take a "break," with or without leaving the office, to think about the couple and to design the input.

The first part of the intervention reflects and validates each partner's complaint. The therapist is careful to speak to each partner separately, using eye contact and body language to join with each person. The input directed to each partner is designed to communicate this message: "I hear your complaint, and I understand how you feel." At the same time, the unspoken message to the other partner is this: "I hear your partner, and I respect his (or her) right to feel that way." Validation statements might begin like this: "I don't blame you, [first partner's name], for feeling distressed. . . . It sounds like it's no fun to . . . .I'm not surprised, [second partner's name], that you feel. . . . "

Compliments comprise the second part of the intervention. Attendance at the appointment, willingness to listen to the other person, recognition of one's own role in problem maintenance, and realizations verbalized during the session can all be highlighted. If pieces of the solution are already happening, the therapist can recognize those achievements. Compliments can be directed to the couple as well as to individuals (e.g., "I'm struck by how thoroughly you both could visualize and describe things that, when you do them, will make so much of a difference," or "It seems remarkable to me that even with the difficulties you've described, you two pulled together to make Michelle's birthday party happen. It's clear to me that you both care about her very deeply").

In addition to any compliments addressed to the couple together, the therapist will usually want to be sure to direct at least one compliment to each individual. Many people come to a first couple's session with some trepidation, expecting or fearing that the "expert" will take the other person's side. This is most apparent for the reluctant partner, but it can also be the secret fear of the person who suggested the therapy. Individual compliments frequently go beyond both validation statements and "dyadic compliments" in countering that fear. To hear admiration from the "expert" from whom one expected censure can be a powerful experience.

Here are some examples of compliments addressed to individuals during a couple's appointment. "I'm struck by the courage and honesty you've shown in here today. What you just told your wife and me wasn't easy to say." "I'm impressed that you care enough about Charles to be here today." "What stands out to me is your ability to recognize that when you did that, Randy ended up feeling suspicious. Not all people that I see take that much responsibility for their own actions."

After the compliment comes the suggestion. Here the basic guideline applies: if something the couple has described is working, the therapist will generally suggest continuing or amplifying it; if the couple's behaviors are not helping, the suggestion will be to do something different. If it is possible to make a specific suggestion, that is usually desirable. If it is still unclear at this point just what is and is not working, a generic suggestion is given.

It is actually fairly common for the therapist to be unclear about specifics to suggest at the end of an initial conjoint appointment. There is so much to assess, with two problems and two solutions; as mentioned, frequently there has not been time for inquiry about attempted solutions. When the therapist does not know what else to suggest, a "skeleton key" suggestion to "do something different" can be surprisingly powerful. The intervention might go like this: "I don't blame you each for feeling distressed. It's no fun to be fighting like you are. . . . I'm impressed that you recognize that when you do . . . , it doesn't work. I don't have a clear sense yet of what will work any better, but we know that whatever it is, it will be different from what you're doing now."

At this point, the therapist might want to tell the couple the little story of the parents who "did something different" to deal with their child's temper tantrums described in Chapter 5. This story is particularly useful with couples, whether or not they are parents, because it describes two small and seemingly random behaviors, each selected independently by the partners, that together lead to positive change.

Joel and Sherry complained that they were fighting too much. The therapist ended their appointment with the temper tantrum story and the generic suggestion to do something different, and the recommendation was for each to come in individually the next time. The therapist asked Joel (whose appointment was first) what was better. "Well," Joel said, "We tried that 'Do something different' thing you suggested." "What did you do?" the therapist asked. Joel replied, "We started to fight, and I said to Sherry, 'I think we're supposed to do something different right now.'" And they stopped fighting! Sherry's version, described in her appointment, was similar, except that she said that *she* was the one who reminded Joel that they were supposed to do "something different."

Couples do not always take this suggestion so literally, of course, but dramatic results are not unusual.

Jill and Nick: "Communication is a Problem"

To illustrate how the components of the initial conjoint appointment fit together, the first session with Jill and Nick will be described in some detail. Jill is a podiatrist, and Nick is an administrator. They have been married for eight years and have no children. Jill called for the appointment, which she said she wanted because "communication is a problem."

The therapist began the appointment by saying that although the form said that Jill had called, it would be useful to clarify whose idea it had been to come in. Both Nick and Jill agreed that counseling was primarily Jill's idea. The first task, the therapist explained, was to understand the problem as each of them saw it. Turning to Jill, the therapist asked, "What's the trouble from your perspective?" Jill's complaint was that Nick worked too late and was too involved in his work. In addition, he did not "share himself enough" when he was at home. He slouched on the sofa and did not talk. The therapist asked Jill which problem distressed her more, "time at work" or "not sharing." "Not sharing," Jill answered immediately. Even if Nick had to work longer, increased talking when he *was* there would make a difference. Had Nick's communication changed recently? No. Then what had led to Jill's calling *now?* Especially when home alone, Jill repeatedly found herself wanting to go out with her single friends and questioning why she was staying married. These thoughts and feelings scared her, and she wanted to "repair the marriage before it was too late."

Nick acknowledged that he was there mainly at Jill's request, but he "guessed" that communication was a problem. He had never been especially verbal about feelings. The therapist asked Nick whether his style would be a problem to him if Jill were not complaining about it. He said that it would not. He just did not like to see Jill so unhappy. It distressed him greatly to think that he might lose her. The therapist said that it seemed as if "communication" per se was not as great a problem from Nick's perspective as Jill's dissatisfaction and complaints about his communication. Nick agreed that this seemed accurate.

The therapist introduced the miracle question, emphasizing that this was a separate question for each of them. Jill volunteered to go first. She said, "Nick would wake up and say, 'I had a strange dream, that my father was still alive.' He would say that he was confused, sad, and that he wanted to share it with me." How would Jill be different as a result of Nick's words? She would feel "connected" to Nick, hopeful and happy. She would hug him, and he would hug her in return. Later, at work, her assistant would notice that she was more outgoing, more talkative. Jill would look forward to coming home. When Nick arrived, she would kiss him hello. She would be quieter during dinner, while he would talk more, about his day or about his feelings. There would be details, descriptions.

"And as a result of those changes, what will be different on the nights when Nick has to work late?" the therapist asked Jill. "I wouldn't feel so lonely," Jill replied. She might leave a friendly "hi" message on Nick's voice mail. She would feel less interested in going out to clubs and bars. How would she spend the evening? "I'd do something else, with a different friend, maybe go to a play or a movie. Or maybe I'd just stay home," Jill said. "I'd feel more normal, more content. And I wouldn't be thinking that I have a bad marriage." When Nick was home but quiet, how would Jill respond? "I'd see it as just temporary. I wouldn't feel so threatened."

Nick answered the miracle question by saying, "Jill will be happy." He would hold her and say, "I'm glad." He would feel "better, have a better attitude." At work, his secretary would notice that he was less grouchy. He would be more pleasant. He would make a point of leaving work on time. Jill would know he was happy to be home. "We'll get closer." "How?" the therapist asked. "By communication and affection. I'd try to be more open."

The therapist asked Nick what would be different on the nights that he did have to work late and then came home exhausted. "She'll understand," Nick said. Jill would sit on the couch, too. Words would not be needed. He would put his head on her shoulder and hold her hand. "She'd realize that I'm tired, I can't think right now; that I feel the conflict: I should work less hours, but I feel torn." Nick would "make it up to her on the weekend. I'd try to use more words, but even if I didn't, Jill would realize that I'm trying to do the things she enjoys, like movies or shopping."

Were pieces of these "miracles" already happening? Both Nick and Jill said that they were. With tears in her eyes, Jill said that she saw that Nick was making a point of doing "things" for her. Nick said that since Jill had told him how unhappy she was, he was attempting to set limits at work and to talk more at home. Jill had held his hand last night. Jill commented that the way Nick "opened up in here" felt like a "piece of the miracle." If he spoke that way at home, it would make a tremendous difference.

The therapist gave the couple this feedback: "I don't blame you each for feeling distressed. It's no fun for you, Jill, to feel that Nick isn't sharing, and then to find yourself wondering why you stay married. And it sure doesn't feel good for you, Nick, to hear Jill say things like that and to see her so unhappy. I'm impressed by the fact that you each seem to care very much about your relationship. You, Jill, cared enough to say, "This isn't okay. I want to do something about it." And you, Nick, cared enough to come here today. And I'm tremendously impressed that pieces of both of your miracles are already happening. What Jill is asking for is exactly what you did in here today, and I'm struck by your clarity, Nick, in expressing the dilemma you feel when you're tired, and you know that

Jill wants words, and you can't even think. And I see your sensitivity, Jill, your capacity to hear the language Nick speaks, that it's often a language of 'doing' rather than a language of words. So, if I were to give you each a suggestion, it would be to do more of what works, and to notice how it makes a difference."

Jill and Nick were seen a few more times. Nick seriously contemplated changing jobs, and Jill decided that when she really wanted "words," she would ask for them. There was still a difference between their styles and languages (words vs. action). There probably always will be such a difference, and that was was acknowledged. But, somehow, it did not matter so much.

Follow-Up: Together or Separately?

As with any case, the plan for additional appointments is tailored to the needs of the couple, and the therapist may tell clients that. The therapist wants to maintain maximum maneuverability, with the freedom to schedule follow-up in a variety of ways. Sometimes the couple's appointment is best seen as a one-time consultation, sometimes the therapist will want to recommend that the partners return together, and sometimes an individual return appointment—for one partner or both—seems like the best idea. As with other decisions in strategic solution focused therapy, there is no rigid formula to apply, but there are some general guidelines that suggest when conjoint or individual follow-up is most likely to be helpful.

Follow-Up Together

Conjoint follow-up may be indicated when "mutual good will" seems to exist between the partners. To assess this, the therapist can consider the following questions. In the appointment together, did the partners appear able to listen to each other, even when they disagreed? Did they seem able to cooperate and to collaborate? Did one or both seem able to build upon what the other said, or upon the interchange between the therapist and the other partner? Perhaps equally important, was the therapist subjectively comfortable being in the room with these two people together? If and when anger flared, did the angry partner(s) seem able to respond to therapist input in the conjoint session so that something could be learned from the anger? If so, there may be reasons to invite the partners back together.

Partners who have the same complaint and are both "customers" for the same thing also may benefit from one or more return visits together. Although "We don't communicate" is not an automatic indication for conjoint follow-up (because that complaint can mean so many different things), communication difficulties sometimes respond quite well to conjoint intervention. There can be continued elaboration of miracle question scenarios where communication is taking place, or of scenarios where one partner "communicates badly" and the other responds so that it does not feel like so much of a problem. The therapist can teach the couple basic communication skills, including speaking in "I-messages," active listening, problem solving, tolerating and enjoying differences, and de-escalation of fighting. Information on common gender differences and developmental stages of relationships may also be useful for the partners to hear together.

Conjoint appointments may also be indicated when the main problem involves managing children or when both partners are concerned about some issue outside the dyad. The partners may have the same goal but disagree on the approach for getting there. Arguments are consistently and predictably about that one topic, with each partner trying to persuade the other that his or her way of handling the situation is the "right one." As described in Chapter 4, the attempt to persuade the partner—or to reach consensus—has become the unsuccessful attempted solution. Here, the therapist might encourage elaboration of a solution scenario where the fact that the partners disagree is, for some reason, not so much a problem. Or to reverse the "We must agree" unsuccessful attempted solution, the therapist might encourage acknowledgment of the disagreement, both within the dyad and to others who may be involved.

Ricardo and Josie, who disagreed on rules for Raphael, their sixteen-year-old son, were seen together and approached in a way suggested by Fisch (1992b). Raphael knew that Mom was the "softy" and Dad "the heavy," and he had learned to play his parents against one another. The therapist said that it seemed that Raphael was a pretty bright kid, who already knew quite well that his parents disagreed. Trying to present a united front was a laudable goal, but, because of strong beliefs that Josie and Ricardo each had, it just was not working. Did the couple want to hear a different idea? Yes.

The therapist suggested that Ricardo and Josie "agree to disagree" in the following way. When Raphael asked Josie if he could do something that was okay with her, but which Ricardo would prohibit, she was to say this: "I have no objection, but you'd better check with your dad" (or, if Ricardo was not around: "Well, you know you'll have to answer to your dad about that"). Ricardo was to take full responsibility for his rules, acknowledging that the standards were his, and it was up to him to enforce them. Josie might assist Ricardo in some way, but she did not have to pretend that the rules were hers or that she agreed with them. Together Ricardo and Josie discussed this approach, and they decided to give it a try. Josie particularly liked the fact that it could teach Raphael "about the real world. Some day he's going to have to work with bosses who have different standards, just like his dad and I do."

Conjoint appointments are also quite useful when the therapist wants to follow up on a suggestion made to the couple together, or when the therapist has an idea for a future intervention that will be most powerful if directed to the couple together. Some common useful sex therapy suggestions are particularly effective if presented in this way. For example, the therapist tells the couple together to "touch without intercourse" to interrupt the common "We must have intercourse" unsuccessful attempted solution.

Finally, there are couples where one or both partners will express strong feelings about wanting to be seen together for all sessions. Sometimes the therapist may not think that this is the best plan, but to pursue a recommendation for individual follow-up too vigorously would counter the client's beliefs about how couples' therapy "should be," thereby weakening the therapist's credibility. Sometimes working with both partners together is not ideal, but things change for the better anyway. If the desired change does not occur with conjoint work, the therapist may then choose to point out that "what we're doing doesn't seem to be helping. Maybe we should do something different." One way of changing things is not meeting with the partners together.

Individual Follow-Up

Most people who specifically seek relationship therapy do not anticipate that they may be seen alone. But working with one or both partners alone frequently produces the desired changes, especially in certain circumstances. One important consideration is whether the partners are "customers" for similar or different things. When two people have distinct complaints, individual sessions may be more effective.

It is fairly common for partners to complain about different things. Amber and Howard both complained of "fighting" and "wanted more domestic harmony." But more thorough problem clarification revealed that Amber's main complaint was that Howard did not socialize enough with other couples, while Howard's complaint was that Amber was "always on my back." Because Amber really wanted "marital therapy together," the therapist attempted to work with them conjointly. Howard and Amber did not fight during the sessions, but the therapy was not particularly helpful. Their views were fixed, and the interaction patterns at home were not changing. When this was acknowledged openly in a session together, Howard and Amber agreed to individual meetings with the therapist, and positive change began.

Not all clients are as amicable as Howard and Amber during conjoint meetings. Sometimes a high degree of animosity is apparent, with interrupting, raised voices and verbal attacks. Not surprisingly, in such an atmosphere both partners have difficulty listening to each other, and they do not hear the therapist very well either. Each partner "digs in his or her heels," becoming increasingly rigid and less open to change. The atmosphere of tension is contagious, affecting the therapist, who may feel like a referee, whose main task seems to be keeping two warring partners off each other's throats. These conditions obviously do not encourage creative thinking on the part of the therapist. On the contrary, they present the *least* positive conditions for therapeutic change that most therapists could imagine.

As Lipchik points out:

It makes no sense to spend more than one session with family members who have entirely different or incompatible goals. Furthermore, when clients get stuck in their problems early in therapy, the therapist can sometimes learn more in private, individual sessions and, in addition, challenge the negative assumptions one client makes about the motives and behavior of another. Finally, when clients get stuck in their problems early in therapy, they feel very defensive and vulnerable in front of each other, afraid to openly express themselves. But clients who can agree on nothing in the emotionally heated atmosphere of joint sessions frequently can agree on principles they hold in common when they are seeing the therapist privately. (Lipchik, 1994, p. 38)

Even when animosity is not marked, individual sessions can be useful in another way. Some interventions are most effective when presented to one or both partners separately. From a systemic perspective, the therapist may sense that if one partner did X and the other did Y, the complaints of both would be significantly reduced. In addition, the therapist may recognize that the partners have different positions. For example, Dorothy is a business executive who values logic and efficiency, while her partner Heather is an artist who values sensitivity. Each of them is likely to be most amenable to change if approached in a way consistent with her individual style.

Linda and Brad: Couple's Therapy in Individual Sessions

The following is an example of a case where the therapist worked individually with each partner. Brad was a dentist and Linda an office manager. Both were in their thirties, married for ten months. They requested a conjoint appointment for "marital problems." Neither partner felt that the other listened, disagreements about little things escalated, and Linda was fed up. Brad became frustrated and angry when Linda nagged and complained. When the therapist attempted to elicit a solution scenario from each partner, Linda had trouble describing anything positive. Brad had difficulty being specific.

During the intervention, the therapist suggested that Linda and Brad each come back for an individual appointment. "Why?" Linda asked. "I'm not here for individual therapy. This is a marital problem." "Yes, it is," said the therapist. "And, you know, it's interesting: people often think that to solve a marital problem, you have to have both people in the room at the same time. They don't realize that sometimes it's more helpful for the therapist to meet with the husband and wife separately. For you two, I'm not sure yet what will be most helpful. But since we've talked together today, I'd like to chat with you each individually the next time." Both Linda and Brad agreed to return alone.

When asked about her biggest complaint, Linda said that she resented Brad's "distractability." During their courtship, Brad had devoted much time and attention to Linda, neglecting various home maintenance and job-related tasks. Almost immediately after the wedding, he began to focus his attention on those tasks, but he was managing them badly, procrastinating, starting one job and then getting distracted by another, and not getting much accomplished. Most distressing, his poor planning led to his not being ready to participate in "couple activities," such as a day trip to the mountains that Linda had planned. Linda wanted more "quality time together."

Part of Linda's attempted solution to the problem of "not enough good couple time" was to make and announce plans for day trips that would give them "quality time together." Then, when Brad "procrastinated," which meant saying, "I have to do something on the computer first," at the time Linda had planned to leave, Linda said, "Why are you doing that now?" and "Brad, you *knew* about this. I told you about it a week ago. This is supposed to help our relationship—why didn't you do that yesterday?" When asked about her rationale for this approach, Linda said that she was trying to "teach Brad to be better organized for the sake of the relationship." When asked if her approach seemed to be working, Linda acknowledged that it was not.

Linda had been quite independent prior to marriage. It was hypothesized that if she could discontinue her "planning couple activities/teaching," she might get more of the couple time she desired. Instead of using her current approach, Linda might casually announce and then implement plans to make a short day trip alone. She might select an activity that she knew Brad enjoyed, but one that she would genuinely enjoy doing on her own as well.

Linda saw Brad's distractability as a psychological flaw that Brad minimized. She could agree with the therapist that at a deeper level Brad must recognize this flaw, and she could see that she might unwittingly be "rubbing salt in the wound" when she asked rhetorical "why" questions that could sound like words of critical teachers from Brad's past. Linda liked the idea of an approach that might make her come across instead as a supportive friend (the person with whom Brad had fallen in love), who was far more interesting than the computer or a broken door hinge.

The plan was for Linda to tell Brad, "You know, I've realized that I've been depending on you too much for my recreation. So this Sunday I'm going to the museum and will be leaving around ten o'clock. Please don't feel any obligation to come along if you're swamped and need the day to catch up."

Brad's chief complaint was Linda's nagging and criticism. He responded to her nagging (e.g., "Why aren't you better organized?") by saying, "Well, I have to get this done—it has a piece that's pretty complicated—but I'll be done by noon." Brad's intent was to explain and justify the delays and to set a goal to be ready for Linda at a certain time. He acknowledged that the time he allotted often turned out to be insufficient. When asked what response on his part would practically guarantee that Linda would nag and criticize, Brad answered, "I could set something up and then make it fall through."

Brad perceived Linda as somewhat spoiled and very accustomed to "getting her own way," especially from her father, who was an efficient handyman (unlike Brad, who was not skilled at household tasks). When the therapist wondered aloud if Linda needed to learn to be less selfish and more empathic, Brad readily agreed. It was suggested that Brad might replace his "justification of delays/promises to finish sooner" with a statement that he recognized that he did have a rather serious problem with procrastination, something he had previously denied. He might add that although he wished he could say that he had licked this problem, he would probably "screw up again."

When seen next, Brad said that the relationship was much improved. He had told Linda that he "tries to fit too much in," and she had responded empathically. However, he told the therapist that he had also resisted the urge to squeeze in one extra errand en route to a date with Linda and had arrived "only three minutes late."

Linda also reported feeling much more positive about the relationship. She said that she had realized that it really was true that she needed to reassume responsibility for her own happiness, and she had told Brad that. She had not really felt like going to the art museum, but on another occasion when there was an opportunity to go sailing with Brad and his friend, she had realized that she really preferred to have Brad go alone; she wanted to spend the day puttering around the house and going for a short walk in the woods. Linda also mentioned that, to her surprise, she had found herself noticing things that Brad was accomplishing around the house, and she was thanking him for them.

In their individual appointments, both partners were complimented on the changes they had begun, and they were also cautioned against initiating additional change too soon. Each was seen again, and when it appeared that the positive changes were "holding," sessions were discontinued.

Individual Sessions in Difficult Situations

Sometimes individual work with the partners is indicated because of the nature of the complaint. When the primary issue involves fidelity, truthfulness, separation, or different degrees of commitment, individual meetings with the partners can be of critical importance. There are "horror stories" of whole courses of "marital therapy" during which one partner continued a relationship with a third party, unbeknownst to either the partner or the therapist. Of course, a deceitful partner could also conceal such a relationship during individual sessions with the therapist, but this is less likely.

Susan sensed that something was wrong with her husband Tom and asked him to see a therapist with her. Reluctantly he agreed. During the conjoint session, Susan said that the problem was that "something is very wrong with Tom. He is withdrawing. It's just not like him." When Tom was asked if he had a complaint, he was vague and somewhat guarded. He denied that he was depressed, and he did not have any particular complaints about Susan. The therapist attempted to validate both Susan's and Tom's feelings. The input to Tom was, "It must feel very uncomfortable to have Susan so distressed, when it's hard for you to put your finger on anything that's wrong from your perspective." The therapist recommended that both partners return individually. Both agreed, but Tom did not keep his individual appointment.

Susan kept hers, using it to express her concern that Tom was involved with another woman. The therapist said that in light of Tom's reaction in the joint appointment, she did not blame Susan for being worried. Together the therapist and Susan agreed that Susan's attempted solution, "If I get Tom to therapy, he'll stop acting strange," was not working. His unusual absences from home during the weekend and his "strange attitude" continued. An alternative was for Susan to recognize that Tom might well be fooling around, even though she did not have evidence, and to build her own support system and to educate herself about finances, in case either of them decided to separate. Susan was able to describe a scenario where she was handling that possibility, even if she did not like thinking about it.

Three months later Susan discovered Tom's relationship with his co-worker and confronted him. Distressed, Tom called the therapist for an appointment. He said that he had not told Susan about his girlfriend because he "did not want to hurt her." He feared (realistically) that Susan might give him an ultimatum, and he did not want to have to choose. The therapist attempted to empathize with Tom's dilemma and to gently point out that his attempts to juggle both relationships and "not hurt Susan" were not working. If he did not choose, either or both of the women in his life might make the decision for him. An alternative was to tell Susan that he had made a grave error in concealing the relationship from her, and that she had a right to feel betrayed. Although he did not want to be kicked out, he would not be surprised if she wanted him to leave, or if she did not trust him. Eventually Susan and Tom did separate.

Therapist Concerns

Therapists sometimes are reluctant to meet with partners separately because they might hear "secrets" like Tom's. In anticipation of that possibility, the therapist should clarify for him- or herself in advance the policy about confidentiality, and it is often useful to be clear with the partners about the policy as well. Different positions can be taken. One stance, described by Fisch (1990, personal communication), involves telling each partner, at the beginning of the first individual appointment, that the therapist will not promise absolute secrecy. Rather, the therapist will use his or her professional discretion about how to use what both partners say. If Tom had kept the first scheduled individual appointment and confided that he was having an affair, and if he had then asked the therapist, "What will you say if Susan asks what I told you?" the therapist's response would be, "I'll tell her that that's something she needs to ask you."

A somewhat different stance, described by Lipchik (1994), promises confidentiality except for child abuse and suicide or homicide threats. Lipchik writes:

> *If a secret affair is revealed, I tell the spouse having the affair that I will not work with a couple if one person's loyalty is divided, although I will offer individual sessions for a time to help him or her make a choice between the two relationships. Then I tell both partners in a conjoint meeting that they need more separate work before I can see them together. If the unknowing partner asks for more detailed reasons, I simply reiterate that sometimes I believe people need to work on separate issues before undertaking joint sessions. In my practice, no couple has ever left therapy because one or the other was dissatisfied with this explanation. (Lipchik, 1994, p. 38)*

In addition to concerns about secrets, therapists sometimes raise other questions about meeting with the partners separately. One question involves the appropriateness of one therapist seeing both partners. In general, if any of the three parties involved—either partner or the therapist—is uncomfortable with the arrangement, the discomfort should be addressed. What is the concern? Clarifying this often provides important information, regardless of whether or not the decision is to continue the arrangement. If someone would prefer that a different therapist see one of the partners, that should be facilitated.

Another question has been raised: what if the partners compare notes? In a situation such as Linda and Brad's, is there not a risk that Linda will tell Brad, "The therapist thinks you have a psychological flaw," and that Brad will tell Linda, "The therapist thinks you're too selfish"? If this occurs, will it be damaging to the couple, and to the therapist's ability to be of assistance?

The answer is "perhaps." However, this difficulty does not arise frequently. The "flaws" of the other person that are discussed in an individual session are selected not so much because the *therapist* thinks they are flaws but because the *client* is already complaining about them. If the client is already complaining about them to the therapist, he or she has probably also used them as "ammunition" against the partner. Any statements suggesting that "the therapist agrees with me that you're a so-and-so" therefore become just another variation on a familiar theme and may be "taken with a grain of salt." However, if the couple does confront the therapist about something that actually was said in an individual session, the therapist can acknowledge that he or she did make such a statement, and that it was done for a reason. In the therapist's professional opinion, that seemed to be the most helpful approach. As Fisch (1990, personal communication) points out, the therapist might say, "I may have erred in not saying it to you together. You two may have more ability to talk together than I initially saw." It is now up to the couple to demonstrate that they can make use of sessions together rather than needing to work separately.

Starting with One Person

Just as therapy that begins with a couple can involve work with individuals, treatment that begins as individual therapy frequently leads to working with the client's partner, individually and/or together with the original client. When the primary complaint in individual therapy involves the client's partner, the therapist may be extremely interested in that partner's perspective, even if the client has not expressed particular interest in involving the partner. The therapist might say, "From what you're saying about [partner], it sounds like he (she) really plays an important part in what you're describing. I'd really like to talk with him (her). If you have no objection, I'd like to invite [partner] to come in and talk with me."

If the client does have some objection, the therapist is inviting him or her to voice it. Clarification of any objection may provide important information, even if the decision is not to invite the partner for an appointment. For example, Nicole said, "Oh, *no*. I haven't told my husband I'm coming here. I don't want him to know how unhappy I am." Her response added important information about the extent to which Nicole was concealing her concerns from her husband.

Some objections become less problematic after they are discussed. For example, Harry said, "My wife refuses to see anyone. She says she doesn't need therapy, because it's my problem." The therapist acknowledged that Harry's wife well might refuse an appointment, but that the therapist planned to use an approach designed to minimize the likelihood of that happening. In this approach, suggested by Fisch (1990, personal communication), the therapist instructs the client to let the partner know that the therapist will be calling. The client is encouraged to specify that "it was the therapist's idea, and I took the liberty of giving him (her) your number." If the partner bristles, asking, "Why should he (she) be calling me?," the client is encouraged to reassure the partner that there is no major crisis (assuming that is an accurate statement). Maybe the therapist "needs some help with me." The message to be *avoided* is that "the therapist thinks *you* have the problem."

After the partner knows that the therapist will be calling, the therapist telephones, saying something like: "Did [original client's name] tell you that I would be calling? I need some help with him (her), and I wondered if you'd be willing to come in for a one-time individual appointment with me? I'd really appreciate your perspective about what's going on with him (her)." When the request is made in this way, most partners are quite willing to come in. Even partners who adamantly insist that they "don't need therapy," individual or marital, for themselves are often willing to assist, in a collateral role, to help "the identified patient." Some are quite eager to offer their views about "what the real trouble is."

In the session, the therapist thanks the partner for coming in and inquires about how he or she sees the situation that led to the original client's appointment. From his or her perspective, what is of greatest importance? Using the same kind of inquiry that is done in any session, the therapist tries to determine if there is any complaint for which this partner would be a "customer." If so, what will be different when this partner can say that this is less of a problem? What has he or she tried to do about this concern? What is important for the therapist to know about the original client—or about the relationship—in order to be of maximum help?

At the end of the session, one or more components of the three-part intervention can frequently be designed for the partner. It is almost always appropriate to compliment the partner about being concerned enough to come in and on sharing a valuable perspective. Sometimes there is also an opportunity to encourage continuation of interactions that have been described as helpful. In other situations, there is an opportunity to suggest a different response, presented in language congruent with the partner's views about the nature and/or etiology of the partner's problem.

The therapist invited Mario for an appointment to share his perspective about his wife, Stephanie. Stephanie had complained of depression, primarily because of her relationship with Mario, whom she described as "macho, cold, and unfeeling." During his appointment, Mario expressed his belief that Stephanie's depression was the result of growing up with an overly critical mother. When asked how he had tried to deal with Stephanie's depression, he said that he had tried to "get her to count her blessings." Mario acknowledged that this approach was not working.

The therapist wondered aloud to Mario if Stephanie's experiences with her mother might somehow lead her to hear his well-intended advice as criticism, too, even though the therapist knew that it was not intended as such. Mario agreed that this could be happening, and he was receptive to a suggestion to tell Stephanie that he perhaps had underestimated the magnitude of her pain. Mario did not see the therapist again, but Stephanie's feedback during her subsequent appointments suggested that her dissatisfaction with their interaction had decreased.

Information from the partner session can also suggest ideas for working with the original client. For example, once the therapist knew that Mario thought in terms of family of origin issues, Stephanie could be encouraged to share with

Mario her feelings of sadness and disappointment about her mother. Without the appointment with Mario, it would not have occurred to the therapist to suggest that Stephanie deliberately discuss these feelings with a man initially portrayed as "unfeeling."

Sometimes material emerges in a partner appointment that the therapist thinks would be helpful for the partner to share with the other person, and there is some reason to believe that the communication would be more powerful if done during a conjoint session. For example, Jonathan told the therapist that he realized that he teased his partner, Alfredo, when he was upset about other things. The therapist suspected that if Jonathan attempted to say this to Alfredo at home, Alfredo would be likely to misinterpret it. On the therapist's suggestion, a conjoint appointment was scheduled. The therapist facilitated the discussion of Jonathan's important realization, maximizing the likelihood that Alfredo would "hear" it accurately. The scheduling of appointments —individual with the original client, individual with the partner, conjoint, followed by individual again, with either or both—must remain flexible, tailored to the needs of the couple.

Sometimes the partner is never seen, either because he or she refuses the therapist's invitation, or because the original client does not want the contact to occur, or for some other reason. The work may be more difficult and may take longer, because the other person's complaints and position must be inferred rather than directly investigated. Nonetheless, desired change in the relationship frequently results from strategic solution focused therapy with one person. Change in one partner's behavior cannot help but influence the larger system.

8

Coping with
Difficult Situations

S ome of psychotherapy's most difficult clients are those who face painful and complicated life situations. Understandably, these clients frequently hope that psychotherapy will eliminate the painful feelings, the uncomfortable circumstances, and the uncertainty they face. Often therapy cannot fulfill that hope. When the goal appears to be unattainable, the therapist's task is to manage the situation and to attempt to transform unattainable goals to achievable solutions. This chapter describes how strategic solution focused therapy approaches that challenge.[1]

Here are some examples of complaints about a situation or state of affairs: "My job is being eliminated," "My husband left me for another woman," "My car was totaled." In these situations, the client is understandably distressed, and he or she may feel powerless to change the situation. The implicit assumption may be. "As long as this undesirable state of affairs exists, I will be distressed."

Sometimes an unwanted feeling is defined as the primary problem. For example, one client says, "I worry too much about AIDS. I have to stop this obsessing." Another says, "I should be over her now, and getting on with my life." Here, the assumption is: "As long as I feel this way, I'm stuck and unable to take the next step."

[1]An earlier version of this chapter was published as "From Unattainable Goals to Achievable Solutions" in *Journal of Systemic Therapies*, 13, 59–64 (1994).

Other clients complain about difficulty tolerating uncertainty. "Will I go crazy if I keep having these feelings?" "I don't have the confidence to apply to law school. I just don't know if I'll make it!" "What if I'm making a bad decision by staying with him?" In these situations, the client wants "certainty" or reassurance—that she will never go crazy, that he can make it as an attorney, or that the decision about the partner is the correct one. Again, the implied assumption is: "As long as uncertainty about this exists, I will feel distressed and unable to take action."

In *Change,* Watzlawick, Weakland, and Fisch quote Robert Ardrey: "While we pursue the unattainable, we make impossible the realizable" (Ardrey, 1970, p. 3). Watzlawick et al. refer to the "utopian syndrome" and assert that the belief that things "should be" a certain way (and not the way they are) is frequently the client's unsuccessful attempted solution (Watzlawick et al., 1974). A number of techniques used in strategic solution focused therapy can help clients to "realize the possible." Many of these attempt to decrease the client's sense of powerlessness, while some emphasize the inability of the therapist to eliminate uncertainty and difficult situations, and others redirect client efforts along different paths.

Clarifying and "Deconstructing" Difficult Problems and Unattainable Goals

The same principles and procedures utilized in any strategic solution focused work are applicable when the client appears to have an unattainable goal. Problem clarification may be particularly important here, as the therapist attempts to define a workable problem. For example, Marjorie called for an appointment because of "county layoff problems." The therapist, who was quite familiar with the political and economic realities of the county, had this thought: "Another tough county situation. I wish I could help but, boy, do I ever feel powerless with these county employees." Nonetheless, the therapist took a deep breath and began the appointment by trying to clarify the problem.

The county government was cutting back personnel in Marjorie's department. Marjorie had not personally been laid off, because she had "high seniority." However, the other person who shared her workload had been laid off, leaving Marjorie twice as much work to do. Although the way in which this would be problematic seemed fairly obvious, the therapist nonetheless asked Marjorie how this was a problem. Marjorie answered, "I know they'll make me come in at seven in the morning to answer the phones. And my son's day-care doesn't open until eight. He's done so well there, and it breaks my heart to think of starting him somewhere else."

The therapist asked Marjorie how much difference it would make if she could somehow know that her son would be able to continue his day-care. "A tremendous amount," Marjorie answered. Thus problem clarification "deconstructed" the complaint. The definition of the problem had shifted from "layoff"—something neither Marjorie nor the therapist could influence—to "concern about child care arrangements." The latter was a far more tangible, limited, and workable problem.

Sometimes questions about how this situation, feeling, or uncertainty is a problem lead to answers emphasizing unpleasant feeling states rather than behavioral excess or deficit. That is, the client says that this is a problem primarily because it is uncomfortable or unpleasant: "I just don't like to feel this way." The therapist may now ask whether the client believes that the intensity and nature of the feeling state are appropriate to the situation or stressor. The therapist may even express surprise that the client is not *more* distressed or disabled, given the magnitude of the stressor. Interventions such as these are used in an attempt to validate and normalize the reaction.

Ben had AIDS and was becoming more debilitated. His partner (who was healthy) was supportive, but he had to work and could not be with Ben all the time, nor could he accompany Ben to his numerous medical appointments. Ben felt increasingly depressed and fearful. The therapist asked if Ben had noticed that his distress varied in intensity. Initially Ben said "No," but as he thought longer, he realized that variations did exist. When did he feel worst? "When I have to go out, to the doctor or even down here (to see the therapist)," Ben replied. Further inquiry about Ben's concerns revealed that as he became weaker, he feared that he would fall or have difficulty using an unfamiliar bathroom. Although he had talked extensively in his AIDS support group about his fears of dying, he had never mentioned the other concerns "because they seemed so mundane." Labeling, validating, and normalizing these very realistic fears facilitated Ben's acceptance and handling of them.

Coping Questions

When a client is experiencing overwhelming pain, too-rapid movement toward relief on the part of the therapist can seem disrespectful. Efron, Clouthier, and Lefcoe (1994) point this out, adding that the therapist who persists in searching for "exceptions to the pain" can come across as if the message about the distress has not been received and acknowledged. In such situations, coping questions (Berg, 1991; Berg and Miller, 1992) can be useful tools.

Coping questions ask how the client manages to go on in the face of the situation. "Given what you've been through in the last year, how *do* you get though the day?" "How do you manage to drive safely through that traffic and then get through a day in that place?" As Berg and Miller point out, clients tend to describe simple behaviors, or they say, "I just do it."

Walter and Peller (1992a) emphasize the meaning conveyed by the wording of the coping question. "How did you get yourself to do that?" and "How did you manage to keep going?" contain presuppositions that invite clients to see themselves as making choices and grasping control. That is, it is not "just by chance" that the client "got through." Even if the coping behavior did not seem at the time to be the result of active choice, the therapist gently is pointing out that the client *did* have a choice, and that he or she selected the "coping" alternative.

Compliments are implicit in inquiry about coping behavior. Phrases such as "That's amazing!" suggest admiration and respect. Sometimes clients respond to "How did you do that?" inquiry by saying, "For my baby (husband, mother, country, etc.)." This response provides an opportunity for the therapist to observe, "You care about him (her, it) very much," another implied compliment.

Coping questions can be valuable with clients who have lived through a variety of traumatic situations, including incest, extreme deprivation, or chronic illness. Shutty and Sheras (1991) describe therapy with chronic pain patients that uses therapist surprise that the patient can walk at all. Dolan (1994) encourages survivors of incest to identify how they got through the difficult times. The debriefing following a trauma or acute crisis emphasizes "You made it through" (Miller, 1991). Questions such as "How did you keep your wits about you?" may be more useful than rushing too quickly to reassure someone that he or she "will be okay." Berg and Miller (1992) highlight what the individual did *personally* to survive. "I'm amazed that somehow you had the good judgment to get yourself out of there. How did you think of that?" A client who has kept an important secret can be asked how he or she managed to live with that information for all this time. With someone who has just chosen to divulge a long-kept secret, the therapist may wonder aloud how the person found the strength or courage to speak.

Coping questions can be extremely valuable with clients who experience suicidal feelings. Suicidal behaviors represent the person's attempt to deal with emotions or situations that seem intolerable. In the terminology of strategic solution focused therapy, the suicidal behavior is an attempted solution. Linehan (1993) uses the term "distress tolerance skills" to describe the alternate solutions clients can develop for managing intensely painful affect. One of the most powerful ways of teaching distress tolerance is through identification of coping behaviors the person has already used successfully. Distraction, self-soothing, anticipation of consequences, and consideration of alternatives are all skills that may already be used by the suicidal person, even if he or she does not realize it.

Janine had struggled with depression, stormy interpersonal relationships, and suicidal thoughts for years, and she had cut her wrists on two occasions. She made an appointment after a much-publicized incident in which a man threatened to jump from a bridge. While driving over that same bridge two days later, Janine thought about how empty her own life seemed. She went home and looked in the medicine cabinet and thought about taking a bottle of pain medicine. Instead, she listened to music for two hours, eventually falling asleep. The next day, when she called the therapist and was seen, Janine felt a little better. She had plans to go to her Spanish class that afternoon and to have dinner with a friend that evening.

"It's truly remarkable that in the midst of all that pain, you were able to see that the music and sleeping would get you through the worst time," the therapist said to Janine. "How did you figure that out?" "I don't know," Janine said. "I just didn't want to think anymore." Together the therapist and Janine talked about the elegance of a solution that had enabled Janine to stop the pain without ending her life in the process.

Amplifying the Coping Response

Once coping skills have been identified, the next therapeutic task is to encourage the continuation and amplification of distress tolerance behavior. As discussed previously in this book, highlighting and complimenting are interventions in themselves. In addition, the therapist can specifically ask the client how he or she can *continue* the behaviors that have been described. After Janine and the therapist had discussed her ability to "sleep off the pain," the therapist asked, "So what will it take for you to do that again?"

Therapist inquiry that invites elaboration of coping responses can be seen as a type of miracle question inquiry. In a "coping miracle question," the future scenario to be described is *not* one where the problem is solved. On the contrary, the therapist attempts to communicate an expectation that the painful situation or affect will still be present, but that the client will somehow be coping. Depending on the client's language and affect, the word "miracle" may deliberately be *omitted*. Efron and Veenendaal (1993) describe a therapist asking a client to consider a scenario where her father was still drinking and being mean, but the family members were learning to treat each other better anyway. The family might still be miserable, but not as miserable as they were now. The authors use the term "minimal misery" to describe the picture they are creating.

Here are some additional examples of questions designed to elicit "minimal misery" scenarios. "If you can't overcome your fate or your past, and you have to live a marginal life, what would at least make it more tolerable?" "What could you do for your children (loved ones, community) that would make you feel your life at least had a little meaning?" "If we can't erase your experiences, and it looks like that will be the case, what goals might you still set anyway?" (Efron and Veenendaal, 1993, p. 16).

Sometimes a client describes an extremely difficult marriage, work situation, or living arrangement. The person says that he or she would like to leave but realistically cannot do so now, because of financial constraints or other restrictions or obligations. The therapist may encourage the client to consider alternatives, but it may soon become apparent that too much encouragement to "find a way to leave anyway" would be counterproductive, becoming an unsuccessful attempted solution. Here the therapist may want to use this kind of coping miracle question: "Since you can't leave now, because of [circumstances], is there something you can do to make your life more comfortable while you're waiting?"

A variation of this question is applicable in a wide range of difficult situations: "Do you have to wait for X (certainty, the economy to improve, your husband to stop drinking, etc.) in order to make things better for you, or are there things you can do to make it better even while you're waiting for X?" (Berg, 1992, personal communication). This is an extremely versatile, useful, and powerful question. The client may answer, "I realize I *do* believe that X must change in order for things to get better." This response clarifies that the client truly may need to take action regarding X, or that he or she may need to give the self permission to be distressed about X, or both. More frequently, however, the client's response reflects an awareness, sometimes a new awareness, that he or she does not need to wait for X in order to make things better. "When you put it that way," Harvey said, "I see that if I wait till I'm over her completely, I'll be waiting forever." Harvey was now ready to elaborate on a scenario where he was still not yet "over" the woman who had left him, but he was coping and seeing things in a different way.

When difficulty tolerating uncertainty is the primary problem, "hypothetical miracle questions" can be useful. The example of Celeste in Chapter 3 illustrates the use of the hypothetical miracle question. This question asks the client: "If you could somehow know [that you'll never die of a heart attack, that your son will never do drugs, etc.], how would that make a difference? What would you do differently as a result of that knowledge?" Frequently the answer reveals adaptive behaviors, things that the person has considered but postponed because of "lack of certainty." Together the therapist and client can reflect on the existential reality that one can *never* know these things in advance and that "waiting for certainty" to proceed becomes an unsuccessful attempted solution. An alternative is "going ahead and living one's life" (driving on the freeway, letting one's son go away to school, etc.), even in the presence of uncertainty.

Coping scenarios can be important therapy tools to use with survivors of sexual abuse. Dolan (1994) encourages clients to create visions of the self as "ex-victims." She describes a technique that she used with a client who was frequently (but not constantly) in a very depressed state. She encouraged the client to write a note to herself when she was in a "coping frame of mind." When she was feeling desperate, the client was to read the "coping message" to herself.

Some clients agonize about whether or not molest actually occurred. Did it "really" happen, or have suggestions or fears begun to seem like reality? Yapko (1994, p. 169) writes: "Given [where] the unbridled need for certainty [about whether or not a molest took place] can lead us, perhaps the most appropriate goal is to *learn to live with the uncertainty and get better anyway*" (italics Yapko's).

Coping scenarios are also useful for couples who are stuck at impasses. Wile (1981) points out that suggestions that the partners "compromise" and "work harder on the relationship" may not help when the partners are already trying— unsuccessfully—to do these very things. "The task in some cases may not be to help partners solve or eliminate problems, but to enable them to acknowledge them, tolerate them, and incorporate them into their relationships" (Wile, 1981, p. 199).

Saul and Maggie predictably repeated their dance of pursuit and withdrawal. The therapist told them that one could imagine Saul and Maggie as characters in a television situation comedy, one which the public followed faithfully, because the protagonists were so predictable and lovable. The viewer could commiserate, laugh, and cry with Saul and Maggie, identifying with their predicament. In every episode, the specifics varied, but the theme was always the same. This couple's task was not so much to alter their pattern as to recognize and tolerate it, without either partner becoming destructive.

Another valuable tool in the development of coping responses uses the process of "externalization," as described by White and Epston (1990). In this process, the therapist and client create a mutually acceptable name for the problem, such as "bulimia," "the economy," or "Dad's Alzheimer's." The therapist wants to convey the message that "the problem is separate from who you are as a person. The problem is not the person; rather, the problem is the problem." Calling the problem by name, the therapist investigates how that problem has been discouraging or dominating the person. Coping questions can elicit information about times when the person has been able to stand up to or escape from the oppression of the problem—and ways that the person can do this again.

Interrupting Unsuccessful Coping Solutions

Sometimes existing coping strategies can be identified and amplified; on other occasions, unsuccessful coping methods need to be interrupted. There are a variety of ways to redirect clients' efforts. The therapist may use reframing in order to disrupt the power of a label that implies limitations. For example, Duncan (1993) describes a woman who was sure that her diagnosis was borderline personality disorder. The client had strong beliefs in doctors' wisdom and wanted to pursue her understanding of borderline functioning. Speaking the client's language, the therapist reviewed possible origins of the problem. This discussion introduced the idea that the borderline diagnosis was one of several possible ways of describing this woman's condition. The therapist asked, "What if the diagnosis were incorrect? What would that mean?" The client answered that she would confront her husband, get a job, and take a class. Eventually the client concluded that she had been misdiagnosed. She wondered what an alternate diagnosis might be. The therapist suggested "dysthymia." Description of herself as "dysthymic" rather than "borderline" offered an opportunity for revision of meaning and deconstruction of the problem.

Redirecting efforts by interrupting unsuccessful attempted solutions has been described extensively throughout this book. People who feel overwhelmed typically receive messages of encouragement, such as "Things will get better" or "Therapy will help." When such messages do not produce the desired change, the strategic solution focused therapist is ready to take a very different stance. "Things may not get better, with or without therapy" is the message conveyed. The therapist may empathize with the magnitude and severity of the problem, expressing skepticism about how much the client—or the therapist—may be able to effect change. As discussed in Chapter 6, this message may be particularly important with clients who do not change in response to straightforward recommendations or encouragement to amplify a solution scenario. In the same way, the therapist may choose this approach with clients who have difficulty visualizing or amplifying "coping" scenarios.

The "pessimistic" stance can elicit several different client responses. On one hand, the client may feel "understood." Someone is finally recognizing the immenseness of the problem. On the other hand, the client may not like being told that the situation is hopeless. Angered and a little insulted by the therapist's pessimistic assumption, the client may think, "So he (she) thinks I can't change? Some therapist! I'll show him (her)!" In that spirit, the client may do something to "prove the therapist wrong," which can only be done by "improving," or changing that which the therapist has just predicted will be unchangeable.

Sometimes clients present for treatment of a problem that has persisted in spite of valiant efforts from an impressive list of previous therapists. As Watzlawick, Weakland, and Fisch (1974, p. 139) point out: "With these antecedents, the therapist soon realizes that his [her] head is destined to become the next addition to the patient's trophy board," and that too much optimism may well exacerbate the persistence of the problem. A message to the client about the unreasonableness of expectations for change can be quite useful.

There are a variety of ways to communicate this pessimism to the client. With some clients, the therapist may choose a rather strong message, such as "I have reason to feel (or "I have a colleague who would say") that your situation is hopeless." The therapist can also be gentler, complimenting the client on his or her persistence in seeking change, but cautioning that he or she may be overestimating what the therapist can accomplish in such a difficult situation.

A therapeutic message that goes beyond "You probably *won't* change" is this: "Even if you *could* change, you probably *shouldn't*." In a case described by Fisch, Weakland, and Segal (1982), the therapist points out the risks or dangers of improvement to the client in the following way: " . . . I wonder if there is something about resolving the problem that might, at some level—unconscious or slightly unaware level—[bring] some hidden threat or danger." Continuation of the status quo, as imperfect as it may seem, might be preferable to problem resolution.

For example, Eleanor complained of "chronic procrastination." She could not get going on her dissertation, and the deadline for completion set by her university was only one year away. The therapist asked Eleanor, "This might sound like a strange question, but if you were to solve your procrastination problem and start writing seriously now, what problem might that bring to your life?" Initially Eleanor could not identify anything. However, as she considered what she would realistically face when she *did* start working on her dissertation, Eleanor realized that her ideas were rather controversial. She would need to defend them to a dissertation committee member who was a vocal proponent of another theory. Of even greater concern, completion of her degree would bring Eleanor to the point of entry into the job market. For years Eleanor had claimed that her goal was a "real job" in her specialty, but now she realized that accepting such a job would require a geographic move from the city where her boyfriend held a tenured university position.

Therapist input that cautions about the dangers of improvement is sometimes useful for clients who complain about "lack of confidence." Frequently the client has had some recent experience—or a more general absence of experience in a particular area—that would make "lack of confidence" a fairly legitimate attitude. If this is the case, there is an opportunity to reframe the client's caution as appropriate rather than pathological. As Fisch (1991, personal communication) has pointed out, confidence grows from the repeated experience of things going well.

When Lars complained about his lack of confidence in applying for jobs, the therapist said to him, "With what you've been through at your last three jobs, I don't blame you for being less than fully confident. In fact, some people would say that after what you've been through, you'd have to be crazy to be confident about work." The message was not just "You probably *won't* be confident" but "You probably *shouldn't* be confident. Lack of confidence is *appropriate* under the circumstances." Following some additional problem clarification, as described in Chapter 2, Lars and the therapist concluded that "lack of confidence" was not the most helpful definition of the problem. "Not having a job" was really the complaint. Lars needed to begin to take some steps towards his vocational goals, even in the presence of legitimate discomfort and hesitancy.

Coping with Indecision

Many difficult life situations involve decisions. People agonize over choices involving commitment to relationships, both entering and leaving them. They struggle with how to deal with family members, whether to have children, how to cope with difficult medical situations, and how to resolve financial, vocational, and ethical dilemmas. When people consult therapists about these hard choices, their indecision is frequently presented as the problem. "I must decide" is frequently the implicit or explicit attempted solution. When telling oneself "to decide" fails to produce resolution, this message becomes an unsuccessful attempted solution. As discussed in Chapter 4, the therapist may attempt to interrupt this response. There are several ways of doing this.

In one approach, the therapist may bring up "the illusion of indecision." This essentially involves pointing out that "one cannot not decide" (Fisch, 1990, personal communication). The "decision" at any point in time "is" the behavior or status quo at that time. The dialogue between therapist and client might go like this:

Alexis: I don't know what to do about my marriage.

Therapist: What is the living arrangement right now?

Alexis: Well, my husband is staying at his brother's, and I'm in the house with the kids.

Therapist: You are separated, then; is that correct?

Alexis: Yes, but I don't know if I should file for divorce or ask him to come back or what.

Therapist: You have not filed for divorce, and you haven't asked him to come back as of now. Have I got that right?

Alexis: Yes, we are just kind of drifting along like this.

Therapist: It sounds to me like you two are separated. You know, many people would say that that's actually the most logical living arrangement for two people who are unsure about the future of their marriage.

The purpose of this intervention is to get "indecision" out of the way as a problem. If that is done, the therapist can attempt to clarify whether "being separated" is a problem. (It may not be; some clients experience relief in response to "therapeutic permission" to reframe a "problem" as a nonproblematic state of affairs.) If it *is* a problem, the therapist will clarify what about it is problematic, and/or how things will be different when it is *not* a problem, and treatment will proceed accordingly.

Sometimes the client directly asks the therapist, "What do you think I should do?" The question may be general, or it may be a request for an opinion on a particular alternative (e.g., "Do you think I should have an abortion?" or "Do you think I should quit my job?"). Using a straightforward approach, the therapist may encourage the client to consider a variety of alternatives and the anticipated consequences, desirable and undesirable, of each one. How would he or she cope with each alternative, and which would be the "lesser of the evils"?

The therapist may also encourage the client to consider the situation in a slightly different way. The client who is considering leaving his wife might be asked, "If *she* left *you*, would that be a problem?" If so, in what way? If not, there may be other obstacles to leaving, and these can be identified.

For the client who asks, "Do you think I should . . . ?" Fisch (1994, personal communication) has suggested the following response: "I don't know, but since you haven't . . . so far [if this is accurate, and if the person has had the opportunity], you must have your reasons, and I'm interested in hearing them." This approach introduces the idea that the client must have legitimate reasons for *not* pursuing the particular alternative under consideration. The therapist may want to encourage the client to take seriously his or her own reservations. Caution to "go slow" before altering the status quo may be used to interrupt an unsuccessful attempted solution of "I must change this." Using an approach suggested by de Shazer (1992, personal communication), the therapist might say, "If you do X, you'll wonder about what would have happened if you'd done Y, and if you do Y, you'll wonder about how your life would have been had you done X. Your confusion may be a good thing, because it keeps you from jumping into a mistake."

Sometimes clients say they *think* they know which alternative they want to pursue, but there is some discomfort, ambivalence, or regret about "the road not taken." Or clients may complain that they cannot take action until they feel sure that they have picked the best alternative. "I want to be positive I'm doing the right thing," the person says. As Walter and Peller (1994) point out, people sometimes think that if they are certain about a decision, that guarantees that things will work out. But this is not always the case. One can be unsure, and the decision can turn out well; conversely, one can feel sure, and it can turn out to be a mistake. Therapeutic intervention here may include asking questions such as: "What would have to happen to reassure you that . . . [you've definitely made the right decision, you'll never go crazy, you'll like that job]?" Whatever the client says, the therapist may gently "play devil's advocate," challenging that "proof." For example, if the client's history includes an instance of once being sure about something (a relationship, a job, health) and subsequently being disappointed, the therapist may point out, "You were certain before, and that didn't turn out the way you expected." This process continues until the client verbalizes the recognition that certainty is impossible; that is, even if the couple stays together for thirty years, there is no way of knowing (in advance) that the partner (or the client himself or herself) will *never* have a midlife crisis, leave, and so on. The goal in this questioning is to facilitate recognition of the fact that "certainty" is, in fact, unattainable, and to get "the pursuit of certainty" out of the way as a therapeutic goal.

This kind of discussion frequently results in the client deciding that he or she does *not* need to wait for "certainty" in order to make a decision or take action. It is now possible to introduce the kind of "coping miracle question" discussed earlier in this chapter. The client might be asked to imagine that he or she has not yet made a final decision, but is feeling "on track" to making a choice that feels comfortable. An alternate coping scenario might involve experiencing the ambivalence but, for some reason, noticing that it does not feel like so much of a problem.

Using Therapist Impotence: "I Can't Make It All Go Away"

Some clients remain distressed. They have come to therapy seeking an "answer" or unambiguous advice, and the therapist is not providing it. "But I *still* don't know what to do about Tony," Kristy wails. "Please tell me. You *must* know." Here the therapist's task is to clearly tell Kristy that being a therapist does *not* mean knowing in advance how things will turn out or what Kristy should do. "Kristy, maybe I should feel flattered that you think I have the ability to know what you should do. What we both know is that you have a tough situation, with no easy answers. But what I *don't* know is what you should do. I'm not clairvoyant, not at all." Using an intervention suggested by Fisch (1989, personal communication), the therapist might add, "My expertise is limited to suggestions about how you might make things less painful with Tony for however long or short you choose to stay with him."

Just as some clients are seeking clear advice about decision making, others have come to therapy hoping that somehow the therapist would take the pain away. Hugh wanted to stop feeling bitter about his experiences in Vietnam. The therapist and Hugh had extensively discussed the normalcy and appropriateness of Hugh's feelings, given what he had experienced. Hugh had (unsuccessfully) attempted to visualize a miracle scenario where the bitterness was gone, and he had extensively elaborated on coping scenarios, where the bitterness was still present, but not so much a problem. Hugh had received homework to experience his bitterness instead of pushing it away, and on several occasions the therapist had asked him to consider the disadvantages of leaving the bitterness behind. None of this helped. Hugh said, "I don't want to 'experience' it, and I don't want to have it but not mind it. I know the bitterness is normal, but I want it *gone*. That's the bottom line of what I want from you."

The therapist asked Hugh how he thought the therapist was supposed to take his bitterness away. With clients like Hugh and Kristy, the therapist needs to be both humble and very frank about what therapists can and cannot do. Therapists cannot make unpleasant situations disappear. Therapists do not have crystal balls that foresee the future. Therapists do not do lobotomies that will make painful experiences painless. Therapists do not make people feel happy about things that genuinely warrant sadness or distress. And if the client insists that the only acceptable outcome is total elimination of the uncertainty, discomfort, or uncomfortable situation, then therapy will not provide what the client is seeking.

After listening to the therapist's acknowledgment of inability to be of much help, Hugh agreed: therapy was *not* going to give him what he wanted. "So what are you going to do?" the therapist asked, gently but matter-of-factly. As Walter and Peller (1992a) point out, this question empathizes with the client's frustration and simultaneously conveys the message that responsibility is ultimately the client's. The question presupposes that the client *will* accept the dilemma and take action of some kind. "I guess I'll just keep doing what I've been doing," Hugh sighed. It should be noted that Hugh did *not* plan to suicide or do anything else drastic.

Most people respond to this kind of "So what will you do?" inquiry much as Hugh did. They say, "Well, I guess I'll . . . [e.g., apply to graduate school anyway, have my savings as a backup in case that doesn't work out]." In other words, the client has gone on to describe a plan of action. The therapist may follow up with questions like: "And how will that make a difference for you? . . . And how will you be coping with the possibility that . . . ?" If these questions elicit responses describing positive change or coping, the therapist may point out how surprising or impressive it is that the client has come up with such reasonable plans. These techniques again encourage the client to shift attention toward what is attainable.

9

Medication and the Model

The systemic therapy literature does not talk much about psychotropic medication. This book (so far, at least) is no exception. Strategic solution focused therapy, like MRI brief strategic therapy and BFTC solution focused therapy, works through verbal interchange between therapist and client. When constructs such as physiological predispositions and chemical imbalances are introduced, they are initially treated like any other construct. The standard inquiry is used: How does this construct become apparent in behavioral and interactional terms? In what way is it a problem? If it were not so problematic, what would be different? Are there already times when its manifestations are not a problem? What has been tried to reduce the influence of this construct? Did that attempted solution work well enough? If not, what approach would be different?

At the same time, the substantial literature on psychopharmacology makes little or no reference to systemic therapy. The Agency for Health Care has published guidelines recommending pharmacology as the first-line treatment for depression (Depression Guideline Panel, 1993). Sometimes the relationship between client and therapist is considered important primarily as the context that supports compliance with the medication regime (Pincus, 1993). There is empirical research that compares the efficacy of psychopharmacology and some therapies, primarily interpersonal and cognitive behavioral in orientation (Blackburn, Eunson, and Bishop, 1986; Elkin, Pilkonis, Docherty, and Sotsky, 1988). However, there is little discussion in the literature of the relationship between medication and strategic or solution focused therapy.

The paucity of dialogue is unfortunate, because both systemic therapy and psychopharmacology are important tools. Moreover, people who consult strategic solution focused psychotherapists often know (or have heard) a good deal about psychotropic medication. They come with a wide range of attitudes and belief systems about psychopharmacology. Some people have heard that "everyone should be on Prozac—it should be in the water." Others relate stories about "it making people suicidal." Positive or negative, these beliefs are position variables that must not be ignored. How strategic solution focused therapy and medication can complement each other is the subject of this chapter.

When the Client Wants Medicine

When a client requests medication (or any specific treatment), the strategic solution focused therapist attempts to clarify the problem for which that treatment is assumed to be the solution. As described in the discussion of problem clarification, the therapist may need to invest considerable time and effort in order to clarify what is most distressing. What complaints are primary? If "sleep" is a problem, in what way? Is the difficulty *falling* asleep or *staying* asleep? Is the anxiety present constantly, or does it come in waves? Is the depression a "wired" or "lethargic" feeling? This kind of information is of great importance to the physician who will be prescribing medicine; it is also of value to nonphysicians who relay information about symptoms to physicians who may prescribe. As continuing developments in pharmacology increase the array of available medications, specificity about the complaint becomes more useful. The health care provider who is skilled in problem clarification inquiry can obtain highly detailed information that has implications for which medication or combination of medications will be used for which symptoms.

Miracle question inquiry can also be useful with clients who request medication. The "specific miracle" may be "that the medication is beginning to work." The therapist might say, "Imagine that we prescribe a medicine for you today, and tonight before you go to bed, you take the first dose. And while you're sleeping, the medicine starts to take effect. Tomorrow morning, when you waken, what will be the first thing that will be different, that will let you know that the medicine is helping you, in just the way you hoped it would?. . .And what will you be doing different as a result of that change?. . .What else?. . .Who in your life will notice that you're different?. . .What will he(she) notice? . . . "

The information elicited through this inquiry can be useful in several different ways. As Cook (1995, personal communication) points out, the client's response can guide the choice of medicine. "That constant anxiety will be starting to go away. I won't be jumping out of my skin," Rodney says. "I'll be calm. Finally I'll relax a little." Rodney's description provides information about the desired effect, and his physician is better able to select the medicine most likely to produce that effect.

The therapist may also follow miracle question inquiry by asking about exceptions. "This calm feeling you're describing, are there times you're already experiencing some of that, these days?" If Rodney says "Yes," the therapist can elaborate, asking how Rodney created that feeling, and what was different as a result of that change. There is also an opportunity for complimenting. "I'm impressed you figured out on your own that taking those deep breaths quiets your body. You didn't need to wait to start the medicine to begin to feel slower, easier inside."

This discussion may result in the client shifting his or her perspective about medicine. If the desired change is already happening without medication, then perhaps medicine is not necessary. Maybe it will be sufficient to give a suggestion to "do more of what works" or to act "as if" the medicine is already taking effect.

Is "not prescribing" desirable? That depends on the person and the circumstances. If it is possible to achieve the desired changes without medication, which always involves some cost and the potential for side effects, many clients (and therapists) would prefer to do so. A nonmedication approach might be the first line of treatment, in the spirit of "do the most straightforward, least intrusive thing first." Many people who initially say that they want medicine are assuming that medicine is the only means to the desired end. Once they realize that there are alternate ways of producing change, and that they are already using these, they may see other possibilities.

For some people, "exceptions" exist, but they are not "good enough." The client does want medication, and the physician may agree that it is entirely appropriate. Here, the information about "exceptions" and suggestions about amplifying them can be used to assist the client while he or she is waiting for the medicine to take effect. The client might also be encouraged to notice when the desired changes are occurring, and what he or she does differently as a result of those changes.

Inquiry about attempted solutions is useful when different medicines have been used in the past. If something "worked" before, might it be prescribed again? Was there, or is there now, some obstacle to using that medicine? Were there side effects that the client could not tolerate, or was the medicine discontinued because it "worked" and was no longer needed? If a certain class of medicine was not helpful, the physician may want to search for "something different."

Position variables and strong attitudes are also important to consider. Some clients come with strong views about a "proposed solution." For example, Natalie wants Prozac. She has two friends whose "lives have turned around" (for the better) since they have taken it, and Natalie is convinced that it will help her, too. The physician will certainly need to evaluate whether Prozac is medically indicated for Natalie. Clearly it will not be given if it is not appropriate, no matter how badly Natalie wants it. But if the evaluation suggests that either Prozac or some other medicine would be equally appropriate, the physician may want to start with Prozac, precisely because Natalie feels so strongly about it.

Strategic solution focused techniques can be quite useful with clients who want to take medicine. However, it is important to note that inquiry about miracle questions, exceptions, and attempted solutions is not universally experienced as useful by clients who expect routine monitoring of their medication. Nylund and Corsiglia (1994) describe a psychiatrist who used a great deal of solution amplification during brief (fifteen- to twenty-minute) medication evaluations; as a result, some of this psychiatrist's clients decided to discontinue their medication. The authors do not specify whether or not the discontinuation of the medication was followed by positive change in the clients' lives. However, the implication is that some of the medication discontinuation was inappropriate and not helpful. In that context, too much solution elaboration was apparently confusing, not empowering. When the client expects and/or wants straightforward monitoring or adjustment of medication, that may well be what is most appropriate. In accordance with the guidelines of this model, the simple, straightforward approach is used first. Shifting to techniques that are too elaborate may be unnecessary and disconcerting when brief, straightforward medication monitoring appointments are sufficient and "working."

When the Client Does Not Want Medicine

Some clients make a point of letting the therapist know that they do not want to take medicine. The very act of mentioning this communicates the message that medication has been considered or suggested as an option at some point. After all, no one makes sure that the psychotherapist knows that "eyeglasses" are not wanted as part of the treatment! Some people expect that medicine will be recommended because they have taken it previously. Others have been advised to try it by friends, relatives, or health care providers. Still others have been influenced by the media or general discussion in such a way that they expect that medication will be suggested by a psychotherapist.

People have a variety of reasons for not wanting to use medicine. Sometimes there are medical contraindications for pharmacology; pregnancy is one example. Some people have had unsatisfactory prior experiences with psychotropic medication, either because of intolerable side effects or because of failure to obtain the desired results. Others have not taken the medicine personally, but they are cautious because of "horror stories" (real or exaggerated) they have heard about side effects, possible dependence, or some other complications. Some people who are involved in twelve-step recovery programs have had so much trouble with drugs in the past that they are extremely reluctant to consider "mind altering" medication of any kind. Some people are concerned about possible repercussions in the workplace if their employers find out they are taking psychotropic medication. And some simply prefer not to use medication as part of the solution for psychological and interpersonal problems. The strength of this preference can vary, from an adamant insistence that one will never put a foreign chemical into the body, on one hand, to a simple preference to use nonpharmacological measures first, on the other.

Strategic solution focused therapy is quite well suited for many people who want an alternative to psychotropic medication, and people who do not want to take medication often use the model quite effectively. Clients whose position and beliefs involve "doing it yourself" can be highly motivated "customers." Sometimes they have specifically sought out a strategic solution focused therapist. They may be actively requesting the kind of input the therapist provides, and they may be very willing to implement homework suggestions. And if the client has some reason to want to "prove wrong" someone who has said or implied that "only medication can solve your problem," that motivation can enhance compliance with the therapist's recommendations.

Sometimes the person who has initially been identified as symptomatic does not want to take medicine, but someone else in the person's life (partner, child, etc.) has strong feelings about the need for a medication solution. In this situation, the therapist may work separately with each part of the system. The concerned family member may be the primary customer, and the therapist certainly wants to meet with the customer. The first step will involve problem clarification: Exactly what is the person doing that is disturbing? The therapist attempts to elicit information about the context and an interactional description of the distressing behavior.

Then a variation of a miracle question may be useful. "If [the person you are concerned about] were to agree to take the medication, and the problem started to diminish, how would that show? What would be the first sign that the medicine was starting to take effect? How will you be different when he (she) does that? How will he (she) know that you're not as worried as you are today?" Next comes the inquiry about exceptions: "Have you noticed that there are any times lately that some pieces of what you've just described are already happening?. . . Are there some brief times when it's almost as if he (she) were already taking medication?" If so, the therapist asks, "How did you do that?"

Inquiry about attempted solutions will also be useful. This inquiry can emphasize either "What have you tried in your best attempt to get the person to take medication?" or "What have you tried in your best attempt to diminish the behavior that concerns you?" The latter question is usually preferable, because if the target behavior were to diminish (for any reason), the concerned other would no longer feel so desperately that medication is absolutely necessary. Moreover, the therapist may want to introduce the notion that medication may not be the only alternative, especially if the identified client does not want to take it. The concerned other may find it useful to consider other approaches.

Input to the concerned "customer" can always validate concern about the distressing behavior, (e.g., "I don't blame you for being worried about Stacy"). Concern and desire to be of help can be complimented. When there are times that the problem behavior is less problematic, a concerned helper can be encouraged to notice how those happen, even without medication, and to create more of those times whenever possible. When the problem remains severe, with few exceptions, the therapist may choose to point out that although it is not yet clear what, if anything, *will* work, there is now increased clarity on what does not, and that is a valuable first step.

Frequently the unsuccessful attempted solution is the message that "you must take medicine." There are a variety of ways of interrupting this message. Some involve the family "backing off" from the "You are sick and therefore need medicine" approach, perhaps by saying "Maybe I'm making too big a deal of [the need for medicine, or the target behavior, or both]." Other approaches involve the concerned person being unpredictable in some other way.

When meeting with the identified client, the therapist will identify what, if anything, is a complaint for that person. The fact that others are "making too big a deal about me" may be a primary concern. Careful problem clarification may reveal that the "fuss" is not equally troublesome at all times; rather, it increases following certain interactions. For example, Stacy acknowledged that Ken's (her husband's) lectures about "You're getting sick again. You need to get back on medicine" usually followed her screaming episodes. The therapist asked Stacy what Ken had done that had led to her screaming. "He talks down to me. He treats me like a two-year-old," Stacy said. Together Stacy and the therapist discussed the fact that when Stacy tried to stop the "talking down" by screaming, her approach backfired. Not only did Ken's condescending tone and words go unchanged and unacknowledged, but now Stacy was "the sick one."

If someone has (unsuccessfully) been pressuring the client to take medicine, the therapist will want to be very careful not to repeat what has already been demonstrated to be an unsuccessful approach. The therapist asked Stacy what she thought about medicine when Ken suggested it. She said that she had taken medicine before, and although it had calmed her down, she had disliked the side effects. The therapist asked Stacy to describe those side effects in detail. "Those sound like a pain," the therapist empathized. Had Ken ever taken similar medicine? He had not, and he could not appreciate what a hassle the side effects were. Eventually Stacy told the therapist that she would like to find out about other medicines that might be available. Maybe there were other possibilities. And even if there were not, it would be nice to feel more stable, and she would like to be able to "tell Ken where to get off without losing it."

Sometimes the therapist may frankly agree with other health care providers or family members that medication would be a good idea. After all, there is a great deal of evidence that behaviors and feeling states associated with schizophrenia and bipolar disorder often respond dramatically to psychopharmacology—and not to psychotherapy. In the spirit of "doing the most straightforward thing first," suggesting drug therapy as a first-line approach is consistent with the strategic solution focused model. In situations where the client's position opposes medication, and the therapist has reason to believe that medication would be helpful, both variables must be considered in planning the approach.

In a discussion of problem solving in psychiatric emergency situations, Perlmutter and Jones (1985) describe a session with a man who displayed paranoid symptomatology. The therapist told the man that medication might relieve some of his distress, but that he might well have some reluctance about taking it. The therapist pointed out that the man had little reason to trust the therapist, who was a total stranger. And how could he know what was "really" in the pills? Therefore, the therapist was "stuck" about what to recommend. The authors report that eventually the man used both psychotherapy and medication. As with some other interventions that include elements of paradox, this therapist's message conveyed the dilemma that a therapist genuinely experiences in this kind of situation. Acknowledging the reality that taking medication does involve potential risks communicates empathy and validates the client's concerns. Freed from the burden of being the lone defender of the cautious position, the client may choose to take the medicine anyway, even in the presence of the risks.

Medication as an Option

In the treatment of some clinical conditions, both medication and psychotherapy have demonstrated efficacy. Both therapists and well-informed clients may recognize that both treatments are options, and respected experts may disagree about which treatment to pursue first. Unlike people who either demand or refuse medication, many clients "could go either way." Many therapists also share that position.

Todd, a high school senior, was mildly but chronically depressed, and he was painfully shy. He worried about how his peers saw him, and he recognized that he was "different," much more sensitive than his classmates. His therapist described Todd's situation in a peer review meeting. Should Todd be referred for a medication consultation? A variety of opinions were expressed.

On one hand, it seemed possible that medication could diminish Todd's anxiety, rumination, and avoidant features, all things that were interfering with his ability to form relationships and prepare for his future. Since medications that could target Todd's symptoms were available, should he not be encouraged to try them now, in preparation for a possible "new start" in college? On the other hand, Todd had not received a "real trial" of psychotherapy, strategic solution focused or otherwise. Was it premature to recommend medication so soon for someone so young?

Therapists who had worked in this setting for many years reflected on the fact that this kind of discussion would not have taken place fifteen years earlier. Then it was a matter of course that one would not rush to medicate a young man struggling with mild depression and characterological problems. The fact that medication was even being considered for Todd seemed to be "a sign of the times," reflecting an increased readiness to consider pharmacology as an option.

The therapist told Todd that medicine was an option, although not one that all experts would recommend. But the therapist wanted Todd to be an "informed consumer" about the alternatives available to him. After thinking about it and discussing the options with his parents, Todd decided to take medication and to participate in psychotherapy. He was still shy, but he was not as distressed about it. Would either strategic solution focused therapy or medication alone have produced the same results? Sometimes Todd and his therapist both wonder.

Louise called for an appointment because she was not functioning very well at work. She could not concentrate, and she felt anxious almost constantly. For five weeks she had been waking early with racing thoughts and could not get back to sleep. The therapist asked what the racing thoughts concerned. Gary, the man Louise loved, was still living with his wife. Louise could not stop thinking about him. She hated being "the other woman," and several months earlier she had given Gary an ultimatum: he needed to "decide" between her and his wife within six months. Now Louise was not sure she could—or wanted to—discontinue seeing Gary, even if he did not leave his wife.

Following strategic solution focused guidelines, the therapist attempted to clarify the part of the problem with which Louise wanted assistance. She answered, "The symptoms, especially not concentrating at work." Louise described a solution scenario (functioning at work, even with the discomfort, spending time with friends, and acting "less needy" with Gary). She described her attempted solutions ("You must keep the ultimatum, now that you've set it," for the "Gary" problem and "You must keep going at work," for the "functioning at work" problem).

In the intervention, the therapist attempted to empathize with Louise's dilemma and to compliment Louise on her ability to visualize change, even in the absence of a final decision about Gary. There were two principal suggestions. One involved noticing times that she was already "acting less needy" and spending time with friends. The other involved telling co-workers to bear with her if she was flaky for a while, because she was going through a tough time in her personal life.

The therapist made sure that Louise knew that she was welcome to request a medication consultation, in addition to any other therapy provided. Louise and the therapist both knew that many people would say that medication evaluation was clearly indicated for Louise's complaints, which included depression, anxiety, early wakening, and decreased concentration of over a month's duration. Louise asked the therapist's opinion. The therapist replied that *either* pursuing medication *or* holding off could be seen as reasonable courses of action. It really depended on Louise's preference.

Louise decided that she did not want to pursue medication now. She was not against *ever* taking it; her attitude was not a rigid rejection, but a preference. She had felt better during her conversation with the therapist, and she wanted to experiment with some of the ideas she and the therapist had discussed. If her sleeping and concentration did not improve, she would reconsider medication.

Louise returned three weeks later saying that she felt much better. She had decided to "listen to my body" and take a week off work. She had spent the week with friends, helping them paint their house. She had also done a lot of thinking about Gary, and she had decided that if she was so uncomfortable with her ultimatum, she did not have to hold herself to it, no matter what her friends advised. Although seeing him while he was living with his wife still was not what she wanted in the long run, maybe the situation did not have to be as limiting as she had made it. If Gary could have Louise and his wife, maybe Louise could have Gary and pursue friendships with other men, as well.

The therapist noticed that Louise had not mentioned sleep, concentration, or how she was functioning at work. When asked about these things, Louise said, "All that fresh air made me sleep like a log." She had been back at work for two weeks and felt that she was doing much better. Louise remarked how glad she was that she had decided to hold off on medication. She and the therapist observed that if Louise had begun medication the day of that first appointment, they might be marveling today about how much better Louise was doing now that she was starting to feel its effects.

"When It Doesn't Work, Do Something Different" and Medicine

The central principles of strategic solution focused therapy stress continuing solutions that are working and changing those that are not. "Medication"—both specific medicines and "pharmacology in general"—are attempted solutions. When a medication approach is not working, or not working well enough, it is time to "do something different."

Following the decision to begin medication, both health care providers and clients will monitor the effects. Based on the symptoms and the specifics of the client's condition, the prescribing physician has obviously made an informed decision about which of the available medicines will provide maximum benefit at the least cost. Sometimes the first choice "works." On other occasions, it does not, either because of intolerable side effects or lack of positive response (or both). In accordance with the principles of this model, the physician who approaches medication management from a strategic solution focused perspective will make necessary adjustments. Taking a pragmatic approach, the client and physician collaborate on making changes and then evaluating whether the new regimen is working better. The fact that one medication, or one dose, is not helping does not mean that *no* medication will help. As with other solutions, a little adjustment or change can sometimes make a big difference. And if there is a need for a major shift, as to a different category of medication, that can be made, too.

As mentioned earlier in this chapter, some clients reject medication altogether as an attempted solution. Although sometimes this decision is based on little or no actual experience with medication, some clients have had such bad experiences that they see psychopharmacology in general as an unsuccessful—or unacceptable—attempted solution. The following example illustrates this situation.

Myron was referred by his internist for "nonpharmacological treatment of severe depression." Myron was widowed and lived in a retirement home; he had several medical conditions that were chronic but not immediately life threatening. Myron's daughters and his sister were extremely concerned about him because he was becoming increasingly despondent and withdrawn. Extensive medical and neuropsychological tests had been conducted, and neither dementia nor other medical conditions appeared to account for the depression. Prozac, Zoloft, Trazodone, and lithium carbonate had all been tried. Myron and his family felt strongly that "medicine only made him worse." They also claimed that previous providers had been too quick to "rush for the pill bottle" without taking the time to talk to him.

The therapist met with Myron, his sister, and his daughters, together and separately, to clarify who was a "customer" for what. All were customers with the same complaint: Myron's despondency. Discussion with Myron in individual sessions clarified what he was upset about and what he did not like about social interaction in the retirement home. With his sister and daughters listening, Myron was able to amplify a solution scenario where it was okay to skip the retirement home movies and bingo games that he did not enjoy anyway. Myron's depression did not disappear, but it was not as extreme. Myron knew that if he wanted medication consultation at any time, that was available, but he did not choose to pursue it.

Just as medication can become an unsuccessful attempted solution, strategic solution focused therapy alone sometimes does not produce the desired results. As discussed in Chapter 6, when one component of the approach is not working well enough, the therapist may decide to emphasize a different part of the model. Another way to "do something different" is to prescribe medication, sometimes in addition to the psychotherapy—and sometimes instead of it.

Sometimes the therapist has made multiple attempts at problem clarification and solution amplification, and there have been a number of suggestions about continuing what works and changing what does not. Nonetheless the problem remains. To continue to search for the "right" problem, the "right" miracle question variation, or the "right" attempted solution becomes "more of the same." Discontinuing therapy altogether, that is, interrupting "working on the problem" in any way, is one option. Seeking a different kind of psychotherapy might be suggested, if the client wants to "keep trying" and if medication is not an option (e.g., in a difficult relationship situation, where the partners are "stuck" but neither individual has psychiatric symptoms).

If medication is a medically appropriate option for the client's symptoms, it may be time to interrupt the unsuccessful strategic solution focused approach by suggesting medication instead of therapy. "While you are being evaluated for medication (or waiting for the medication to work), don't deliberately do anything else to try and solve the problem," the therapist might say. Sessions with the therapist might be discontinued, or if the client wants to continue to meet, the therapist might stress that, for the time being, the purpose is solely to "let me know how you are doing," rather than to "do therapy" in any other way.

Another approach, probably more common, involves using medication in combination with the psychotherapy. In this approach, discontinuing strategic solution focused work is neither necessary nor desirable. On the contrary, the assumption is that if the medication decreases symptoms, the client will be better able to participate in problem clarification, solution amplification, and implementation of suggestions. The following example illustrates the combined approach.

Jessica had taken the last semester off from college because of depression and bulimia. She had spent the last four months living with her parents in her home state. She had seen a therapist there one time but had not followed up "because I'm going back to school." Now she was back in town, ready to return to college, and she "wanted therapy." Jessica said that she only binged and purged "once in a while," much less than she had done previously. Her main complaint was "feeling horrible." She stayed in her dorm room and did not go out with her roommates because she was "sure she would ruin their fun." Jessica was able to elaborate a solution scenario where she felt a little better. She could describe going out a little more, sometimes with her roommates and sometimes alone, even if she did not feel wonderful. Were there any times that she was already doing this? Yes, she had done so once in the previous week. The therapist's intervention included a suggestion to do so again.

When Jessica returned for a follow-up appointment two weeks later, she said that she was feeling worse. To do her therapy homework, she had attempted to go out with her roommates, but she had felt so terrible that suicide had crossed her mind as a possibility. She was attending her classes but going nowhere else. What the therapist had suggested was not helping.

Faced with the need to "do something different," the therapist could have used strategic solution focused therapy in a number of different ways. The session could have been devoted to detailed inquiry about the context in which the homework was done and exactly what happened to precipitate the suicidal thoughts. Or the attempted solution "Go out" could have been reversed to "Stay home—don't force yourself." Or most of the session could have been spent on detailed elaboration of how Jessica coped with the suicidal thoughts without acting on them. The therapist spent a little time on the latter option (asking coping questions) and checking for suicidal risk (Jessica denied both plan and intent), and then took a different approach.

"Jessica, what I suggested to you last time obviously hasn't worked," the therapist said. "And I'm aware that there's a very different approach that some of my colleagues would be saying that you and I ought to be seriously considering right now. And that's antidepressant medicine." Jessica said that her gynecologist had recommended medicine to her three months ago, and that she had not liked the doctor's idea. But now she was feeling worse, and she agreed with the therapist that it was time to try something different. With twenty minutes of the appointment time remaining, the therapist decided to use that time to arrange a medication consultation rather than to continue conversation with Jessica. Jessica would continue to meet with the therapist, and she started taking antidepressant medication that day.

Two weeks later, Jessica was starting to feel better. Now the therapist returned to several parts of strategic solution focused therapy that had not been pursued during the prior session. Exactly what had happened when Jessica tried to go out and became upset? In nine sessions over the next four months, Jessica and the therapist discovered Jessica's unsuccessful attempted solution: "Leave what's bad behind." Jessica was telling herself that two weeks without bingeing or purging meant that her bulimia should be "cured." She also told herself that she "should enjoy" going out. Interventions with Jessica included "planning" occasional binges and "stay-at-home nights." There was homework to "deliberately have a 'so-so' time at a Super Bowl party."

Jessica described a variety of miracle scenarios. In one she told her parents about her plans for after graduation and tolerated their anticipated disapproval. In another she imagined coping with suicidal impulses after a relapse of her bulimia. When she graduated and moved away, Jessica was still taking the medication. She planned to stay on it for a while and to seek additional psychotherapy in her home state.

When the Client Is Already Taking Medicine

"To take or not to take medicine" may not be a question or issue at all. Some clients who come for therapy are already using psychotropic medication, and they simply assume that they will continue to do so. They are not requesting an alternate approach or seeking an "opinion" about the appropriateness of medicine. The therapy is sought as an adjunct to the medication, which presumably will be continued independent of whatever happens in the therapy. In this kind of situation, "being on medicine" can be seen as part of the client's position. Like any other position variable, it will be accepted, incorporated into the treatment, and utilized whenever possible.

In some settings, people who take psychotropic medication are encouraged (or required) to participate in "supportive psychotherapy." Supportive psychotherapy can mean many different things, depending on the treatment setting, the therapist, and the client. The task implicitly or explicitly assigned by the treatment setting may be for the client to provide an update to the therapist about how things are going. The client may visit monthly (or at some other predetermined interval) because it is time for a visit, not because there is a specific complaint.

In this situation, the strategic solution focused therapist can easily inquire if there does happen to be any problem or issue with which the client wants assistance today. The therapist can directly explain that the client is not "required" to produce a problem; it is fine to simply "check in." Over time, there will probably be some appointments that are "routine checkups." These usually provide an opportunity for encouraging continuation of whatever is working well enough to enable the client to say that there is no particular problem. At other appointments, the client may have a concern to discuss, and the therapist can proceed with problem clarification, solution amplification, and clarification of attempted solutions, as in any case.

Gersten (1988) describes an approach used in addition to medication with a client who was distressed about visual hallucinations. The therapist encouraged the client to enhance his feelings of control over the experience by spending ten minutes "waiting for" the hallucinations at the time they were most likely to appear. This suggestion reversed the typical attempted solution, "I must keep my hallucinations away." Gersten emphasizes that this procedure was used in combination with neuroleptic medication. It was not intended to replace it, and the therapist neither directly suggested nor indirectly implied that the client should discontinue the medicine.

When coping questions are used to ask how someone got through a difficult time, clients who take medicine may make reference to that medication. "I knew that since the medicine has kicked in, the flutter wouldn't build to a full-blown panic attack," Peter said. "It would just be a flutter and then drift away." "How did knowing that help you?" the therapist asked. "It helped me keep my eyes on the road," Peter answered. "I just told myself, 'You're on 150 milligrams of Imipramine. So you can do it.' " Later, as part of the intervention, the therapist told Peter, "What strikes me is your capacity to trust the medicine, to know from your own experience that when you're on it, the sensations just pass." Peter could be encouraged to continue what worked.

Knowing how much the medicine helped him also helped Peter to cope with its side effects. Sometimes he experienced dry mouth or constipation, and these reactions were a nuisance. Remembering how effectively the medicine blocked the panic attacks enabled Peter to tolerate the discomfort. Sometimes he had the urge to skip his nightly dose. "Not all people tolerate those unpleasant side effects. How do you manage to keep taking your medicine, even when the side effects are such a pain?" the therapist asked. "I just remember that being a little dry is a heck of a lot better than thinking you're going to lose it," Peter answered emphatically.

Molly had been on Prozac for five years for "chronic dysthymia." She had tried other medicines, and she had tried to discontinue medicine altogether. She and her physician agreed that Prozac was the best choice for her, or at least "the lesser of the evils." Molly's complaint concerned her orgasms, which were less intense since she had been taking the medicine. She wondered if "sex therapy" could make her sexual experiences more enjoyable.

Molly had never been fully comfortable asking for the kind of touch she enjoyed. Her therapy began with some of the straightforward suggestions generally used with women who have this complaint. Molly was encouraged to notice what her body wanted and to practice masturbating, initially without any expectation that she would experience orgasm. When Molly's treatment progressed to the point that she did want to experience more sensation, the therapist cautioned that because of the Prozac, Molly probably would not experience sensations that were extremely intense. Since Molly knew that, she should not try to produce what was probably unachievable. Instead, she might notice any mildly pleasurable sensations that occurred in the absence of full orgasms.

Molly came to the next session with a "discovery": that the sensations did not have to be intense to be enjoyable. With the therapist's encouragement, Molly was able to tell her husband that she had learned in her therapy that she needed certain kinds of touch to compensate for the effect of the Prozac. To help her compensate, would he be willing to cup his hands around her breasts and to move his thigh against her clitoris? He was quite willing to be of assistance, and Molly found that even if the orgasms were less intense, she was feeling closer to her husband and enjoying sex more. Molly also spontaneously reported that other things in her life could be "less than ideal and still be nice." She observed that she did not work on her acrylic painting hobby as much as she wanted to, but that now seemed like less of a problem.

Some people experience distress episodically and have histories of symptoms that have reliably decreased in response to medication. Medication has therefore been a successful attempted solution, and it is fully reasonable for the client, and others, to hope and expect that it will succeed again. In some settings therapists take a "case manager" role with such clients, assuring that they are triaged for appropriate medication follow-up. Unlike the "supportive psychotherapist" role, the "case manager" role may not involve regular contact. Rather, the case manager assesses the situation, makes a disposition, and is "on call" if further service is needed.

The case manager who uses strategic solution focused principles may arrange the medication follow-up—and make it clear that if the client ever wants to address a specific problem, the case manager is available. The consultation will not replace the medication; it will be in addition to it. The message conveyed is this: "You tell me that you have an episodic condition that responds to psychotropic medication. Therefore, our first order of business is to get your medication taken care of. I know that your medicine helps you. At the same time, I do not assume that taking medicine will solve or prevent all life issue and relationship problems. If and when one arises, I'm available."

Antonio was a "case management" client. He had experienced recurrent depressions since his return from Vietnam, and each one cleared in response to antidepressant treatment. Now Antonio was becoming depressed again. He had consulted his internist, who wrote an initial prescription for antidepressant medicine (the same one Antonio had used four years earlier) and referred Antonio for follow-up in the psychiatry department. The case manager's task was to arrange that follow-up, along with any other care that was needed.

During the evaluation, the case manager asked Antonio what he was sad about. Antonio did not know. Nothing was different at home or at work, although he observed that he had been dissatisfied with work "for years." His work (landscaping supervisor) was no longer challenging, "But at my age, what else can I do?" Antonio shrugged. Antonio was not a "customer" for psychotherapy, for the work problem or anything else. He simply knew that he had to "get into the system" so that his next prescription could be written. He fully expected that work would not bother him so much after a month or so on the medicine. (That was part of his answer to the miracle question.) The therapist complimented Antonio on pursuing what he knew he needed and arranged the medication follow-up. As Antonio rose to leave the appointment, he asked, "After I'm on the medicine, if work is still a problem, what do you think I should do?" The answer was: "Set up another appointment with me, and we'll talk about it." Antonio appeared to have heard the message: some problems may persist, even when the medication is working.

Brief Therapy
Problems and Solutions in Managed Care

"**M**anaged care" is increasingly affecting the work of psychotherapists. Once seen as a specialized service, brief treatment is becoming a standard model of care. According to Austad and Hoyt (1992), most insurers cover their subscribers for somewhere between six and twenty sessions. Discussions of managed care can contain enough acronyms to fill a hearty alphabet soup. There are HMOs (Health Maintenance Organizations), PPOs (Preferred Provider Organizations), EAPs (Employee Assistance Providers), PCNs (Primary Care Networks), MCOs (Managed Care Organizations), and IPAs (Individual Practitioner Associations). This chapter addresses how strategic solution focused therapy approaches the issues raised by managed care.

Cost Containment Issues

Skyrocketing costs of health care have led to scrutiny of where the money is spent, both in mental health care and in health care in general. Resnick and DeLeon (1995) report the following information about health care cost problems and attempted solutions. As much as twenty percent of medical expenses may go for services that may be unnecessary, inappropriate, or inefficient, according to the projections of some health care experts. Fraud and abuse have been projected to account for another ten percent of health care dollars spent. Managed care attempts to solve these health care expenditure problems by assuring that only the most appropriate and cost effective services are provided. Resnick and DeLeon assert that this way of delivering health care has been considered since the 1930s. Later, in the 1970s, Nixon's health care reform proposals again emphasized managed care, as have most federal proposals made since then.

A managed care approach described by Cummings (1995) uses the term "catalyst model" to describe the therapist's role and tasks. In the catalyst model, many clients are seen, for brief episodes and often in nontraditional ways. The therapist is like a "catalyst" for change, like the "yeast for growth outside therapy." The emphasis is on restoring a natural drive for development that has gone awry. After an episode of therapist–client contact, therapy is not terminated but interrupted. In the catalyst model, every available healing resource is mobilized. Treatment is not limited to therapist–client contact in the therapist's office. Cummings asserts that some resources are more effective than office visits; certain conditions respond better to group therapy or psychoeducational approaches.

Managing limited benefits requires skill on the part of the therapist or case manager. When a resource is limited, people sometimes value it more highly than they would if it were freely available. This concept has been called "psychological reactance" (Brehm, 1966). Some ways of presenting a benefit that minimize psychological reactance will be discussed later in this chapter.

In response to benefit limitations, both therapists and clients display psychological reactance. Some protests are raised by therapists, most frequently therapists who believe that significant change occurs only in the context of longer-term therapy, often psychoanalytic in orientation. These therapists may see initial complaints as surface manifestations of underlying psychopathology. Some therapists have even taken the position that clients who want "real psychotherapy" cannot find it in the managed care arena (Karon, 1995). Other protests are raised by clients, often those who are specifically seeking longer-term, insight-oriented psychotherapy. Some of these people have had this kind of treatment before, some have heard that "real therapy requires an investment of time," and some are themselves therapists seeking personal treatment.

However, as Hoyt points out, "Many (if not most) patients want the most parsimonious and least expensive treatment that will help" (Hoyt, Rosenbaum, and Talmon, 1992, p. 80). Pekarik (in Chubb and Evans, 1987) noted that more than two-thirds of the clients sampled expected therapy to last less than ten sessions, and they expected to see improvement in five. Pekarik observed that many clients expected treatment to end even sooner, and they hoped to focus on direct problem resolution.

Not only does brief therapy appear to be what most clients prefer, but it also seems to be what they receive, regardless of the therapist's orientation or the initial treatment plan. Research studies on duration of treatment indicate that clients tend to stay in therapy for about six to ten sessions (Garfield, 1978, and Gurman, 1981, in de Shazer, 1985). Moreover, there is outcome research that demonstrates that efficient therapy can be effective therapy (Bennett, 1994).

The following sequence of events described by Chubb and Evans (1987) provides one example of the efficacy of brief therapy. These authors worked in a Northern California Kaiser Permanante psychiatry clinic. Before 1979, approximately one-third of the Kaiser subscribers received mental health services as a benefit. Those services were provided by experienced therapists, who conducted primarily longer-term, psychoanalytically oriented therapy. When the 1979 Health Maintenance Organization Act mandated extension of mental health coverage to all plan members, staffing was increased. However, costs rose and access deteriorated. In the early 1980s, the clinic administration began to encourage measures to decrease the length of treatment and to improve access. Different approaches were used in different facilities.

One facility was staffed with providers who were trained to conduct MRI brief strategic therapy. During most of 1985 and 1986, routine cases were seen within one week. At a neighboring clinic, therapists averaged more direct treatment hours, but routine cases were waiting an average of twenty-two weeks for an initial appointment. At the clinic using strategic therapy, the rate of hospitalization was the lowest of any facility in the region, and member satisfaction was above ninety percent.

A Model That "Works" in Managed Care

As emphasized throughout this book, the goals of strategic solution focused therapy are the resolution of clients' problems and the development of solutions that work. "Brevity" is not particularly a goal, in and of itself; nor is "popularity" with managed care companies. However, therapy based on the premises described in this book often does turn out to be brief. As Weakland, Fisch, Watzlawick, and Bodin (1974) point out in their discussion of brief strategic therapy, even when brevity is not the primary *aim*, it can be a *consequence* of using certain methods.

Strategic solution focused therapy "works" in managed care. It "fits" well with the catalyst model, despite the fact that neither strategic solution focused therapy nor its parent models were designed for the purpose of satisfying health care administrators. "Benefit limitations" regarding number of allowable sessions seem less restrictive to practice when most courses of therapy will naturally be completed within the designated number of appointments anyway. From the therapist's perspective, requirements for paperwork or administrative needs may seem like nuisances or annoyances at times, but they do not tend to be major obstacles that would preclude use of the model. Compared with therapists who find that the regulations block their ability to use their models in the intended way, strategic solution focused therapists typically experience less frustration and anger. The system generally supports (or at least allows) the therapist to do what seems to be clinically indicated. Experiencing the system as supportive, or at least benign, leaves more therapist energy available for doing therapy creatively.

Many of strategic solution focused therapy's component parts are especially useful if therapy must be brief. As noted in Chapter 2, the problem clarification phase of treatment, in which the therapist narrows in on the primary complaint, helps to guide the therapy and to assure that it is relevant. Therefore, problem clarification is extremely important, regardless of treatment's length. But in brief treatment, identification of a single focal issue is more than useful. Clarifying the problem, and in what way it is a problem, can be of critical importance. The therapist does not have time to conduct a four-session "evaluation phase." Nor does the brief therapist have the luxury of following free association, letting the conversation meander where it will, confident that eventually there will be an opportunity to integrate multiple themes and issues into the bigger picture. The "time might be up" before the central issue is addressed.

In the same way, the solution elaboration phase of strategic solution focused therapy rapidly leads to identification of goals, both the "initial miracle" and the details of how that solution will be manifest in daily interaction. Miracle question amplification and subsequent specification of exceptions can begin right away. Well before the end of a first session, the therapist and client often have identified both final goals and "first steps in the right direction." Direct inquiry about attempted solutions identifies what has been tried, while identifying what does not work immediately lets the therapist know what approaches or suggestions should probably be avoided.

By the end of a single appointment conducted in this way, the therapist has collected much essential information. In the process, there have been multiple opportunities for deconstructing, reframing, and other process interventions. During the intervention phase, the therapist summarizes the central complaint, validates the client's feelings, compliments strengths, and offers homework, advice, or suggestions. Significant therapeutic work has been done, sometimes so much that only a little follow-up is required. On some occasions the client is satisfied with a single session and does not need to reschedule at all. (Single-session therapy will be discussed in more detail later in this chapter.) The therapy is brief, not because of benefit limitations, but because what is needed for now has been completed.

Intermittent Care: "The Family Practice Model"

For now, the needed work has been done, and the problem has been resolved or appears to be resolving to the client's satisfaction. One reason that the therapist can be so comfortable and casual about stopping is that "the door remains open" for additional service, when and if it is needed. As Budman, Friedman, and Hoyt (1992) point out, therapy may be considered to be "time sensitive" rather than simply "brief." Treatment may involve a number of episodes of care spaced over time. Cummings and VandenBos (1979) call this "brief, intermittent psychotherapy throughout the life cycle." The therapist's practice is more like that of a general practitioner than like that of a psychoanalyst (Heath and Ayers, 1991; Cummings and VandenBos, 1979).

Heath and Ayers write the following about MRI strategic therapy, but their statement is fully applicable to strategic solution focused therapy, as well:

> *Clients are seen as entering and leaving therapy just as they would begin and end a series of consultations with their physicians. They go to the doctor when they hurt and stop going when they begin to feel better. Thus MRI therapists see clients over short intervals, consider cases open indefinitely, encourage people to stop therapy when specific problems end and return if other problems occur, interpret returns by clients as statements of their satisfaction, and expect that life goes on before, during and after therapy. (Heath and Ayers, 1991, p. 60)*

Using a different analogy, Bergman (1985) compares the therapist to the car mechanic. Just as one brings one's car in for specific repairs or a general tune-up, the strategic solution focused therapist can be a tune-up expert who does whatever is needed to "get the car back on the road." The car mechanic analogy is very different from that of guru, spiritual guide, poet, or mentor. Of course, some therapists may not like the idea of being compared to car mechanics!

Whatever the analogy, intermittent care offers maximum flexibility, and that flexibility is an asset when the therapist works with a large number of clients who present with a wide variety of complaints. When there are limited resources (staff, time), an intermittent care model becomes immensely practical. Kreilkamp (1989) writes about the application of an intermittent care model in a large staff HMO. Intermittent care works particularly well in a system where there are many consultants in many specialties (not just psychiatry) and where there is emergency room backup. Clients are accustomed to receiving consultations, with feedback given to the referring provider. However, Kreilkamp emphasizes that the model's utility is neither specific nor limited to HMOs, because intermittent care can be useful in any setting where many people require access to limited resources. Cummings and VandenBos (1979, p. 12) write that "brief intermittent psychotherapy throughout the life cycle has now been empirically studied for more than thirty years and has been shown to be more efficient and effective than keeping the patient in treatment beyond the resolution of the life problem presented."

When care is expected to be intermittent, it follows that "termination" is not viewed as a special event. On the contrary, its significance may be minimized. There is no implication that discontinuation of sessions means "graduation" from therapy, that underlying problems have been elegantly resolved, or that difficulties will not recur. As Fisch, Weakland, and Segal (1982) point out, the therapist may want to end with a recommendation that the client "go slow" and refrain from further improvement "for the time being." The therapist may predict or anticipate "relapse," and as part of the "coping strategy" for dealing with that relapse, there may be direct or indirect suggestions to return for "booster sessions" or a new course of brief therapy. Clients who are learning to manage anxiety are instructed to recognize that they are "body reactors," who will probably re-experience their "body reactions" when they hit "bumps on the road of life" (Quick, 1990a). When sessions are ending and the problem has *not* been resolved, Fisch, Weakland, and Segal recommend taking what they call a "gracious one-down position." Here, the therapist openly acknowledges that the therapy has not been as helpful as was hoped.

How Many Sessions? "Not One More Than Necessary"

A frequently asked question about strategic solution focused therapy addresses how many times clients are seen. The answer must be: "It depends." As de Shazer (in Simon, 1993) puts it: the answer to the question "How brief is brief (therapy)?" is: "Not one session more than necessary." This is especially true for clients who have experienced extremely difficult life situations. Simon also quotes Dolan (in Simon, 1993): "Therapy that is longer than necessary, especially for people who have suffered abuse or pain for a long time, adds to the abuse." Voicing the same sentiment, Berg (1991) has pointed out that "having to go for therapy" is or can become an additional problem. Therapy requires time and effort, and often there are financial and transportation costs. It is hoped that there will be benefits, too, of course, but for most people, "going for therapy" is a bit like going to the dentist. Therapy is a necessary procedure to "get over with" as quickly as possible, so that one "does not have to go back."

Some brief therapy protocols and managed care systems attempt to plan in advance how many appointments will take place. Therapists are sometimes encouraged to "contract" for a fixed number of visits. For example, when the managed care benefit specifies that clients may have six appointments, therapists frequently recommend six-session courses of treatment. However, as therapists who attempt to do this quickly discover, not all clients who receive this recommendation receive exactly six appointments. Many receive fewer, and some may receive more (when the system allows it).

The client's initial request is also an unreliable predictor of the length of therapy. When experiencing acute distress, a person may feel sure that he or she wants "long-term therapy to resolve the underlying issues that got me into this mess." However, when initial symptom relief occurs, motivation for that long-term treatment may diminish considerably. Conversely, someone who initially seeks or is referred for a single appointment may discover that the experience is extremely helpful in unanticipated ways, and the person may wish to return for more, if cost and benefit parameters make this possible. As de Shazer (1994, p. 274) points out,

> *The details and specifics of where clients want to go and what they wish for frequently change in the course of therapy, much to the surprise of both client and therapist. . . . For therapists to expect clients to know at the beginning of therapy exactly where they want to go is unrealistic; if they did, they probably would not need therapy.*

Rigidly specifying a fixed number of sessions in advance can be counterproductive in different ways for different people. Some clients (and therapists) see the last session as a "deadline" and worry (sometimes appropriately) that the initial problem will not be fully resolved by then, or that some new complaint will emerge. Other clients (and therapists) may act as if "having six sessions means that you can wait until the last one" to get to work. As Walter and Peller (1992b) have said, "If you want to do therapy briefly, approach each session as if it were the last or only time you will see that client."

From the perspective of strategic solution focused therapy, it is not surprising that length of therapy is so difficult to predict. Because the model emphasizes flexibility, it is expected that interventions, number of appointments, and who should come to the next appointment will constantly be shifting, in accordance with client position and with what is (or is not) working. Therefore, the strategic solution focused therapist frequently does not contract at the beginning for a specific number of sessions.

Spacing Sessions

The spacing of sessions, or the interval between appointments, is also individually tailored to the needs of the client and the situation. Like other intermittent care models, strategic solution focused therapy does not automatically assume that the therapist and client will meet weekly, or at *any* regular, predetermined interval. This often surprises clients who expect such an arrangement, either because of previous therapy experiences or because of what they have read or heard. Client preferences are position variables that will definitely be taken into account when the spacing of sessions is planned, but they are by no means the only consideration.

The following guidelines about spacing of sessions can be articulated. Intervals shorter than one week may be appropriate when a client is experiencing an acute crisis. One-week intervals are often useful between a first and second appointment or when there is a specific homework task. Somewhat longer intervals (two or three weeks) are useful when positive change has begun and the task is either continuation of that change or "restraint from further change." Still longer intervals are appropriate when the task is maintenance of change, as opposed to initiation of change. Fisch et al. (1982) recommend that the therapist suggest a break of some kind between sessions when the client reports that the initial problem has been resolved, and work on a second issue is requested. Taking some time before moving to the next problem can consolidate the learning involved in the resolution of the initial complaint.

Specific recommendations for longer intervals (after shorter intervals earlier in treatment) promote client confidence and independence. The recommendation for more time between appointments communicates this message: "I think you are on track. I do not see you as so fragile that you 'need me every week' to continue what you have begun." In managed care, where there may be a limited number of sessions, longer intervals between appointments can also help the therapy to "last longer." For example, six sessions held weekly are "used up" in six weeks. Those same six sessions may last eight months or longer if there is a one-week interval between the first and second, a two-week interval between the second and third, and monthly or longer intervals after that.

Longer intervals can also be followed by shorter intervals. Unless there is some particular reason not to do so, the client is welcome to return sooner if there is a need. In the same way, the therapist who has recommended previous intervals of one month may recommend a shorter time until the next appointment when there is a reason to do so. This recommendation punctuates the therapy, communicating a message like this: "Given what you've [told me today and/or what I'm suggesting that you do], I'd like to see you back sooner next time, if you're agreeable." Longer intervals may then be resumed after the crisis or new development has passed.

Follow-Up Sessions

Like initial sessions, follow-up sessions in managed care have a focus and generally do not invite free association or open-ended conversation. Follow-up sessions in strategic solution focused therapy can be structured in several different ways. Sometimes the therapist may want to inquire about a homework assignment given during the previous appointment. On other occasions, the follow-up session might begin with an inquiry suggested by Walter and Peller (1992b): "What's better?" A variation of that inquiry asks "What's better—or different?" Although either of these questions may initially seem to invite more open-ended responses than might be expected in a focused model, both versions actually convey a pre-supposition (that something *will* be better or different) consistent with the strategic solution focused approach.

Of course, the therapist needs to consider the client's demeanor and the context of the appointment before communicating a presupposition that "something is better." If the client is tearful or has requested an emergency extra session, a cheery "What's better?" is clearly unempathic and inappropriate. Similarly, as Dolan (1994) points out, if a client has described a history of severe trauma, a more neutral question, such as "How are you doing?" might be used to begin a follow-up session.

If a client responds to the initial follow-up inquiry by describing positive change, the strategic solution focused therapist can respond by asking, "How did you do that?" Behaviors that "worked" can be identified. If the client says that nothing has improved or changed, the therapist can ask, "How did you keep things from getting worse?" This question is a process intervention that invites identification of client action that at least kept matters from deteriorating.

If "things are worse," the therapist wants to know "In what way?" Exactly what happened that led to that conclusion? Sometimes more detailed discussion reveals that although things seemed "worse last night," there were also examples of significant positive change since the last appointment. When things became worse, exactly what did the client do (or not do) that produced that result? Careful clarification here may result in better understanding of what does not work. If previous successes have occurred, the therapist might ask, "What did you forget to do?" As Walter and Peller (1992b) have pointed out, a relapse can be defined as forgetting to do what worked. The therapist may want to convey the message that a relapse is not a terrible, unforgivable event; it is simply that one did not apply the successful solution.

If a suggestion was made at the last appointment, the therapist wants to assess how the client interpreted or implemented it. If the behaviors and words used were not what the therapist had in mind, then suggestions still might be useful if implemented differently. Was the therapist unclear about what to do or say? Did the client forget, choose a different behavior, or both? Was there some obstacle to implementing the suggestion? Here the therapist wants to determine if the suggestion should be discarded (as an unsuccessful attempted solution) or whether it is "worth another try."

If positive change is reported, continuation or amplification is usually desired. The therapist may compliment and highlight the change by expressing surprise about how much the client achieved, given the difficulties previously described. However, the therapist will usually not rush in with glowing praise, assurances that the client can "keep up the good work," or exhortations to strive for still higher goals. On the contrary, the therapist knows that because of "regression toward the mean," positive change is frequently followed by a setback. Therefore, the therapist may point out that in view of how much has been achieved, the client might expect a little backsliding. He or she certainly can continue what works but should take sufficient time to consolidate the changes, not rushing into additional change too quickly.

To convey a similar message, the therapist may ask clients to rate their confidence about their ability to continue the new behaviors. If the client voices some caution, the therapist can reinforce that uncertainty. "I don't blame you for being a little unsure," the therapist might say. "This is still pretty new and unfamiliar to you." If the client expresses a high degree of confidence, the therapist usually will not immediately agree and offer congratulations. Instead, some skepticism might be introduced. "I'm not quite as confident as you are," the therapist may say. "You have done this only twice so far. And I think about sixteen-year-olds who've been driving for two weeks. . . . After a victory, it's so easy to get overconfident and forget how easy it is to slide back. But I hope you're right."

"Termination" in Intermittent Care

When care is brief and/or intermittent, how does the therapist decide when to discontinue sessions? As noted, "termination" is not a weighty issue for therapy that is based on an intermittent care/family practice model. When the presenting complaint is resolved to the client's satisfaction, appointments can stop, and service can always be resumed if problems occur—either the same problem or a new one. But how is "problem resolution" to be defined, especially for difficult issues and situations that do not seem to be fully "solvable"? de Shazer (1991) asks clients to consider the current situation and to judge whether "if it stays like this, will that be good enough?" Similarly, Walter and Peller (1994) point out that the concept of being "on track" is useful in keeping therapy brief. That is, being "on track" to a goal or coping "well enough" with a difficult situation may be sufficient. Therapy may not need to continue until the final goal is reached or the problem totally eliminated.

The kind of "confidence" inquiry previously described can also be used in preparation for discontinuing appointments. The therapist might ask questions like these: "On a zero to ten scale, where ten is total confidence that you can continue the changes you've begun, and zero is 'the change was a fluke or pure luck—I could be back where I started tomorrow,' how confident do you feel that you can keep up what you're describing?" "What will you have to do to stay at a six?" "How would your husband answer that question?" "Is a six good enough?" "What will be different when you're able to say that you're confident at a seven?"

Walter and Peller (1992b) have observed that in therapy as they conduct it, every session is either a first or a last session. This statement also applies well to strategic solution focused therapy. Either the therapist is essentially saying, "Keep doing what works, go slow on additional change, and you know where I am if you need me" (a "last-session message"), or the therapist is clarifying the problem, exploring desired solutions, and inquiring about attempted solutions ("first-session behavior"). In single-session therapy the appointment is *both* a first and a last session.

Practical Considerations

Therapists who are accustomed to using the first (or first few) appointments for history gathering sometimes ask if and when background information is collected in strategic solution focused therapy and other intermittent care models. Is a complete mental status examination conducted? Is a multi-axial diagnosis given? Are intake reports written and progress notes kept? The answers to these questions vary greatly depending on the treatment setting. Nearly every system requires documentation of some kind. If insurance or organizational requirements specify that certain kinds of information will be collected, the therapist will collect what is necessary. Several ways of gathering required information will be described.

In any psychotherapy setting, the therapist must remain alert to the possibility of dangerous behavior. When anyone's safety is a concern, that will be directly and carefully assessed. If hospitalization must be arranged, or if the police or Child Protective Services must be contacted, the therapist takes care of these things first. When an emergency is the problem, dealing with it directly must be the first step in building a solution. If that "uses up the session time," and there is not time for further problem clarification or solution amplification, so be it.

However, most initial psychotherapy appointments *do* leave time to begin strategic solution focused therapy, especially if the therapist has some information beforehand. Often there is information from the original request for service, usually through a telephone call or a written referral. Many individual therapists and treatment settings ask clients to complete some paperwork or questionnaires prior to the initial appointment. If a questionnaire is well constructed, it can save time by providing significant information about psychiatric symptomatology, family background, and medical issues, as well as about the current difficulties. Review of this material can alert the therapist about areas that require more detailed inquiry. In the treatment setting where the author works, an experiment is being tried where therapists (rather than clerical staff) are gathering a fair amount of background information (as well as "beginning the therapy," in some cases) during the initial telephone call. By the time the client is seen, much (although not all) of the initial evaluation has been completed.

Sometimes the strategic solution focused therapist faces the following situation at the beginning of an initial appointment. Some information that is not directly related to problem clarification or solution amplification must be collected. The therapist would like to gather that information without conveying the message that this topic will therefore be the main focus of the therapy. To set the preliminary information apart from the rest of the interview a bit, the therapist might say, "Before we get into what you're here about, I need to ask you a few questions for [the agency, my forms, the insurance, etc.]. So let's take care of that first." After the necessary information is collected, the therapist may "punctuate" the interview by setting some papers aside, shifting tone of voice or position or saying, "Okay. Now, tell me what the trouble is that you're here about today." This way of gathering required information has been suggested by Fisch (1990, personal communication).

Information about fees, procedures, and benefit guidelines needs to be communicated to the client. If there are limitations, how they are presented can make a great deal of difference in how they are perceived. For example, the author works in a setting where clients receive a brief written description of the mental health benefit. That description specifies that "up to six individual, family, or couple sessions" may be provided, with some additional service available, subject to administrative review. One *could* present this information with emphasis on the fact that *only* brief treatment is provided, implying (or stating) that difficult or long-standing problems are unlikely to be resolved in such a setting.

An alternate approach is to downplay the importance of the limitation. The therapist can say, "As you know, your benefit says that we can meet up to six times. But 'six' isn't written in concrete. Frankly, I'm not as interested in counting appointments as I am in your resolving your problem. After all, I'm sure you wouldn't object if that happened in *less* than six times. And, on the other hand, if we have a need to meet more than six times, that probably can be arranged (*if* that is true). There also isn't an obligation to come back. It's perfectly appropriate to use today as a one-time consultation and leave me 'on call.' In practice, the number of times I get together with anyone, and how much time we leave between appointments, we tailor to what's going on."

This approach makes explicit the family practice model. The client may be directly encouraged to view the therapist as an available resource. "You know how you go to family practice if you have a sore throat? Maybe you go a time or two," the therapist might say. "There's no implication that you'll *never* have another sore throat. When you do, you go back, and the doctor and the patient try to remember, 'Gee, what did we do about this last time?' Or maybe you go in when you have a sore toe—that's still your doctor, whatever the problem. I guess what I'm saying is that I want you to feel free to use me that way, kind of like your family practice person, for the problems we see here."

The therapist does not automatically assume that the client will schedule a return visit. At the conclusion of a first appointment, after delivering the intervention, the therapist may ask, "So, what would you like to do as a next step?" (In the setting where the author works, a variety of options are available and have been offered. These possibilities include groups, classes, medication consultation, and individual follow-up, as appropriate.) The therapist may make a suggestion, of course. If the client wants individual follow-up, the therapist may inquire what interval the client had in mind. There is no automatic assumption about returning in one week, although again the therapist may suggest an interval. Clients often surprise their therapists by suggesting *longer* intervals than the therapist would have anticipated. Over time, few clients repeatedly request weekly appointments. Those who do frequently are themselves therapists or people who have had therapy before. Unless one has been socialized to expect weekly appointments, most people do not plan on seeing the therapist every week.

Some clients do anticipate that the interval between appointments (whatever its length) will always be the same. This expectation is a "position" variable that the therapist will certainly want to consider. Clients often readily agree with the idea of tailoring the interval to the situation. For example, when a client says, "I'd like to come every two weeks for a while," the therapist might say, "Okay. Let's schedule our next appointment two weeks from now. But after that, I'd like to leave open the option of us being real flexible. I can imagine a time when we might want to get together *sooner* than two weeks, or we might have a reason to go longer than that. Would that be okay, to set it up as we go along?"

Single-Session Therapy

Many clients who consult psychotherapists are seen for one appointment only. This phenomenon is not new. However, it has received more attention recently, as a number of authors have described the possibilities of "single-session therapy." Rather than representing "dropouts" or "premature terminators," clients who complete a single session often report both improvement in the presenting problem and other positive "ripple effects" (Hoyt, Rosenbaum, and Talmon, 1992). Follette and Cummings (1967, 1976, in Hoyt et al., 1992) reported medical utilization to be reduced by sixty percent over a five-year period for clients who received a single session of psychotherapy.

As Hoyt (1994) points out, therapists should not be particularly surprised by the fact that a single session can make a difference. After all, *clinicians* make frequent use of one-time consultations with colleagues when they want some ideas for working with a particular problem. "Once may be enough"—for now. Most effective single-session therapy is not rigidly "time limited"; rather, it is open ended. The client stops coming not because the benefit ends but because he or she received what was needed. This is a common phenomenon in strategic solution focused therapy.

Hoyt et al. (1994) describe a number of different types of clients likely to benefit from a single session. One type includes people who present with a specific problem for which a solution is within their control. A little problem solving, brainstorming, and clarification can make a big difference. Other clients who make excellent use of a single appointment are those who are experiencing normal reactions to loss, stress, or life transition. Reassurance about the normalcy and appropriateness of one's response can bring great relief. For other people, a single session provides the opportunity for referral to specific resources other than psychotherapy. Clients who have not yet utilized nonpsychotherapy support and community resources generally can be encouraged to do so before engaging in more psychotherapy.

Sometimes more extensive treatment can exacerbate the very problem the client is seeking to eliminate, and *preventing* additional treatment can be of value. This can occur when a normal transition is labeled as pathological. Jones (1985) gives an example of a family that presents with a concern about their previously cheerful and talkative thirteen-year-old, who is now sharing fewer secrets and spending more time in her room with the door closed. Her behavior could be labeled as "depression," and more extensive treatment could be offered. However, if, after an evaluation, the therapist perceives that this is normal adolescent development, brief education about adolescence might be the most useful treatment. Jones describes "no further treatment" as the amplification of confidence.

Treatment can also make things worse if it creates or maintains an illusion that an unresolvable problem can be resolved. Jones (1985) and Hoyt (1994) both assert that people who have had extensive previous psychotherapy without good results would frequently be better off without additional treatment. Some clinicians might say that if significant psychopathology can be detected, then treatment is still indicated. However, in some situations, additional treatment is unlikely to produce the desired results. Jones (1985) gives the following example. Sometimes "therapy" is sought in an interpersonal struggle to convince someone (a specific person, community resource, agency) that a "problem" is being eliminated. If, for whatever reason, that problem is likely to continue to be present, even with therapy, it may be more helpful not to collude with the viewpoint that the therapy will make a significant difference. As Chubb and Evans (1985) point out, continuing open-ended therapy can engender a false hope or sense of security that simply "being in therapy" will take care of the problem. Clarifying that risk may be the most effective intervention the therapist can provide.

In a description of the techniques used in single session therapy, Hoyt et al. (1994) include the following: focusing on pivotal problems, practicing solutions, giving feedback, and leaving the door open for future service. These methods involve many of the procedures used in strategic solution focused therapy. In single-session therapy, return to treatment in the future in no way implies that anything was "wrong" with the treatment given previously. It is simply time for another episode of "brief intermittent psychotherapy."

There are also problems for which single session therapy is less likely to be helpful. Hoyt et al. (1994) describe the following problems and clients that may require "more" or different treatment. When the client is psychotic, a single session may be insufficient. Chronic pain and somatization may require additional resources. Clients who need medication or hospitalization require access to those services. And those who are specifically requesting long-term psychotherapy will not be satisfied with a single session—or with several sessions of brief, intermittent psychotherapy, either.

Caveats in Brief Therapy and Managed Care

Managed care systems are not all alike, and as they proliferate, so do potential problems. As discussed earlier in this chapter, managed care was originally designed to eliminate unnecessary, costly procedures, while retaining effective and appropriate measures. In addition, as Karon (1995) points out, some early managed care proposals were innovative and creative, stressing primary prevention as a major component. Over time, however, Karon asserts that for both general medical care and mental health care, cost cutting has become so extreme that the quality of care has sometimes deteriorated. He states that in practice, many managed care systems have spent little or no money on prevention, they have replaced health care staff with less experienced personnel, and they have cut back health services that were previously provided. The aim of some managed care companies is not to save money over time (over five, ten, or twenty years) but in the *current* year. From the standpoint of some managed care systems, the person who "gives up" on treatment or seeks service elsewhere is a financial success.

It is all too easy for managed care administrators (who frequently are not themselves psychotherapists) to establish standard treatment protocols. While these can be useful guidelines, *no* single system works for every client or every clinical problem. As stressed throughout this book, remaining flexible is a central tenet of strategic solution focused therapy. Cummings (1995) takes a similar position when he states that standard protocols fit approximately thirty to thirty-five percent of a client population; the remaining sixty-five to seventy percent require additional clinical acumen and individualized treatment planning. There may be some clients who will not be assertive enough to request follow-up, and they may "fall through the cracks." Some of these may be people who, if actively encouraged to continue treatment, would have done so, perhaps with positive results.

Nylund and Corsiglia (1994) point out that in managed care settings, the pressure to provide efficient, cost-effective service may subtly influence therapists to misuse approaches such as those discussed in this book. They describe a client who perceived discussion of "how you will know when you don't need to come back" as an attempt on the part of the therapist to "push her out the door faster." The "How will you know when we're done?" inquiry may enhance brevity, but it does *not* automatically enhance rapport unless used with clinical skill and sensitivity.

In addition, some therapists who work in managed care may be forced by management to learn approaches such as strategic solution focused therapy "because they are supposed to be efficient." Other therapists are genuinely interested in brief therapy, but their backgrounds have emphasized psychodynamic or cognitive behavioral models, and they have little grounding in the vast literature on systemic therapy, the work of Milton Erickson, and so on. A therapist who lacks this background and tries to implement specific techniques without understanding larger systemic issues can more easily misinterpret or misuse the model (Nylund and Corsiglia, 1994).

For the therapist who genuinely wants to practice briefly or to demonstrate that a brief therapy model "works," there is the risk of focusing so much on the approach that the person who is the client is not truly seen. The therapist may forget to use empathy, validation, and pacing. As Nylund and Corsiglia (1994) emphasize, it is far too easy to "follow a formula," and the result can be inappropriate, rapid-fire questions, without pacing or noticing and responding to the client's body language and tone.

Commenting on the same theme, Lipchik (1994) writes that in an age of managed care, therapy will need to be clear, goal directed, and brief—or it may not be done at all. However, therapy that meets these criteria does *not* need to be depersonalized or mechanized. On the contrary, the effectiveness of models such as strategic solution focused therapy *requires* recognizing idiosyncrasies and adapting the treatment accordingly.

One potential "danger" of brief therapy involves the financial cost to the therapist, particularly the therapist in private practice who is paid by the session. Writing about the "disadvantages" of working briefly, Haley (1990) has described how brief therapy can create hardship for the therapist. In the first session, the brief therapist gives a suggestion. In the second, the therapist fine-tunes it and cautions the client to "go slow on additional change." In the third session, the client "terminates." And during the time that would have been the fourth session, the therapist is out giving another talk to the PTA or the EAPs, trying to drum up some more business! There is an element of satire in this description, and therapy obviously does not always proceed this way, but there is also a grain of truth. Writing about the same phenomenon, Miller (1992b) points out that to compensate for lost private practice income, brief therapists may resort to teaching others to do brief treatment. The same approach that makes a large service area caseload manageable becomes "a heck of a way to run a private practice."

Extensions for the Future?

Can, or should, brief therapy become even shorter? Can, or should, the therapy appointment be limited altogether? As Weiner-Davis, de Shazer, and Gingerich (1987) point out, clinically observable changes frequently occur between the time service is requested and the time the client attends a first session. It appears that this effect can be further enhanced by specifically encouraging the client to notice the changes that occur during this interval (Miller, 1992b). Miller also reports that therapists at BFTC have observed a steady decline in the number of sessions clients receive.

This phenomenon is of particular interest to managed care organizations that do a good deal of intake work by telephone. A Kaiser clinic in Colorado is reported to do so much intervention by telephone that up to one-fifth of the clients that call for service do not need any in-person appointments (Blasi, 1995, personal communication; Cheadle, 1995). As noted, the clinic where the author works is experimenting with telephone intake work. If single-session therapy is reduced to "telephone therapy," is this a desirable phenomenon? Or can therapy become "too brief"? The answers to these questions remain unclear.

Can, or should, strategic solution focused therapy become a "psychoeducational approach"? Can, or should, clients be instructed in the principles outlined here, so that they can apply the principles to themselves in a variety of situations? In a book addressed to a lay audience, Weiner-Davis (1992) advises people to construct their own "180-degree changes." She warns that doing so may defy common sense and require a leap of faith, and she predicts that people will fear changing "because the worst may happen." She writes, "I can't guarantee that this will work, but I can guarantee that if you keep doing what you've been doing, it will make things worse" (Weiner-Davis, 1992, pp. 163–164).

The idea of teaching clients to apply the principles to themselves raises the question of how effectively this can be done. Certainly therapists who are familiar with the principles attempt to apply them to their own situations at times. How effectively can one deconstruct one's own problem, amplify one's own miracle, or reverse one's own unsuccessful attempted solution? Watzlawick (1987) has suggested that some of the input may need to come from outside, in the same way that "tickling oneself does not produce the same reaction as being tickled." However, many other approaches that began as externally applied therapy models have been extended, with at least partial success, to psychoeducational classes and self-help books and groups. How much this will occur with strategic solution focused therapy remains to be seen.

Case Examples
Intermittent Care

Harriet: "I Guess I Come When I Need You"

Harriet was fifty-nine years old when she first called for an appointment. She was experiencing occasional "claustrophobia" since her husband's retirement six months earlier. Harriet felt "closed in" by having to spend more time with her husband, who had been "domineering and difficult" for many years. The therapist validated Harriet's concerns, emphasizing that this *was* going to be a difficult time, given the fact that conditions like claustrophobia tend to flare up when things are stressful. Harriet said that "learning I'm not crazy" was helpful. She did not feel she needed to come back, either for individual follow-up or for a class on anxiety.

Five years later, Harriet returned, this time on the suggestion of a nurse practitioner. She had gone to Family Practice because of various infections, and she had told the nurse practitioner that she thought her "resistance was down because things were not going well at home." Her husband was now chronically ill, and he had become cantankerous and disagreeable. Were there times when her husband's attitude was *not* problematic? Yes, he was on "good behavior" when "high-powered, hotshot women" were visiting. Harriet liked the idea of acting a little more independent herself—like some of the women her husband "tried to impress." She was encouraged to notice "how she did it" when she got her husband to be "more pleasant."

Harriet came to two more appointments. As she observed her husband's behavior, she noticed that he was less cranky when she was unpredictable, "like making off-the-wall comments about weird things on TV and in the paper, instead of listening to him drone on about his aches and pains."

Harriet was next seen two years later, following the death of her husband. Now she was having panic attacks, mostly at dusk, and only on days when she was home alone. The symptoms did *not* occur when she had company. Harriet and the therapist readily identified Harriet's unsuccessful attempted solution: a message to herself that "you must not have panic attacks." Harriet was willing to experiment with the opposite: to *anticipate* that she would have them on the evenings that she was home alone. This time Harriet agreed to attend a two-session class on anxiety, the same class that she had declined when it had been offered eight years earlier.

Four months after completing the class, Harriet returned. "I just can't seem to apply what I've learned," she said. Her friends were encouraging her to take in a housemate, since evenings alone were so difficult for her, but Harriet was not comfortable with this. She feared sharing her house with a stranger, who would be an "unknown quantity." The therapist validated Harriet's caution and encouraged her to take all the time she needed before implementing additional change.

Harriet made her next appointment ten months later. She told the therapist that she had made *many* changes since her last visit. She had bought new clothes, in bright colors, she was taking a dance class, and she had joined a bridge group. Now she had a new complaint: "I think I suppressed my true feelings during the forty years of my marriage." Harriet had a new male friend, and she found herself "suppressing herself" with him—that is, not speaking up directly when she disagreed with him. Could Harriet describe a scenario where "suppressing herself" was less of a problem? She could. In her scenario, she told her friend, "Sometimes I act phony—but I'm working on it." She also mentioned that she would have more time for bridge "because I'd have my cleaning lady come an extra day." Was there any obstacle to arranging the extra day of cleaning? No, there was not. Harriet did not want to arrange a follow-up appointment. "I guess I come when I need you," she smiled.

Kevin: A Week Away from Work

Kevin was referred to the Psychiatry Department by his internist. One year earlier, Kevin's partner of sixteen years had died of AIDS. Since then, Kevin had been in a brief relationship with a new man; that new partner broke it off. (Kevin was in good health, was HIV negative, and claimed that he used safer sex practices and was tested regularly.) Kevin had gone to his internist after he had taken a week of vacation. Upon his return to work, he told his supervisor that he "just sat around, didn't do anything, and didn't sleep much for a couple of nights." His supervisor told Kevin that he must be depressed and should "get some help."

Kevin's internist prescribed an antidepressant and made a referral for psychotherapy. Kevin never took the medicine, but he said that he felt better anyway. He was also sleeping better, and he was back into his routine at work. He was here primarily because the doctor had told him to come; he really did not have a complaint. As is customary with "visitors," the therapist complimented Kevin on taking care of his sleep problem (whatever its cause) and getting back to work on his own. Kevin was welcome to return if he ever wanted to.

Eight months later Kevin returned. Again he had taken a week off from work. This time, however, he had not let his supervisor know that he was doing this. After two days' absence, the supervisor called Kevin at home to find out what was going on. Kevin told him, "I'm feeling a little blah—I think I'll take a week of vacation." Now Kevin was back at work, and again his supervisor told him, "You really need to talk to someone about this."

The therapist inquired how Kevin was functioning. He was not suicidal; he was eating and sleeping adequately; he was in good health; he was socializing, although he did not have a committed relationship; and he was functioning well at work (other than not notifying his supervisor in advance about the time off). Now that he was here, was there anything Kevin wanted to discuss or anything with which he wanted assistance? Kevin thought for a minute. "Not really," he replied.

The therapist asked Kevin the miracle question and received a response instantly. "I wouldn't have to go to work," Kevin grinned. What would he do instead? He would go on a trip around the world, with a friend (he was not sure who). How would he be different after that? "I'd be ready to go back to work." What would his supervisor notice about him? "I'd look rested." How would the supervisor be different as a result of Kevin's looking rested? "He wouldn't be bugging me about what's wrong with me." What *would* the supervisor be saying? "He'd ask me about my trip." What else? "Oh, we'd just get the bugs out of the [computer] system." And so on.

Kevin liked to take a week off work every so often, preferably in July or December. But the *way* he was going about it—staying home, waiting for his supervisor to call, and then saying he felt "blah"—was getting his supervisor on his back. That is, his attempted solution was not working. Kevin and the therapist talked about how Kevin could plan to take a week in advance now and then, maybe not to go around the world right now, but to "hang out." If Kevin felt "blah" during that time, it was not his supervisor's business; Kevin was not obligated to tell his supervisor about his personal life. Kevin had a right to use his earned vacation time without his boss breathing down his neck about it.

Kevin said he liked the idea of "planning vacation," not right away, since he had just used a week of leave, but the next time he was ready for some time away from "that place." He declined the therapist's offer of a follow-up appointment, but he said that he knew that he was free to come back.

Kevin did so five months later. The issue was the same. In December he was ready for some time off again, and once more he took three days off work without giving advance notice. This time, however, Kevin's supervisor told him that his attendance *was* affecting his job performance. If problems continued, Kevin's job might be in jeopardy. From now on, if Kevin was absent without notice, he needed a "doctor's excuse."

Again the therapist inquired about suicidal and homicidal ideation, health, vegetative signs of depression, general functioning, relationships, and stress at work. Kevin acknowledged that he became a little lonely at holiday time, but that if his job were not in jeopardy, he would not be here. He just liked to have a few days without "having to deal with people" every once in a while. What would it take to accomplish this? "I guess I'll need the doctor's excuse," Kevin said. He asked the therapist to complete one for that day's appointment.

"Kevin, let me ask you this," the therapist said. "If you were to call my office and get an off-work slip when you wanted to have a day like that, how much difference would that make to your supervisor?" "A lot," Kevin said. Was there any obstacle to making such a call? Kevin acknowledged that there was. On days that he did not want to "deal with people," he did not want to talk to a doctor's office, a therapist, or anyone else. He just wanted a day alone, and then he would be okay.

The therapist attempted to empathize with Kevin's dilemma. He was being asked to hassle with a doctor's office at the very times he *least* felt like doing so! What was he going to do? Kevin did not know. Had he ever done something even if he "didn't feel like it" at the time? Kevin guessed that he had. He would "just have to do it," he said.

Again Kevin declined offers of a follow-up visit with the therapist and of various psychoeducational groups and classes. However, over the next year, he called twice for "off-work slips" and made two appointments. On each occasion the therapist told Kevin how impressive it was that he was calling and coming in when he least wanted to do so. Kevin was still not a "customer" for psychotherapy for any of the many issues that could have been addressed, but his job was no longer in jeopardy.

Gail: "Rage Attacks Forever"

"I get depressed. I have rage attacks. I think about killing myself. I'm furious with my husband. But it's not just him. I've been like this forever." Gail, then thirty-four, wrote this on the form that asked why she was requesting therapy. Gail had felt like cutting her wrists the night before, when Neal, her husband (of four months) was watching a pornographic video. Gail had been feeling hopeless about her life. She had left her ex-husband and a higher-paying job in Kansas City for Neal—and now, he was watching that trash! She felt guilty about the car she had totaled when drunk seven months ago (but she had six months sobriety now). She deeply regretted her four abortions, and she feared that she would never have a child. Neal, twelve years older than she, already had three children from his previous marriage, and he had told her from the start that he probably would not want more children. With bitterness, Gail said, "He dispenses my [birth control] pill every night."

Gail's main complaint was how Neal "degraded" her. However, it quickly became clear that Gail had a way of dealing with Neal's "degrading" words that was quite effective—when she used it. Even while feeling rage during the "pornographic video incident," Gail had somehow managed to do three remarkable things. She had labeled what she was upset about, she had identified what she wanted, and she had asked for it directly. Neal had turned off the video, they had "snuggled," and Gail had felt better. The therapist complimented Gail on her ability to do these three important tasks, even when her rage was intense. Continuing to do what worked was Gail's homework.

Gail came for four more appointments over the next three months. She continued to have episodes of feeling furious at Neal. According to Gail, he eyed other women in restaurants. He did not want to pay for her to return to school. He did not want to go shopping for drapes. Gail could not always recognize what she was upset about at the moment the rage emerged. But as soon as she labeled a precipitant, she was able to apologize to Neal for her outburst and to tell him what she wanted. He did not always comply with her requests. When she asked him not to eye other women, he complied—for about ten minutes. Nonetheless, he acknowledged her feelings, and Gail felt better. Neal did agree that Gail could return to school. As she took classes, and did well there, Gail began to feel better about herself.

The therapist asked about calling Neal to invite him for an appointment. Gail agreed, and Neal made an appointment. However, he canceled it because of business obligations and did not reschedule. Gail came three more times. She continued to practice labeling what she wanted and asking for it, in school and at work, as well as at home. This worked reliably—when she did it. Gail felt ready to stop meeting for a while.

One year later Gail returned, on referral from the hospital Emergency Room. She had thrown a lamp at Neal and become "hysterical," and Neal had called Emergency. The precipitant had been Neal's plan to have dinner with a former girlfriend, who was passing through town. Gail had told Neal, and herself, that this dinner was okay with her. Belatedly she had realized that it was really *not* okay. "It's the same thing we talked about last year," Gail said. "I have to realize what I'm feeling."

Gail did not really want more therapy now. She had resumed taking an anti-depressant, similar to one she had taken five years earlier. At Gail's request, the medicine was prescribed by her family practice doctor. After the lamp incident, the family practitioner wanted Gail to have a consultation with a psychiatrist, and the therapist arranged that consultation. The psychiatrist told Gail that a low-dose neuroleptic could be used as needed along with the antidepressant if Gail wanted it, but she did not. She wanted to stay on the antidepressant, and she wanted the family practitioner to prescribe it.

Gail called the therapist again six months later. An incident at work had led to her feeling "betrayed," and she wanted to discuss this. However, by the day of the appointment, the work problem had "taken care of itself." "How did you get it to do that?" the therapist asked. "I told my manager I didn't agree with how he'd handled the incident," Gail answered. "And it was amazing. He told me I had a good point. And he took care of it."

"But since I'm here, there's something else I want to tell you about," Gail said. "I've been dreaming about Kansas City. I think I'm falling in love with my ex-husband again. I've been planning a trip to Kansas City. I'm telling Neal I'm going to see my sister. But I'm afraid I really want to check out my ex." "What are you afraid will happen?" the therapist asked. "I'm afraid Neal will find out what I'm planning," Gail said. "I guess I want you to tell me to be honest with Neal. That I just need to get this out of my system." "It sounds like you don't need *me* to tell you that," the therapist said. "It seems like you figured that out for yourself."

Two years later, Gail called to ask if she and Neal could come in together, "because we're having trouble communicating." When Gail and Neal were seen, it was evident that both were speaking and hearing each other quite clearly. Gail, now thirty-eight, was saying clearly that she wanted to start a family. Neal was equally clear: he did *not* want another child. If Gail badly wanted one, he would go along with it, but he would not be particularly enthusiastic, and Gail would have to realize that this would be primarily "her" project. Gail said that this was no way to have a child, and that what Neal was conceding was "not enough."

Articulately, and with humor and affection, both Gail and Neal could say how this dilemma might not be solvable, and that Gail might decide to leave Neal because of it. How did they hope the therapist might help? "Make that miracle happen," Gail smiled. "Get him to change his mind." But in the absence of that, they both would "settle" for "keeping the eruptions shorter," for however long or short they stayed together.

Eighteen months later, Gail returned (alone). "I think I might need to leave Neal," Gail sighed. "I'm so furious with him. He doesn't help one bit around the house. He won't even call the pool service to fix the filters. He *knows* how much that pool means to me. And I can't even use it the way it is now." Having a child did not seem so important now, Gail added.

"Gail, if you had the pool fixed, how much difference would that make in how you feel about Neal?" the therapist asked. "A lot," Gail answered tearfully. "I know it doesn't make sense. But that's how I feel."

The therapist told Gail, "Over the years, it seems to me that labeling what you feel and going for it has worked for you as well as anything I've seen. So maybe, if you feel that strongly about it, you might go ahead and get the pool fixed before giving up on the marriage. Is there any obstacle to your getting the service people lined up?" "No, not really," Gail sighed. "Probably I should do that. Neal won't care, as long as he doesn't have to fuss with it. Besides, if we split up and sell the house, having a pool that works is a good idea."

The therapist empathized with Gail's dilemma. Then Gail smiled. "Remember how you told us, for however long or short we stay together, we might as well keep the eruptions shorter? Well, I think I just decided: for however long we stay together, we're going to do it with a pool that works."

Jeffrey and Claudia: Sex Drive Differences

Jeffrey wanted to see a therapist because of his difficulty "recommitting." His girlfriend, Claudia, was sweet and attentive, but Jeffrey feared getting too close. He had been deeply hurt when his ex-wife had left him for another man two years earlier, and he feared that if he trusted someone new, he would be betrayed and hurt again. There were no overt "danger signals" in Claudia's behavior, but after his painful divorce, Jeffrey questioned his judgment about women. He also wondered if he was really lovable; would any woman eventually leave him?

Jeffrey came for several sessions, during which he discussed some additional concerns. Jeffrey's "sex drive" had never been high, and he believed that this could have contributed to his ex-wife's "looking for it elsewhere." He was very attracted to Claudia now, but he feared that his sex drive might eventually diminish with her, too.

The therapist empathized with Jeffrey's concerns. Given how badly he had been hurt, it was not at all surprising that he would be cautious about trusting again. Loving Claudia now would not guarantee that his sex drive would never diminish or that she would never leave him. Jeffrey had paid spousal support, so he knew that failed marriages could be costly as well as painful. "Recommitting" certainly entailed risk, and the therapist agreed that although Claudia sounded like a good woman, no one could guarantee that if Jeffrey married her, he would not be hurt again. Jeffrey said that his appointments were helpful. He was still unsure about making a definite commitment to Claudia, but he now felt that his hesitancy was appropriate.

Three years later, Claudia called to schedule an appointment for Jeffrey and herself. They had been married for one and a half years. Claudia was concerned because Jeffrey's sex drive, never as strong as hers, was not increasing as she had hoped and assumed that it would after marriage. Jeffrey and Claudia had sex about once a week. After sex, Claudia was happy, but she felt rejected and sad when four or five days went by without Jeffrey initiating, or when she initiated and Jeffrey was not in the mood. *How* Jeffrey said "no" did not matter; any "no" felt like a rejection. Claudia's "miracle" emphasized increased frequency of sexual contact.

Jeffrey was distressed by Claudia's reaction, and he feared that his "worst-case scenario" was beginning to unfold. He felt frustrated by Claudia's difficulty recognizing how much he loved her. In Jeffrey's miracle, Claudia was just as loving and funny "without sex" as she was after sexual contact.

How much Jeffrey and Claudia cared about each other was immediately apparent, and the therapist told the couple so. The therapist also pointed out that they each seemed to have the same "worst fear": rejection by the other. Because both had become so predictable, it was suggested that each "do something different." The therapist also recommended that each partner come in alone for the next appointment.

During Claudia's individual appointment, the therapist focused on clarifying the meaning of "four days without sex." As Claudia thought about this, she realized that sex meant "closeness" and "being wanted." What was she doing in her best attempt to create closeness? Quickly Claudia realized that dramatically sighing "It's been four days" was not producing the desired results; on the contrary, it elicited exactly the opposite effect. She decided that when she wanted to feel close to Jeffrey she would "reach for his hand instead of other parts of his anatomy."

Jeffrey's appointment revealed his deep fear of losing Claudia. The therapist wanted to know if Jeffrey still felt attracted to her. He said that he did, and he tried hard to "fulfill her needs." However, he was usually half asleep by Claudia's bedtime, when *she* became amorous. Jeffrey got up at 4:00 A.M to go to work, while Claudia worked until midevening. Jeffrey often felt desire at 3:30 A.M., but, of course, Claudia was fast asleep then. The therapist wondered aloud whether Jeffrey might be working so hard to "fulfill Claudia's needs" that he was neglecting his own. Jeffrey suddenly remembered one morning when he "just couldn't help himself" and pulled Claudia to him "selfishly." How had she reacted? She had been "silly and fun" all the next day. Jeffrey decided that he would "be selfish a little more," after checking out with Claudia if that would be okay.

It was more than okay. Jeffrey did not return, but Claudia had two more individual appointments, during which she described seeing things in a new way. "Now I see how much he cares," Claudia said. "I guess I was being pretty selfish." Fifteen months later she sent the therapist a picture of their new daughter and a thank you note that said, "I can't say that our sex life is all that active, with the new baby and all, but I'm very, very happy."

Two years later, Claudia returned. "Do you think I was molested when I was a child?," she asked. "Is that why I think about sex so much?" Claudia had no conscious memories of being molested, but her sister had just told her that she (the sister) had been touched inappropriately by an uncle, and Claudia wondered if the uncle had touched her, too. "If we could somehow know, for sure, that you had been molested, how would that make a difference for you?" the therapist asked. "I'm not sure," Claudia replied. "Maybe I'd understand why I base so much of my self-esteem on whether I'm being seen as sexually desirable." "And if you understood that," the therapist continued, "what would you be doing differently?"

"This is just coming into my mind now," Claudia said, speaking slowly. "You know, I had to stop working at the restaurant when I had back surgery two months ago. It's really time to go back now, but I don't want to. Guys there make comments about my legs in those little shorts we have to wear. I used to get a kick out of that. Now the thought of them doing that makes me want to smack them. But there's nothing else I'm trained to do. I always thought there's not much else I'm smart enough to do, either, but maybe that's not true. Maybe I could go back to school."

"And if you could know for sure that you were *not* molested," the therapist asked, "how would that make a difference in your plans for the future?" Claudia smiled. "I *still* don't want to be a waitress all my life," she said.

Claudia and the therapist discussed the fact that Claudia might never know for sure whether she had been molested. Whether she had or not, however, she planned to be very cautious when her own daughter had occasion to be around that uncle. She also planned to get some information about community college schedules and to discuss with Jeffrey what was financially realistic for them. Claudia did not feel a need to schedule follow-up for now.

12

Excerpts
Single-Session Therapy

Mary's Miracle

Mary, age fifty, was divorced; she worked as a nurse's aide. She was feeling depressed, she was having trouble sleeping, and she found herself tearful. Mary consulted her family practice doctor, who prescribed antidepressant medicine and referred her for a Psychiatry Department appointment. This excerpt, early in that appointment, illustrates the therapist's attempts to determine who is the "customer" and what is the complaint.

Therapist: I understand that Dr. Calhoun asked us to call you and schedule an appointment.

Mary: That's right.

Therapist: Maybe I should check out how you two decided you ought to come talk to us. I can't tell from the forms she sent over how much this appointment was her idea or yours.

Mary: It was hers, really. You know, she asked me to do this a few months ago.

Therapist: No, I didn't know that. What happened with that?

Mary: I didn't come. She also gave me some pills.

Therapist:	Are you taking them?
Mary:	No. Well, yes. Now I am. Back then I didn't, though. I took them for a few days, and I didn't like them. When I saw her last week, she told me to take them again, and to come over and talk to you.
Therapist:	So, you started them again?
Mary:	Yes.
Therapist:	What are they called?
Mary:	Imipramine, I think. They must be working this time.
Therapist:	That's good. Any side effects so far?
Mary:	No.
Therapist:	Okay. Well, then maybe you can tell me what the trouble is you're hoping I might help you with.
Mary:	Well, it's compounded. It's my children, my job. It's emotional. I get in a slump. Crying, not too much eating, but, like I said, I'm better this week.
Therapist:	Are you aware how you did that, how you got yourself better since last week?
Mary:	No, I don't know. Maybe the pills. No, I don't know. I don't think the pills are supposed to work that fast.
Therapist:	So that's still a puzzle. Anyway, to get back to the problem you're here for . . .
Mary:	I don't know, to be honest. I harbor feelings. Maybe I hold things in too much.
Therapist:	Maybe I should back up a bit, because maybe I'm jumping the gun in assuming that there *is* a problem you want my help with. Let me ask you this. If Dr. Calhoun had called you yesterday and said, "I know I told you to go to Psychiatry, but I was thinking about it, and the medicine should be enough. You don't need to keep that appointment," would you still have kept this appointment today?
Mary:	Yes, I would have.
Therapist:	Why?
Mary:	I must need an outlet. I don't have an outlet. I isolate. And I was

abused. I was in a relationship for twenty years, until I came here [to the current city, five years ago]. He's back in Atlanta. He's the father of my children. He would never let me have my freedom. I honestly believe it has a lot to do with how I am now. Now that I have my freedom, I still have a lot of those things inside me. I stay in my house. I just go to work. I take care of business. See, I wasn't allowed to go out, or let people come in, or go to visit. And I just do the same thing now. I isolate.

Therapist: Is that a problem for you now?

Mary: No, it hasn't been. I don't know if it is or not. Actually I kind of like my privacy. I like it the way it is.

Therapist: It sounds like sometimes you have different feelings about keeping to yourself. Is that the problem you were hoping I might help you with?

Mary: No, not really. Now, I was stressed at work yesterday.

Therapist: What happened?

Mary: Well, some cookies were left in a drawer, and my boss—well, she's not really my boss, but she acts like she is—she came in and said to me, in front of these two other ladies, "You wash that out." I said, "Okay," but it was eating at me.

Therapist: What did you do?

Mary: Afterwards I went over to her, and I took her aside, and I said to her, "Don't you *do* that anymore. That's unprofessional."

Therapist: What was different after you told her that?

Mary: I felt better.

Therapist: Interesting. How'd you decide how to handle that?

Mary: Well, I had some help.

Therapist: From whom?

Mary: One of my associates. I don't know, I worry about my children, too. My daughter, she's still back in Atlanta. And she's not doing so good. And I can't go back to help her, because the children's daddy is still back there. So I get headaches. And I worry.

Therapist: It sounds like there are a bunch of things going on for you: your kids, your experiences back in Atlanta, your isolating, your holding in your feelings, your headaches, the stress at work—although I'm actually rather impressed about how you handled that one—your feeling in a slump, crying, not eating so good. I guess the piece I'm still foggy about—and I know I'm going to sound like a broken record here—is what the problem is that you're hoping I might help with.

Mary: I don't know. I wish I knew.

The therapist's attempts to clarify Mary's primary complaint are not working. At this point it seems unlikely that "more of the same" will make things much clearer, so it is time to shift gears. The therapist decides to ask the miracle question.

Therapist: Let me ask you a different kind of question. I want you to pretend, for a moment, that after we get done talking today, and you go back to work, or do whatever you're going to do the rest of today, and then go home tonight, and fall asleep, that while you're sleeping tonight, a miracle happens. And the miracle is that the problem you're here about today is solved. Because you're sleeping, you don't know that happened, but it has. You wake up tomorrow morning. What will be the first thing that will be different, that will let you know that this isn't such a problem any more?

Mary: Hmm. What would I do that would let me know it was not a problem any more?

Therapist: Yes.

Mary: Well, that God gave me another chance, this next day. I open my eyes, and I have breath in my body, and I have another chance to do His will and not my own. I'm a religious person, you see.

Therapist: And as a result of realizing that God has given you another opportunity, how will you be different?

Mary: How could I be different tomorrow?

Therapist: Yes. And I'm being very concrete, tomorrow, Saturday.

Mary: I'll be grateful. It will be a grateful day.

Therapist: Yes. So if there were a fly on your wall, and flies could think and talk and stuff like that, what would you be doing different that would make that fly say, "Boy, she's different today"?

Mary:	If I get up and start cleaning. [Both laugh.] That would be a surprise.
Therapist:	What would you clean?
Mary:	First thing, my kitchen.
Therapist:	Your kitchen. And how will you be different as a result of having cleaned your kitchen?
Mary:	It'll be clean, sanitized, spray the roaches. I can't get rid of them. But I will attempt to do so. And hold my cat. Give him a bath.
Therapist:	And how will that make a difference for you, that you've done that?
Mary:	Just that I won't be so into myself, thinking about myself. Maybe I might even have a guest tomorrow. Who knows?
Therapist:	Who?
Mary:	I don't know. I'm just hoping, maybe.
Therapist:	Well, if you did know?
Mary:	Maybe my friend, you know, the one I talked to, about the cookies in the drawer thing. Actually, he probably *would* come. Of course, I'd have to invite him.
Therapist:	How would you do that?
Mary:	Pick up the phone. Say, "Would you come and have lunch with me, have a bite to eat?" Instead of him eating alone and me eating alone.
Therapist:	And what will he notice about you?
Mary:	Maybe a smile. That I don't seem so serious. I'm always so serious. It's hard to make me smile or laugh. [She smiles a little.]
Therapist:	A smile like that?
Mary:	[smiling broadly] Yeah, I guess. You made that smile come.
Therapist:	What else?
Mary:	If I can wake up tomorrow, and be thankful for the day, instead of having worry and concern on my face, that would be very good.
Therapist:	Who else will notice that you are different?

Miracle question elaboration continues. Mary's cousin, whom she plans to see tomorrow evening, will also notice that Mary is different. They will talk about church, they will go window shopping, or they will see a movie—"anything but worrying about our children." Back at work, on Monday, Mary's co-workers will notice that she is more alert, more "on top of things." She and her co-workers will go to coffee together. The "cookie incident" will seem less significant. Miracle question elaboration does not always continue through so much of the session, but Mary is responding so fully that the therapist decides to continue what seems to be "working."

Therapist:	Now, this problem with your daughter, back in Atlanta, how will your attitude toward that be different, as a result of all these other changes you've described?
Mary:	Well, I'd realize there's nothing I can do to help her, unless she wants the help. God will do what He has to do, in taking care of her. I'll stop—what's the word?—underestimating God.
Therapist:	And as a result of not underestimating God, and letting Him take care of her, how will you be different?
Mary:	I'll be—oh, what's the word? It was right there—released, yes, released to do what I have to do for me.
Therapist:	Which is what?
Mary:	Enjoy life. Take one day at a time. Do what's in front of me, and not try to look in back of me.
Therapist:	And how will you do that?
Mary:	Keep moving forward.
Therapist:	And how would this problem of not having an outlet be different, as a result of you keeping going forward?
Mary:	I'll have to get me an outlet.
Therapist:	How will you do that?
Mary:	Well, just be more . . . don't be so afraid of people. I just look at 'em. I go to church, I'm in the choir, I've been doing that for almost two years, but I have not made a single friend.
Therapist:	So how will you be different at choir when you're ready to . . .
Mary:	Talk more. I'll get some telephone numbers.
Therapist:	How will you do that?

Mary:	Ask them. Just ask them. Say, "I would like to call and talk with you some time. May I have your number?" And I'll give them mine. They don't have to call me. I'll call them.
Therapist:	You really know how you'll do this. And this problem of holding in your feelings, like you sometimes do, what will be different about that, as a result of your having more outlets?
Mary:	Well, I'll be testing the waters.

The therapist is ready to inquire about "exceptions" to the problem. Mary has already described one "piece of the miracle that already happened" in her response to the cookie incident. The therapist expects that there will be others as well.

Therapist:	This miracle—are there any little pieces of it that are already happening, lately?
Mary:	Yeah, right now, talking to you. I haven't really let anyone get close to me.
Therapist:	So it was a tremendous step for you to be willing to be here, to be talking to a total stranger.
Mary:	Well, it's different. People I work with, people at church, they could use things against me. You know, church is supposed to be a place of God, and they are the most terrible people of all sometimes.
Therapist:	Any other little pieces of your miracle that are happening lately?
Mary:	Yes. I'm relaxing. Maybe it's the medicine. I've been, like I said, sleeping better, functioning well.
Therapist:	I want to ask you about something you said a little bit ago. Remember you said you took your co-worker aside and said, "Don't do that anymore"? Is that a little piece of the miracle?
Mary:	Yes. It is.
Therapist:	And did you say you confided in your co-worker, and used him as an outlet?
Mary:	Yes. Yes.
Therapist:	Wow. What else, now that we're talking about those kinds of things?

Mary:	When I sing in the choir, that's an outlet, because I really enjoy it, and it's something I never did in my whole life before.
Therapist:	I want to ask you a scaling question, zero to ten. Zero is when this problem, whatever it is, was at its very worst. Ten is when it's solved to your satisfaction. Miracle's happened. You don't need to come back and talk to me or anyone else, because it's not a problem anymore. I want you to give me a number between zero and ten that best describes where you are right now.
Mary:	Hmm. I'd say about eight.
Therapist:	Eight? Where ten is the solved end? How'd you get all the way up to an eight?
Mary:	Well, I felt much better, but I still kept this appointment, so I could call Dr. Calhoun, or maybe you could call her, whatever, and tell her what you think, so she won't worry. I know she has a lot of patients, and I don't want her to worry.
Therapist:	So how did you get up to an eight?
Mary:	Oh, with this incident at work yesterday, that I handled it, and it worked. And I came here, and I'm letting out some things I haven't expressed to anyone else. Now, for me to make an evaluation of myself, I don't think I'm that sick, but I know that I *have* been sick, very deeply sick, where I was very, very sad.
Therapist:	Now, how confident are you that you can stay at an eight?
Mary:	I could stay at an eight. Yeah, I can stay here. I feel pretty good.
Therapist:	What do you need to do in order to stay at an eight?
Mary:	Keep remembering—miracles do happen. [Both laugh.]
Therapist:	And what do you need to keep doing in order to keep that miracle happening?
Mary:	Keep having outlets.
Therapist:	If you can stay at an eight for a while longer, will that be good enough?
Mary:	Um, improvement, I could take a little bit of improvement. What's wrong with wanting to be a ten?
Therapist:	Okay, what will have to be different for you to be able to say you're at a nine?

Mary:	Uh, things will be better at work. I'll be more resourceful.
Therapist:	What do you need to do to make that happen?
Mary:	Pay attention. Pick up and notice things. Be observant. As far as the children are concerned, as long as they don't call me with their negativity, I'm fine.
Therapist:	Hmm. Do you need them never to call you with negativity in order to stay at an eight or a nine, or can you stay up there even if they call you with some negativity in their lives?
Mary:	It depends on what it is.
Therapist:	How likely is it that they'll never call you with their negativity?
Mary:	Well, it's almost the end of the month. One of them is going to call me for some rent money.
Therapist:	So—you need them never to call you for rent money? Or can you keep things good for you even when they call?
Mary:	I can keep it good.
Therapist:	How will you do that?
Mary:	If I have it, I'll send it. But if I don't have it, "Baby, I'm sorry. I don't have it."
Therapist:	Wow.

The appointment time is ending, and there is not time to inquire about attempted solutions. Nor has a primary complaint been identified. But those things do not particularly matter at this point. Mary has described some powerful realizations, along with changes that she has already begun. The therapist delivers an intervention designed to validate Mary's experience and to encourage "more of what works."

Therapist:	Well, I have a bunch of things I want to say to you. First of all, I sure don't blame you for feeling distressed. You've had a tremendous amount going on for you, between the abuse back in Atlanta, your kids, the stress at work, feeling like you isolate and don't have outlets. I'm impressed that even with all of that going on, you managed to join the choir; you were able to do what needed to be done at work yesterday; that you were able to reach out to your associate; that there are pieces of your miracle already happening. I'm impressed that you recognize that when you get

some phone numbers from people at church, and go out to coffee with your co-workers, it will make a difference for you. I'm impressed that you recognize, on a deeper level, that when you stop underestimating God, and you let God take care of your kids, that kind of frees you up to live your life one day at a time, and that will make a difference. And with all those pieces of the miracle already happening—I'm a believer in "If something works, do more of it"—what can I say? You've discovered some things that work. If I had any suggestion, it would be to keep doing those things, and notice how that makes a difference for you.

Mary: I believe by you using that word "miracle," and I'm, like I say, a deeply religious person, that was a connection for me to you.

Therapist: Yes. I think you know some things that, when you do them, they make a difference.

The therapist reviewed the treatment options available to Mary. Mary wanted Dr. Calhoun to continue to prescribe her medication. Mary did not feel that she needed an individual follow-up appointment, but she expressed interest in joining a women's group. Several weeks later, when offered an appointment to begin that group, Mary declined it, leaving the message, "Doing fine. Don't need it."

Review of Mary's medical chart one year later showed that she had stayed on the medicine for four months. She had two additional appointments with Dr. Calhoun (for medical complaints). One of Dr. Calhoun's chart notes says, "Cheerful. No longer depressed."

Liz: "I Blow Up at Him"

Liz was a forty-three-year-old, divorced college administrator who called for an appointment for "relationship problems." This excerpt begins early in the first session, after the therapist has collected some preliminary information for forms that must be completed.

Therapist: Okay, that's what I need for my forms. Now, what's the trouble you called about?

Liz: Well, I feel like I need some help.

Therapist: With what?

Liz: Coping with—well, I'm not sure what the problem is. I'm disappointed with myself, with my ability to be patient. I'm a perfectionist, and I get cynical and insecure when other people don't give me the same kind of consideration I give them. I had a fight with my boyfriend this weekend. My boyfriend is a sweet man, and he suggested that since we have so many blowups, maybe I have deep-seated problems. He said that maybe rather than just saying, "You're full of it," I have to think: maybe I push people away from me.

Therapist:	What happened?
Liz:	Well, it's an accumulation of things. But specifically, I was angry he didn't tell me that this woman came to his house to take his kids to Sea World. I had to find out from them. I felt like something was going on. I was pissed, and I confronted him, at which point he told me, "You're insecure. You're always accusing me." I said, "That's right, I *am* accusing you. I don't think it's appropriate for you to have other women at your house. I know how women are—they use kids to get one foot in the door with a guy. And I'd have appreciated it if you'd told me. I don't think you'd have liked it if you found out I had some other guy here with my kids."
Therapist:	And you said it pretty much like you just said it to me?
Liz:	Yes. I told him I don't want to just pretend everything is okay, so it blew up into a discussion of all the other times he's done things.
Therapist:	Blew up? How did you blow it up?
Liz:	Well, we had a two-hour discussion on the phone. I said, "I don't trust you, and I don't want to be in a relationship with you." But, see, I don't *really* want to end it. I mean, I really love Harrison, but the fact that he doesn't tell me things just makes me suspicious.
Therapist:	Would you say you have a right to feel suspicious?
Liz:	Well, *I* think I do—but Harrison doesn't. He says I just automatically assume the worst about people. But I'm perceptive. I predict the end of a movie, and I'm usually right.
Therapist:	You have a real accurate sense of intuition.
Liz:	I do, even in personal relationships.
Therapist:	So what does your intuition tell you about Harrison?

Here Liz describes in some detail her hunch that Harrison is hypersensitive to being "smothered," as he was by his demanding ex-wife. She believes that Harrison resists having to explain his actions. Liz thinks that Harrison loves her, and she does not think that he is involved with anyone else currently. However, she also knows that Harrison was unfaithful to his ex-wife, and she does not want to be "mindlessly trusting and pretend these things don't happen."

At this point the problem with which Liz wants assistance is not fully clear. Three issues have been identified. First, Liz does not like the fact that Harrison brought the other woman to his home. Second, she does not like the fact that he did not tell her about the woman's visit. Third, she does not like her own reaction, what she calls "blowing up." Which problem is primary will make a difference for the therapy. In the next section of the interview, the therapist attempts to clarify the complaint.

Liz:	See, he knows from his past experience with me that I'm really going to get uptight. So of course he doesn't tell me things.
Therapist:	So it becomes sort of a vicious circle.
Liz:	Yeah. He doesn't tell me because he doesn't want me to be mad, and then when I find out, I'm pissed even more.
Therapist:	If Harrison had this woman come and take his kids places, and he mentioned to you that she was coming, how much difference would that make for you?
Liz:	Some, but still, in my heart, I don't see him having a lot of women friends. The bottom line is, I'm dubious about how much a platonic friendship can stay platonic.
Therapist:	So the problem you're hoping I might help you with, is it more Harrison's behavior or your reaction to Harrison's behavior?
Liz:	It's more me, I think.
Therapist:	So even if he were still having women come over, and even if he weren't telling you, if you weren't reacting the way you do, that would make more difference than Harrison's getting rid of the women coming over, or the not telling you?
Liz:	Yeah. Because it's not just the women. If it's not one thing, it'll be another. See, it keeps coming up. Like Harrison said on the phone, "It happens all the time. You're judgmental. Maybe there's something in your past you need to address."
Therapist:	What do you think about that?
Liz:	Well, I'm not sure what it is in my past. But I guess I *do* react that

way. When I get mad, or think something's going on, I just get totally unable to think rationally about it. I almost get sick to my stomach, it's so painful to hold in. And I say the first thing that comes to mind, without thinking, cruel things, hurtful, judgmental things. Especially in the area of jealousy, or suspicion. It's complex. I think I'm insecure. And cynical. And I think I cause people to avoid telling me the truth. When I go ballistic, they're afraid of me.

Therapist: So when you react that way, it makes Harrison less likely to say, "Oh, by the way, so-and-so is stopping over."

Liz: Yeah, like he says, he doesn't know how to tell me.

Therapist: It's the way you react, how you say it?

Liz: Yeah, that I sound sinister.

Problem clarification continues a bit longer, as the therapist wants to be sure whether Liz is more distressed about what she *feels* or how she *expresses* those feelings. Liz says that her girlfriends would be jealous, too, but they would not react aloud as strongly as she does. She recognizes that although she does not like experiencing the jealousy, as an "intuitive person," she *will* be suspicious at times. The problem is what she *says* when she expresses those feelings. Once that is clear, the therapist wants to clarify Liz's expectation about how the therapist will help.

Therapist: What is your hope of how I might help with this problem?

Liz: I need coping skills, so that rather than being confrontational, which I have to be in my job, I'll be able to express things in a nonthreatening, nonjudgmental way.

That is clear enough. The therapist decides to ask the miracle question now.

Therapist: Okay. Let me ask you to imagine something, then. I want you to pretend that after you leave here today, and go back to work, and then go home, and go to bed tonight, and fall asleep, a miracle happens. And the miracle is that you've acquired the ability to express feelings like jealousy in a nonjudgmental way. The miracle has not made your cynicism go away, because we'll assume that the cynicism is the product of good, sensitive intuition. So you still have some skepticism, but now you have the ability to talk about it in a way that won't get the other person so defensive. What will be

	the first thing that will be different, that will let you know that how you put it isn't so much a problem?
Liz:	Well, if I could do that, and Harrison understood how I felt, things would be much better. If I was mad, I'd just tell him so, calmly. I wouldn't lose it.
Therapist:	How would you put it?
Liz:	Hmm . . . I don't know.
Therapist:	How would your girlfriend say it?
Liz:	Well, she probably *wouldn't* say anything right then. Instead, she'd say—or I'd say—"Give me a call later."
Therapist:	And then later?
Liz:	I'd say, "Harrison, in the past you've not mentioned certain things. You know I love you, and we need to build our relationship, but what you need to understand is that when you don't tell me things, it makes me wonder. Please just tell me. It will make me be not suspicious."
Therapist:	And how will Harrison respond?
Liz:	He'll probably respond positively.
Therapist:	What will he say?
Liz:	He'd say, "Okay, I didn't tell you this time, because I know when you hear about some woman, you're gonna freak out. I just wanted my kids to go to Sea World. They're here all summer, and I feel guilty that I have to work every day."
Therapist:	And how will you respond?
Liz:	"Okay, I don't mind that they went to Sea World with her, but I *do* want you to understand that I don't trust her, like her real motives, at this point. And listen, Harrison, if you ever want someone else, I want to be the first to know."
Therapist:	And he'll say?
Liz:	"It's not going to happen, but if it ever did, I told you I'd do that. I promise you'd be the first to know."
Therapist:	And what else will be different?
Liz:	Hopefully we won't be fighting so much. And we'll be more affec-

tionate. See, we don't spend a lot of time together, because of both of our schedules. We both have really demanding careers.

Liz digresses a bit, and the therapist allows her to do so. (This may be an error, because more detailed elaboration of the miracle scenario is not elicited, and the miracle remains somewhat narrowly defined. Therapy does not always follow the guidelines!) Liz talks about how she and Harrison actually spend very little time together during the week. When they try to squeeze in more time together, they are both tired, it is not "quality time," and they just fall asleep. The only thing that Liz can imagine giving them more time together would be living together, and Liz is not willing to do that "for moral reasons." Liz says that having so little "quality time together," which is "neither of our faults," further increases her sensitivity to the possibility that Harrison might become interested in someone else. The therapist attempts to empathize with her difficult situation, and then to return to the picture of Liz's miracle, and whether any pieces of it are already happening.

Therapist:	So you guys are in a real bind.
Liz:	We're in a horrible bind. If we try to get together mid-week, it's just not worth it.
Therapist:	Going back for a minute to that miracle question I asked you before, where you're telling Harrison in a calm tone that you don't like something—are there any pieces of that picture that are already happening?
Liz:	No. Well, maybe. No, actually, no. See, what happens is, we have a crisis, and instead of going back and readdressing that issue which we're calm, we just leave it.
Therapist:	So, no pieces of that scenario are happening yet.
Liz:	No, because I always make a big deal of it. But I try not to. Do I ever try. Every time, I say to myself, "Why can't you just say it calmly the next time?" It's what I always hope for. I say in my mind, "The next time something like this happens, don't react that way." I tell myself, "You do it at work. You know how to talk calmly. Why can't you do it in relationships?"
Therapist:	You tell yourself, "I'll do it differently next time."
Liz:	Yeah, that's exactly what I say.
Therapist:	And what happens?

Liz: Nothing good. I overreact in exactly the same way. I just lose it. Every time. And I tell myself, "You screwed up again."

This is important. Liz has spontaneously described her unsuccessful attempted solution, which is essentially the same thing as her primary response to the miracle question. Therefore, this is *not* a time to suggest that Liz act "as if" pieces of her miracle were happening. On the contrary, Liz's response guides the therapist to move in the opposite direction.

Therapist: So you're saying it doesn't work to tell yourself, "I won't overreact."

Liz: No, it doesn't.

Therapist: Well, we don't know yet what, if anything, will *stop* the overreacting, but, you know, we've clarified one important thing in the last few minutes. We know that telling yourself, "Take it easy; say it calmly" *doesn't* work. Have I got that right?

Liz: Yeah.

Therapist: So if *anything* is going to work, it'll be something real different from that.

Liz: Do you have any suggestions?

Therapist: Actually there *is* a thought coming into my mind as we talk about this, about something you might say to Harrison. Does he know, by the way, that you had this appointment here today?

Liz: Yes.

Therapist: Okay. You could say something like this: "Harrison, remember how you told me I'm insecure, that I need to address some things in myself? Well, I've been doing a lot of thinking about it. And I went and talked to a therapist about it last week. And I think you were right, I do come on too strong sometimes. And I *am* insecure. And I think that when we don't spend a lot of time together, my insecurity gets even worse, and I freak out if I think you might be spending time with some other lady. And I frankly can't blame you for not wanting to tell me about it, since I have a cow when you do. Anyway, I wish I could tell you that after my therapy appointment, I now understand all of this, and I won't ever do it again. But, if I'm real, real honest with myself, and with you, I have to say I probably *will* overreact. So when I do, all I can say is: I apologize in advance—not for my feeling of not liking it—that's real, and I'm entitled to it—but for the volume of the attacks and stuff. So, please ignore that part, and bear with me.

Liz: I see what you mean. It's worth a try.

The session time is almost up. The therapist has already made a suggestion; nonetheless, it seems useful to summarize what has taken place. The therapist takes a short break to construct an intervention for Liz.

Therapist: Well, I don't blame you for not liking to find out in an offhand way that Harrison has had some lady over. Your intuition tells you that it just doesn't seem right for her to be there. You call it "insecurity," but some people would say that most women, frankly, aren't cynical enough about all the women out there trying to steal their man. And when you're not spending a lot of time together, it certainly doesn't increase your confidence in Harrison to hear that, for whatever reason, this gal was at his place. But I also hear you saying that there's something about the way you put it when you say things that ends up making things worse. And that's the main thing you want to change at this point. You know that when you raise your voice and say things in anger, then he's less likely to tell you about it next time. And that doesn't exactly enhance a person's feelings of security. I'm impressed that you could come up with a scenario where you could say it differently, the same content, "Harrison, I don't like it," but with different words and tone. And you recognize that, if you could do that, it would make a real difference. But even more, Liz, I'm impressed with your self-knowledge. You recognize that it's a heck of a lot easier to say it like that in here, with me, than with Harrison, and you know that when you've tried to do that, it hasn't worked. So, it wouldn't be much help to you if I were to say, "Go talk to Harrison the way you did in here," because you know, and I know, that you've already tried that, and it hasn't worked. So, like I said before, I think your best shot may be to warn Harrison, in advance, that you'll probably overreact to certain things, and when you do, would he please bear with you.

Liz: Yeah, that makes sense. I'm going to do that.

Therapist: Where shall we go from here, you and I? Do you want to make a follow-up appointment, or leave it open ended, or what?

Liz: I think I want to leave it open ended for now. Can I come back later if I need to?

Therapist: Absolutely.

Liz: Thanks. I'm glad I came in.

Therapist: I am, too. I'll see you whenever.

As this chapter is being written, it has been ten months since Liz's appointment. She has not returned, and there is no information about what happened after her single session.

13

Excerpts
Brief Therapy

Megan: "Problems with My Father"

Megan, age twenty-four, was a student and a waitress; she lived with her boyfriend, Oliver. Megan came in complaining about "problems with my father." What were those problems? Her father had lied to Megan, he was always critical, and he had been verbally abusive. When did this happen? It had gone on "for years." Was Megan financially dependent on her father? No. Did she have frequent contact with him? No. In fact, for eight months there had been no contact whatsoever.

How was Megan's relationship with her father a problem for her *now*? "Well, I thought it would all go away if I didn't see him, but it didn't." (Megan was describing an unsuccessful attempted solution, although the problem she was trying to solve was not yet clear.) What was the "it" Megan hoped would go away? "How it's affecting my relationships." "Any relationship in particular?" the therapist asked. "Yes, my relationship with Oliver," Megan said. The following excerpt from the first session begins with the therapist's request for elaboration and Megan's response.

Therapist: You said that your feelings about your dad are affecting your relationship with Oliver. In what way?

Megan: We constantly argue.

Therapist:	Can you give me an example of that?
Megan:	Um, we have a cat. If Oliver doesn't clean the cat litter, I get extremely upset.
Therapist:	If I had a video segment of how that goes . . .
Megan:	Oh, you'd laugh. It's ridiculous.
Therapist:	Help me see it.
Megan:	I would say, um, "You haven't cleaned the cat litter. Are you going to clean the cat litter?" He'll say, "I'll get to it when I have time." And I'll say, "Well, the time is now." He'll keep saying, "I don't have time." And I say, "Well, I don't like the smell. You procrastinate constantly." And then it gets to a procrastination argument. And then he starts trying to hold his own, to not give in to me. And so it's a battle.
Therapist:	What does he say?
Megan:	He says, "I know it needs to be cleaned; I'll do it in my own time." And then I say, "Well, let's just get rid of the cat." That's what I find myself doing a lot. Or, "Well, I'll just move out. I'm moving out." And when I first heard myself saying that, I thought I should go get some help.
Therapist:	You're saying that it was your thinking about moving out that led to your being here now?
Megan:	Yes. It scared me.
Therapist:	What scared you about thinking that?
Megan:	The trying to solve the problem by moving out. My dad used to do that. And the "why now" part—well, we had ants in our kitchen last week. And I was doing all the work. He wasn't taking an active part, and actually getting down on his hands and knees and helping. So I got very angry. I did everything. And I do a lot anyway, you know, all the housework, the laundry, the cooking. I take care of everything, and now the ants. I was really bitter. Sometimes I do wonder if I should have moved in with him without getting married. Because I didn't realize it would be so much work, and I don't get any help. I feel like a trapped housewife, and I'm not a housewife.
Therapist:	The fact that Oliver's not doing his share, is that the main thing you're angry at him about?

Megan: Yes. I mean, I'm still a student. I shouldn't have to do all this.

Therapist: Let me ask you this. Do you think it's legitimate to be angry about this?

Megan: I do.

Therapist: And do you think it's legitimate to be angry about doing more than your share of the work, apart from what's going on with your father? I mean, even if you had a nice, normal father, would you still say it's legitimate to be angry about doing more than your share?

Megan: I probably would, yeah. Because I'd want it to be equal, straight down the middle.

Therapist: So are you saying you might be having feelings of resentment toward Oliver apart from your experiences with your dad?

Megan: Possibly, yeah. I just think the problems I'm having with my dad start interfering and making these little things worse.

Therapist: In what way?

Megan: Well, I automatically say I'm leaving and moving out. Oliver comes from a very normal family—well, I don't really know what normal is—but very supportive family. His parents are still married, very nice people, and he hasn't had to be as independent as I've had to be.

Therapist: So you think that because of some of your experiences with your dad, with his taking the drastic approach of saying, "I'm out of here," that you do the same thing with Oliver, even though you don't really think that's the best way to approach it?

Megan: Mm-hmm.

Therapist: How does Oliver react, by the way, when you say, "I'm moving out"?

Megan: Well, of course, the first time I said it, he took it very seriously, and then I think each time we get into these things—because our relationship, as I see it, has ups and downs; I call it the hills and valleys—the valleys are bad, and the hills are good. And lately the valleys have been getting longer and longer before we get up to the good again. And when I say these things, he knows it's coming. I don't know, I haven't asked him, but I believe he knows it's coming, from the way I react to him.

Therapist:	I'm not sure I'm clear on how Oliver reacts *now* when you say you're moving out. You said the first time he took it real seriously.
Megan:	Yeah, he was very upset.
Therapist:	Did he start cleaning up?
Megan:	Yeah, he did, for the first two weeks, and then it goes back to how it was before.
Therapist:	And what do you do when it goes back to how it was before?
Megan:	Get upset.
Therapist:	What do you do or say?
Megan:	Well, I don't usually say anything. I just take it on. You know, the floor needs to be cleaned, so I'll clean the floor, and I'll clean the windows, and I'll vacuum. And then I'll get upset, really angry, because I'm doing it all again. And I catch myself taking care of everything.
Therapist:	And then what happens?
Megan:	I get angry. Yell at him.
Therapist:	What do you say?
Megan:	"Here we go again. It's happening again. You told me this would change, and it's not changing."
Therapist:	So the way you're handling it right now, when he goes back to letting you carry more of the load, is that you go ahead and do it, and you get angry inside, and then you yell at him, "Here we go again."
Megan:	Mm-hmm.
Therapist:	Is that pattern working in getting Oliver to do more?
Megan:	Well, it's doing okay now, because we just had that fight about the cat litter. So he's been doing his stuff the last two days, but I know that pretty soon it's going to go back to exactly where it was before.
Therapist:	Let me ask you this question. I want you to pretend, for a moment, that whatever issues you had with your dad are resolved. Whether through therapy, or whatever, you've made peace with those. The "magic wand" has not changed Oliver, who still is who he is, a little lazy at times; he'll slip into his slovenly ways, waiting

for you to take care of the cat, the dishes, etc. But the one piece that's different is that you're not now responding from the part of you that's messed up because of your dad. You're responding from the perspective of those issues being resolved. What will be different about how you'll handle it when Oliver doesn't do the dishes?

Megan responds that she will be more relaxed. Specks on the carpet will not bother her so much. She will calmly remind Oliver to do "his thing," but she anticipates that he will continue to procrastinate. Megan can imagine the following dialogue.

Megan:	He'll say, "I'll do it when I feel like it." And I'll say, "Will you please do it now?" He'll say, "Well, I'm going surfing now." He'll always have something else to do.
Therapist:	And how will you be handling that?
Megan:	I don't know.
Therapist:	So would it be accurate to say, then, that this is a dilemma you'll face, with or without your dad's stuff: that right now you're in a relationship with a man who doesn't do his share?
Megan:	Probably, yeah. It really will.
Therapist:	What will Oliver notice about you when your feelings about your father are resolved?
Megan:	Well, I'd probably be more relaxed, less stressed out.
Therapist:	And when you're more relaxed, what else will be different?
Megan:	Well, if he wants to do something and I don't want to, I'd say, "I don't particularly *like* doing what we're planning to do, but I'll do it for you."
Therapist:	So you'll be saying, sort of, "It's not really my thing, but, yeah, we can do it." How will Oliver be different when you convey that attitude?
Megan:	He won't be stressed out.

In the next segment, the therapist inquires about "exceptions" to the problem.

Therapist:	This scenario, are there any pieces of it already happening?

Megan:	That's what I've been working on a lot lately, like trying to hold calm conversations with Oliver. Like last week, when he wanted to go to this party, and I didn't, I told him that I'd go, but I wasn't really into it. And we did go, but we left early, and it really turned out to be okay.
Therapist:	What you said made a difference. What else?
Megan:	Um, trying not to hold everything in when I get upset. See, what I've always done is when anyone gets me upset, I just hold it in, and take it, and just do whatever needs to be dealt with, take on the responsibility, and get things done.
Therapist:	So you're saying there are some times when you're not doing that now?
Megan:	Um, once in a while.
Therapist:	Really? Give me an example.
Megan:	Well, Oliver left his wet suit in the bathroom. It was all full of salt and slime. I told him he'd better wash the salt out of it. He didn't, and I was all dressed to go to school, and I just left it there.
Therapist:	What happened to the wet suit?
Megan:	He must have hosed it off. I don't know for sure, but it was gone by the time I got home.
Therapist:	Interesting.

In the next section, the therapist asks about Megan's expectations about how therapy will help.

Megan:	I'm hoping you can help me sort out what's going on with me. Help me solve this. Maybe give me some reasons why I feel the way I do. I mean, I have my own theory about it.
Therapist:	And your theory is?
Megan:	Well, I always equate it with my dad. I mean, my family went through hell with him. I've been taking care of things forever. Taking responsibility has been my job ever since I was eight, nine years old: getting my sister up, making my brother's lunch, getting him off to school, all that. But maybe that's completely inaccurate.

Therapist: What makes you think your theory might be incorrect?

Megan: Well, cutting off all contact with my dad sure didn't fix things.

Megan appeared to be open to viewing and approaching the problem in a different way. After validating Megan's feelings and complimenting her on changes already begun, the therapist introduced the possibility that Megan was "letting Oliver off the hook." The combination of Megan "yelling" about—but then doing—Oliver's "dirty work" left only one aversive consequence for Oliver to face: Megan's anger, not the mess. Megan decided to pick some task that she could tolerate being undone for a while, if necessary. She would ask Oliver to do it, and if he did not, she would "let him deal with the mold, or whatever." Megan and the therapist agreed that the therapist would contact Oliver to invite him in for an individual appointment; after that, Megan would return.

Oliver was quite willing to come in. He said that Megan "worries about anything and everything," and her "nit-picking" him about chores was one example of this. Oliver acknowledged that Megan did many more household tasks then he did, partly because their "standards of neatness" were very different, with his standards much more relaxed. Oliver's attempts to soothe Megan involved making general promises to take care of tasks that did not really seem important to him.

Oliver knew about Megan's distress about her father, and he readily agreed that his general promises, made in an attempt to help her, resulted in her feeling "lied to" by him, just as she had been lied to by her father in the past. Oliver decided that he would not be so quick to volunteer for a task that he honestly knew that he did not care enough about to complete. He also planned to respond to Megan's "yelling" in a different way. Rather than trying to convince her "logically" not to worry about the mess, he would say, "You're right. I didn't do it, and I said I would. I can be a real slob, and a real procrastinator, at times."

When Megan returned two weeks later, she said that she felt calmer. Oliver had told her directly that he did not see certain household tasks as high priority, and that he probably had not been honest with either Megan or himself about how much he would be willing to do around the house. Both of them agreed that Megan would still "bug him" at times. Megan had done a lot of thinking about Oliver's "selfishness" and her ambivalence about the relationship. She recognized that Oliver was pretty "self-centered," maybe too much like her father. At the same time, she cared about him, he cared about her, and they enjoyed many activities together. Megan was not sure that she wanted to stay with Oliver "forever," but she accepted that dilemma and wanted to "just live with it for a while—at least until our lease is up" (three months later). She would practice asking for what she wanted, leaving his "messes," and paying attention to what she discovered.

Two months later Megan came in again. She had to make a decision about attending a fiftieth birthday party for her father that his current wife was giving, and she did not want to go. The therapist asked how Megan hoped that a therapy appointment would help, since Megan was obviously quite aware of her feelings already. Megan said, "I guess I want you to reaffirm that my feelings about my dad are normal, after everything I went through with him. I need to get on with my life."

Oliver's messiness and the arguing were no longer major problems. In fact, Megan said that she and Oliver were doing "great." Oliver was still a "slob," but Megan felt that he was now doing his share. They joked about being "the slob, the neatnik—and the cat," and they planned to renew their lease for another six months.

Jack: Trichotillomania

Jack, age twenty-eight, a married computer scientist, called requesting "nonmedication therapy" for his trichotillomania, a problem of six years' duration. Jack had requested service now after reading an article on trichotillomania that referred him to a national Obsessive Compulsive Disorders foundation. He had written to that group and had received information about medication and behavior therapy. The following excerpt begins during the problem clarification stage of Jack's first appointment.

Therapist:	How is it a problem that you do this from time to time?
Jack:	Well, when I pull hair out from different parts of my head, it's just disquieting, and I notice hair all over the place, and seeing how much is there.
Therapist:	And when you say it's disquieting, you mean . . .
Jack:	It bothers me.
Therapist:	It bothers you. Okay, the fact that you're pulling your hair, is it interfering with your functioning in any tangible way?
Jack:	I don't think so. I don't think it's a problem with my peers. I do notice that once some of the programmers asked me why I was getting bald at twenty-five.
Therapist:	What did you answer?
Jack:	I just sort of mumbled, "Oh it's one of those things," but it was sort of embarrassing. One person did take me aside and asked

me, "Why are you bald, and is it stress related?" I said, "I don't know if it's stress related."

Therapist: Was it a problem that he asked you that? For some people it feels kind of nice to be asked, and for some people that feels embarrassing.

Jack: Yeah, it was nice he noticed, but I also didn't like having something so apparent. But, you know, other people's reactions aren't really that big a deal to me.

Therapist: Is there any other way it's a problem?

Jack: Well, one problem is I get cramps in my elbow doing this while I'm on the computer. But that's not really a big deal.

Therapist: Let me ask you this about baldness. If you were getting bald just because you were balding early and not because you pulled your hair, how much of a difference would that make to you?

Jack: I don't know, since there have been times I've actually shaved my head, so I wouldn't have to bother with my hair.

Therapist: You wanted to not have to comb it, or to not have to pull it?

Jack: To not have to wash it on a backpacking trip. I don't know, baldness *would* probably bother me.

Therapist: If you were bald just because you were balding, how would you respond to questions like "Why are you bald?"

Jack: I'd say, "It happened." Or if my head was shaved for backpacking, and someone asked, I'd tell them, "Would *you* want to have dirty hair for five weeks?"

Therapist: Interesting. So there are some situations where it's actually an advantage to not have hair. Okay. Can I take it that the main way the hair pulling is a problem is that it's disquieting and it bothers you?

Jack: Yes. I just don't like it.

The next section is the inquiry about attempted solutions.

Therapist: I want to make sure that I understand clearly what all you've tried in your best attempts to solve this. Actually you've already told me some things already. You've used gloves; you've squeezed a bean bag; is that right?

Jack:	Yes.
Therapist:	Just to make sure I understand, what has been your rationale about how those things were supposed to help?
Jack:	Well, for the bean bag, the rationale was that if I could keep my hands occupied, then I wouldn't be wanting to pull my hair. With the gloves, you supposedly can't grasp a single hair with gloves on.
Therapist:	And did you say before that all those things seemed to work a little bit, but they didn't work well enough?
Jack:	Yes, that's right.
Therapist:	What else have you tried?
Jack:	Well, I've sat on my hands. When I'm with my wife, she holds my hand.
Therapist:	And what happens when she does that?
Jack:	She holds it pretty tight.
Therapist:	Well, would you say that works well enough?
Jack:	Well—
Therapist:	You hesitated.
Jack:	No, because I still pick it. Like, when we're both watching a movie, my hand just creeps back to my head.

The therapist realizes that Jack's wife may be more of a "customer" than Jack for this problem and inquires about this possibility.

Therapist:	Let me digress for a moment from "What have you tried?" back to "How is this a problem?" I know some of the things you've said involved your wife. Is this more of a problem for her or for you?
Jack:	Um, she loves my hair. She's said that much. I'd say it bothers us about the same.
Therapist:	Let me ask you this as a hypothetical question. If your wife were to say to you, "You know, I've made too much of a big deal about the hair thing; I have my habits, too—it's not a big deal," how much difference would that make in how much of a problem this was?
Jack:	It would still be somewhat of a problem, maybe not as much, but

I'd say on a scale of one to ten, it would still be seven, instead of the eight it is now.

Jack seems to be "enough of a customer" to proceed. The interview returns to clarification of attempted solutions.

Therapist:	Okay, let's go back to what all you've tried: gloves, bean bags, keeping your hand occupied, sitting on your hands, your wife holding your hands—what else?
Jack:	I've tried a crew cut. I had one when I was in the Navy. And once in a while I get one in the summer, because it's hot.
Therapist:	So, does a crew cut work?
Jack:	Yeah, I would say because of how short the hair is, I can't grasp it.
Therapist:	Okay. So, some people might say, if a crew cut works, the solution to this is no farther than your barber's chair. Obviously I'm a therapist and not a hairdresser. Just for my information, what's the obstacle to having a crew cut all the time?
Jack:	I kind of like having longer hair. Also, if I get a crew cut every week, it starts to get expensive. If I just cut my hair every six weeks, it's pretty darn cheap.
Therapist:	So that in terms of both convenience and preference, you like longer hair better. If I were to push you, which one—preference or convenience and cost—is the more important reason?
Jack:	Preference.
Therapist:	Okay. You just like longer hair.
Jack:	Yes.
Therapist:	What else have you tried, or what else has been suggested?
Jack:	Well, one of my friends suggested I put so much styling gel in my hair that it would feel gross to put my hand there.
Therapist:	Did you try that?
Jack:	No, I never did. I just don't like gel.
Therapist:	One of the things I thought I heard you say before was that people have said to you, "If you're pulling your hair, you must be stressed." The implication in that is "Do something to relieve the stress." Has anyone said anything like that to you?

Jack:	Yes.
Therapist:	What along those lines have you tried?
Jack:	Well, I cycle, and I surf.
Therapist:	Do you do those things in an attempt to not pull your hair, or do you do them because you like them?
Jack:	Because I like surfing. I like bicycling, too.
Therapist:	Okay. So you haven't done those things specifically in an attempt to not pull your hair, although other people have suggested that.
Jack:	No, I've never done anything like that specifically for hair pulling.
Therapist:	You said you wrote to the OCD association, and they sent you some information. I'm curious if they had any suggestions.
Jack:	Well, they suggested some things to look at. For instance, they suggested that I check out the fillings in my teeth, if there's any mercury there, because some research found some connection.
Therapist:	Have you done that?
Jack:	No, I haven't, but I do have a lot of fillings. Maybe I'll talk to my dentist about it. But I don't know if there's really a connection.
Therapist:	You sound skeptical.
Jack:	I sound skeptical, but then again, I don't know all the research, and it's worth asking about. Of course they also suggested taking medicine for it. And they suggested going to behavior modification, which I'm seeking right now. Those are the three main suggestions I remember.
Therapist:	You said you're seeking behavior modification.
Jack:	Yes.
Therapist:	Maybe that comes down to the question of your being here now. What specifically is your hope about how I'll be able to help you with this problem?
Jack:	Well, I have pretty strong feelings about not wanting to put chemicals into my body. So I hope you can help me modify my actions.
Therapist:	By doing what? I want to make sure I understand what your hope is that I'm going to do that will help you modify your actions.
Jack:	Um, through suggesting and helping me do behavior modifica-

tion, by giving me a guided way of doing it, because I feel like I've already been doing it in an unstructured way.

Therapist: Oh, so you feel you *have* been doing some of it on your own?

Jack: Yeah, the bean bag and all that, but it's not the same as maybe my perception of what a psychologist would suggest.

Therapist: Okay.

The therapist has not asked a miracle question and at this point decides not to do so. The unsuccessful attempted solution seems reasonably clear, and the therapist has an idea for a "behavioral suggestion," which is what Jack is requesting. After a short break, the therapist continues with the following intervention.

Therapist: Well, there are several things I want to say to you, Jack. I hear you saying pretty clearly that you don't like your hair pulling, and you find it disquieting. Frankly, I'm impressed that even with the hair pulling you've managed to function at school, and now at work, and to get married, and you cope with the questions like "Why are you bald?" And I'm also impressed that you know your own mind, that you really don't want to take medicine if you can avoid it. And you know that if nothing else works, a crew cut could make a difference, even though it's not your personal preference and it's kind of a pain, in terms of money and hassle to go for it— although it's interesting to wonder whether if it came to a choice, that would be a lesser evil than medication. Nonetheless, I hear you saying you don't like pulling your hair, and you want to try something different. Actually, you've already tried a number of things: gloves, bean bags, sitting on your hands, and so on. I think what all of those things have in common is that they're a way of saying "Keep your hands occupied. Keep your hands away from your scalp. *Don't do it.*" Am I hearing that right?

Jack: Yes.

Therapist: And I think that what all of those things also have in common is that they haven't worked, or they haven't worked well enough.

Jack: Yes, that's right. They haven't.

Therapist: So, I think that if you and I come up with some suggestion that's kind of "more of the same"—don't do it, keep your hands off— we're probably going to get the same results you got before. Now, one of the central tenets of behavior modification is this: if something doesn't work, don't keep doing it. I've also heard you say that sometimes you pull your hair outside of awareness; you're not aware of the behavior. Now, sometimes one of the best ways to grasp control of a behavior involves making yourself *very* aware of it. What you have tried to do to solve the problem is telling yourself, "Don't do it." One very different approach might be to *extend* the behavior a bit. What that might mean is that when you find yourself taking your hand toward your hair, to consciously, deliberately, in full awareness, keep your hand on that hair for an extra second, to extend the period of time the hand is on the hair. This means being fully aware of what you're doing, and noticing how that makes a difference.

Jack:	Okay.
Therapist:	Is that something you're willing to experiment with, to see if you can grasp control of it?
Jack:	That sounds reasonable. I never thought of doing something like that.
Therapist:	We need to stop in a moment. Do you want to set up a follow-up appointment to tell me what you discover from this?
Jack:	Yes.

Jack wanted to return in three weeks. When seen then, he said that he had sometimes "held on" to the hairs when he reached to pull them. He felt a little more aware of the pulling. When his hand was on a hair, he thought: "Do I want to pull this one?" Sometimes he briefly debated the "pros and cons": "Don't pull; you'll go bald" versus "Go ahead and relieve the tension. Get it out." Sometimes Jack decided to pull; sometimes he decided to let go. Perhaps there were fewer strands of hair on his computer, but the change was not dramatic. The therapist complimented Jack on his increased awareness of his behavior and cautioned him to refrain from additional change.

One month later Jack returned. He said that sometimes he "held on" to the hairs before he pulled them, while sometimes he did not. He still pulled, but his barber had told him that his hair seemed to be "thicker, growing in on top." The therapist asked Jack a scaling question: where zero was when the problem was at its worst and ten was when it was solved, where was he now? "Six," Jack answered. Where would Jack say he had been, on that same scale, when he first came in? "Two" was the answer. If Jack could stay at a "six" for a while longer, would that be good enough? Jack replied that it would. How confident was he that he could stay at a "six"? "About a six or a seven," Jack replied. To be confident at a "seven or eight," he would need to "do this a little longer." Jack's home-work was to do just that, and again to "go slow" on additional change.

Jack returned in another month. His rating of the "pulling problem" was still at "six," and he felt confident "at a seven and a half" that he could continue at that level. The therapist asked Jack how he managed to continue to pay attention to his behavior. Jack replied that he knew a great deal about continued practice from his experience in athletics.

Jack also mentioned that he had read an article on trichotillomania that sug-gested that this was a biological condition. If he could know for certain that the condition was "biologically based," how would that make a difference for him? Jack answered that he would accept it—"and do what I need to do to keep it un-der control." Jack compared his trichotillomania to his eczema, another "physi-cal condition" that he accepted, and chose to manage without medication. Jack's homework was to "continue practice," and to watch how hair pulling, like eczema, could vary in intensity without being a problem. Jack did not feel a need to schedule a definite follow-up appointment. He would return as needed.

Gloria: The Inconsistent Overeater[1]

Gloria was thirty-one years old, a city employee and part-time student. She had been separated from her husband for three years, and she had an eight-year-old daughter. She called requesting therapy for her "eating disorder."

Gloria was 185 pounds overweight. She felt inferior and inadequate because of her size, and she did not like herself. Why was she here now? There had not been any recent increase in either her weight or her distress about it. She was seeking help now simply because "it's summer and I have the time."

For many years Gloria had tried to lose weight. She started liquid diet pro-grams three times, and each time she dropped out. She sought therapy once be-fore. The therapist told her she was depressed and should take Prozac. She did not think the Prozac made any difference, and she stopped taking it.

Gloria's own attempted solutions were variations on the theme of "Don't eat." "Don't eat early in the day." "Fat people shouldn't be seen eating in public." "Don't eat what you like." She acknowledged that none of this worked very well, because she usually binged later in the day and felt ashamed and disgusted. She said, "I eat to pacify myself. I wasn't pacified enough when I was a child." She hoped that therapy would help her to understand why she ate so much.

Gloria answered the miracle question by saying that she would fix her daugh-ter breakfast. The girl would be surprised and pleased by this. Getting her off to school would be more relaxed. Gloria would not care so much if her daughter's

---

[1]An earlier version of this section was published in *News of the Difference* (Quick, 1993).

hair was perfectly combed. Gloria said nothing much would be different during her work day. Later, she would plan a dinner for the two of them, chicken or hamburgers, maybe, and she would eat with her daughter. She would "put the leftovers up." She would feel "uplifted." She would soothe herself by praying. She would understand why she eats.

When asked about times that pieces of her miracle were already happening, Gloria said that sometimes she felt "positive." This occurred when she felt she had some glimmer of understanding about why she ate. On a zero to ten scale, she was at a "four." She emphasized that she really wanted more understanding about why she ate and why she kept "falling back."

The therapist complimented Gloria on her awareness that when eating was less of a problem, she would be planning meals. Since she knew that trying to understand the problem through liquid diets and Prozac had not worked, perhaps she was ready to understand the problem in a different way. Maybe she would even understand more about that tough part, the falling back. The therapist wondered if Gloria might consider fixing a meal, but before actually doing so, she might pause to understand what problem that might bring into her life, and how she would go about solving it.

At the next appointment, Gloria said that she had thought about things differently. She said, "If I was thin, I'd never know if people like me for being thin or for who I really am." She would have to face "my loneliness." When asked what she is doing now about her loneliness, she answered, "Not much. I guess I'm waiting." She was waiting to be thin, waiting for someone to come along. She acknowledged that, so far, this was not working. The therapist asked Gloria how she managed in other areas of her life (work, school), even though she was still overweight. She said, "I just do it."

Gloria came to the next session with more new understanding. She said, "This 'Don't eat' stuff doesn't work. You have to eat anyway." She talked about how she might plan and savor a meal just as she does "a good bargain." (When asked what she already genuinely enjoyed, Gloria said that she was an avid shopper.) The therapist asked how Gloria's daughter would know that Gloria was enjoying a meal. She said, "If we ate inside at Burger King instead of getting takeout." Gloria had just discovered her homework.

Over the next few weeks, Gloria ate inside at fast food restaurants a few times. At Disneyland she considered "just watching" her daughter ride, as she had done in the past, since "fat people don't go on rides," but she decided she did not have to wait to be thin to do what she had paid for. The therapist asked Gloria how she would view "dieting" if she were not waiting to be thin to live her life. She said, "I'd just eat healthy food, a little less of it, and exercise." Was there any obstacle to doing that now? "I don't do it because I'm afraid I might stop."

The therapist asked Gloria how she walked around Disneyland. She replied, "I just did it." Then she said, "What if eating healthy or walking wasn't a project, but just something I did today?" The therapist wondered aloud whether it might actually be an advantage to do those things just once in a while, inconsistently. The therapist added that the word "inconsistent" made her wonder what it would be like to be an "inconsistent overeater." Gloria liked that phrase and wrote it down.

Over the next few weeks, Gloria parked at the far end of the parking lot at the mall a few times, and she ate breakfast once in a while. She also mentioned that she had filed for divorce, something she had not previously bothered to do, even though she had been separated for three years. Together Gloria and the therapist talked about how "waiting to be totally sure you're doing the right thing means waiting forever." Gloria agreed that if this "being inconsistent" stuff works for her, she might as well keep doing it.

Gloria had six appointments over three months. The following excerpt begins in her final appointment, following the therapist's question about what Gloria will "take with her" from her appointments.

Gloria: I'm not having obsessive thoughts about having to diet. And like I said, they do come fleetingly, when you don't see pounds shedding visibly, minute by minute, but, they're much less. So that's one thing I'll be able to take with me. And also the idea of food as a pleasurable experience. Um, I'm kind of realizing when it's not pleasurable, I should pay attention to other things, and myself, or feelings, or whatever. I guess I'm trying not to use food as a crutch. But if you're going to eat or whatever, enjoy. You know, it's okay.

Therapist: And how does it make a difference for you when you can say, "It's okay to enjoy it"?

Gloria: Well, when I'm able to do that, I'm able to—I don't know what the word is—I don't have to make it into a negative experience and overeat to the point of delirium. It's okay to stop, because you want it to be a good feeling when you're done, as well.

Therapist: Exactly.

Gloria: So I think, just kind of, regulation. When it gets to be unpleasant, you can stop.

Therapist: Who in your life do you think is noticing that you're different, with these changes?

Gloria: Besides myself? Um, I don't know, I don't make a point of talking about myself. Well, I guess my daughter is noticing. We're going to have a family dinner out, a nice dinner, the two of us out together.

Therapist:	What else is different?
Gloria:	I don't know if I would attribute it to just eating habits, or maybe just being out of my marriage, or just being able to focus on my actual desires and needs, but it helps a lot. I think that helps, trying to alleviate the need to overindulge in food.
Therapist:	And as a result of focusing on your own desires and needs, what are you discovering?
Gloria:	Um, well, they vary from day to day. It's like, one day, I might want to just sit home, and you know, read or whatever. Another day I'll feel like, you know, let's get out and do something exciting. So just realizing that, and just being okay with it, is good. I told you before how everything was just "Hurry up and do it; you're late." Now I think there's time to do things in a leisurely manner and not feel rushed. So it's helping me to realize I can do that, without having to wait till you're ten minutes late, and then do it.
Therapist:	The other thing I'm remembering that you talked about was being able to be inconsistent, and this sounds like an example of that: how one day, you ladies can stay home, and another, you can go out and do stuff. And it *is* different day to day, and when you listen to what you're interested in, you discover that.
Gloria:	Yeah.
Therapist:	What else have you been able to be inconsistent with?
Gloria:	Um, having done little bits of exercise. I've considered, and maybe this is wrong, walking around the mall, even though I'm not at the track or whatever, that's okay. And I can count it. That's a way for you to get some exercise. And it's not something rigid, to say I've failed, if I'm in a hurry and do park at the front, so it's not a rigid thing.
Therapist:	Of course. When you're in a hurry, you'll park near the front.
Gloria:	Right, exactly. So that's kind of an inconsistent thing for me. I mean, I used to circle that parking lot till I got one of the closest ones. Now I'm like, well, let me just park. And that's okay. And then, it's a positive stroke, in that, gosh, you got ten extra steps of exercise that you normally wouldn't have gotten in.
Therapist:	Let me ask you this. On my zero to ten scale, where ten is where this problem you came here about is solved to your satisfaction,

and zero is when it was at its very worst, where would you say you are now?

Gloria: Hmm, I don't know if you're allowed to go to a ten, so I won't do that.

Therapist: You're allowed to do anything you want. This is your scale.

Gloria: Well, I don't think it's totally solved, because I just don't. I probably won't think that until I'm physically fit. But I feel closer to working through things. So I would say a nine. I feel closer to just being honest, and, um, I don't know. I mean, it's not perfect, but I feel like I'm thinking about things differently. So that's good for me. And it's certainly not a zero. I mean, I don't think I came in at a zero.

Therapist: Do you remember what you told me when I asked you that question the day we first talked?

Gloria: No. I don't remember. What, a four, five?

Therapist: Well, let's look. [Looking through chart] You said that you were at a four. That's less than three months ago, that you've moved from a four to a nine. How did you do that?

Gloria: I think the thought process has helped a lot, just to be real. I don't have to be hiding behind "You don't eat in public." And if I can come to grips with sitting down and eating, it's not an elaborate meal, just a fast food meal, that was a plus for me. And even when I have thoughts of fasting, it's like, "Well, be realistic."

Therapist: So what I hear you saying is that you got yourself from a four to a nine by saying, "It's okay to eat in public, a fast food meal," and that when you have, as you said before, those fleeting thoughts of fasting, to say, "Be realistic. You don't have to do that."

Gloria: Mm-hmm. And then I think, too, just remember, too, and this is one of the most excellent exercises, that a lot of the things you do, you do even at the weight you are. And that you continue to function, maybe not at the optimal level, but you do continue. And that was a plus for me, just to realize that. It makes it easier.

Therapist: When you said that thing about doing things at the weight you are, I was thinking about what you said last time about how change is continuous.

Gloria: Yeah, I used to always have this thing, it used to be, about "stop and start." And I realize now that life just goes on, and you continue. It's not that firm division between what you do today and what you do tomorrow. And I can't just say, "Don't overeat today; don't ever overeat again," because it's not going to happen. You still wear shorts even though it's fall. "Don't you know it's fall?" But that's how life continues. Because, you know, as long as the weather's nice, wear what you want to wear. When it's raining, put on a sweatsuit; that's okay. Just go with the flow; just kind of monitor it.

Therapist: Exactly. I want to ask you another question on my zero to ten scale. How confident do you feel about staying where you are now, where ten is "I'm totally confident," and zero is "I'm not confident at all; it's a pure fluke"?

Gloria: Hmm, let's see. I feel pretty confident, because I think about it a lot. I think about different things, and it's not something you just forget. I think it'll be pretty much with me to continue to think about things, to evaluate: what are you going to do now? Are you going to run though here, real quick, stuff your face, and then feel bad, or, how about, "Hmm, sit down a minute, you can slowly eat your food, enjoy it." And I realize I don't even need that much. And that's what's been happening. It's a continuous thing, reevaluate, every day. So I feel confident at about a nine. I don't even know how much I'm going to lose. But yeah, I can keep this up. At least a nine.

Therapist: A nine.

Gloria: You know, I had this thought the other day: You know what? What if you were at your ideal weight, because that's a number I can see on the scale, what would you do? Would you eat like you usually eat, till you get sick, or what? What would you do? It was like, you know what, I might stop eating when I get full. I might even think about being full sooner, you know. And it was like, why can't you live like that?

Therapist: Sort of like, maybe you don't have to wait until you're at the ideal weight to stop eating when you're full.

Gloria: Right.

Therapist: Interesting.

Gloria: It was pretty neat. It was like, gosh, if you did that, I wonder what would happen?

Therapist: Hmm. So, when you had that thought, were you eating at the time?

Gloria: Um, I was thinking about it. It was like, I'm gonna go get something to eat; how do I want to do this? So it was like—why don't you try it? When you're full, stop. And it was like, well, okay.

Therapist: And what happened?

Gloria: Well, I did, and it was, like, okay, I honestly admit I ordered more than I needed. It was like, gosh darn, that was way too much.

Therapist: What did you do with it?

Gloria: So it was like, well, I don't have to eat this. You can save it or something. It was like, well, stop. And it felt good. And I know I use food for emotional reasons sometimes, and I don't know if I can do it at those times, but it felt good that day. And I thought, "Hmm, I can still walk around, and I don't have to go lay down." So it felt good.

Therapist: Wow.

Gloria: Yeah.

Therapist: Those are pretty significant changes.

Gloria: Yeah, I think so.

Therapist: Well, I wonder whether—you said you just made this discovery yesterday?

Gloria: Yeah. I said, let's try this at this particular meal, and like, okay.

Therapist: I wonder if nine is a little high in confidence for something you just discovered yesterday?

Gloria: Yeah, I know I've been thinking about it, but I haven't had much time to use it.

Therapist: Well, I'm also thinking that confidence is something that you gain from the repeated experience of doing something. Like the only way you're going to be more confident on that one is to do it for a while?

Gloria: Right. I know I'll keep the ideas, but as far as the actual changes, I know I'm going to overeat again.

Therapist: Of course.

Gloria: I already know that. So I'm not under the illusion that I'm never going to overeat. I'm just going to be more attuned to what is pleasurable. If I want to be sick today, I'll just do that. But not all the time.

Therapist: You can be inconsistent in where you park, and when you go out and when you stay at home, and when you overeat, too.

Gloria: Exactly. Because when I think about it, I always have this idea, you know: you're overweight, so you're a person who eats a lot. Or the opposite: you're overweight, so you have to fast.

Therapist: They're the two extremes. And sometimes you can eat a lot, and sometimes you can fast, and sometimes you can eat the way you'll eat when you're thin, eating till you're full and then stopping.

Gloria: Exactly.

Therapist: Just being deliciously inconsistent.

Gloria: Yeah, that'll be excellent. Then you don't have to feel like, "Oh, I failed at this, or I failed at that." Because there's no one way.

Therapist: It's kind of funny. The way we're talking about it, the only way you could fail at being inconsistent would be by being too consistent.

Gloria: Yeah, and it doesn't sound like the way I used to think, you know: have a consistent program, diet, exercise.

Therapist: And if I'm remembering right, that was what you tried before that didn't work for you, when you said, "I have to stay on this program all the time."

Gloria: Yeah, it didn't work. That rigid living doesn't work.

Therapist: Exactly. Gloria, if you were going to plan a relapse, how would you go about doing it?

Gloria: Hmm.

Therapist: I'm not suggesting you should, but just theoretically.

Gloria: I'd go call the diet program, and I'd go, and say "Now you'll stay on it." And every morning I'd get up with the idea:"You are not going to eat today, because if you eat today, you are a total failure." And I'd go all day without eating, probably until about four o'clock, till I start swimming in the head by then, dizzy. And then I'd run in somewhere, to some drive through, and eat it so fast, so no one saw me. And then dinner time would come, and I'd wait as late as possible, so no one saw me, and I'd eat so much that I'd almost pass out. That's a relapse for me. That's kind of like the extremes from both ends.

Therapist: So you know how to plan a relapse, if you ever wanted to have one. And, again, I'm not suggesting you should. But it's useful to know.

Gloria: Hmm. So I could plan one? So I could avoid one? So I'd know when I'm there?

Therapist: What do you think?

Gloria: Hmm. All of the above, maybe? If I could see it coming, that would be the best thing for me. That's part of the inconsistency, that I don't have to stay there.

Therapist: You could relapse inconsistently.

Gloria: Right.

Therapist: Interesting. How could you have an inconsistent relapse?

Gloria: That when I realize that this is the old process that kept me—I want to say, bound—I realize, I don't have to continue with that. I just don't. To be inconsistent, what's wrong with that? Okay, that was yesterday. And I guess that's part of the continuing saga of life. That was yesterday, this is today, and you can do something different. It doesn't have to be the same. And that's okay. I can't even describe what it will be, but it will be different.

Therapist: So not only do you know how to overeat and diet inconsistently, but you even know how to have a relapse inconsistently.

Gloria: Relapse just says there was a break in the pattern.

Therapist: Like—what did I forget to do? Or what do I want to go back and do again?

Gloria: That's good. That's excellent. What do you call a relapse in other areas? I mean, like in other things in my life, if I'm doing something that doesn't feel good, I could change it and be inconsistent.

Therapist: And do something different from what you were doing before. Playing with the idea of doing something different, or the opposite, maybe, of what didn't work.

Gloria: It's sad, in a way. I wish I could have known that before. And not wasted so much time.

Therapist: Like someone should tell us these things before. So we don't spend all this time on stuff that doesn't work.

Gloria: Like I wasted all that time telling myself, "I'm waiting to be thin."

Therapist: It's sort of like two sides of the same coin. One side is feeling sad that the time is wasted. And the other is realizing that I don't have to waste more time from this point forward.

Gloria: Yeah. I appreciate your saying that. Because I was going to get deep into a path I couldn't do anything about. I'll tell you, it will make a big difference, just thinking that. Thinking different.

Therapist: You and I are going to need to wind down in a couple of minutes. The feedback I want to give you—I've kind of been giving it to you as we're going along—is that the amount of change you've made in the last couple of months is really amazing. If anything, it's so huge that the homework I want to give you is: don't make too much additional change, with the magnitude of what you're doing and what you've described. What can I say? If you've found some things that work, keep doing them, but just don't push yourself to do too much extra. Maybe you can just practice being inconsistent, and notice how that makes a difference for you.

Gloria: Okay. I'll do that. The inconsistency. I really like that.

Therapist: Good. Let us stop, for now, then. You know where I am if you need me, in the future. I can be sort of like your family practice doctor. You know, you go in if you have a sore throat, and maybe you go a few times, and if things are on track, you can stop, but there's no implication that at some point in the future, you won't have another sore throat. And if you come back, the doctor and the patient kind of scratch their heads and say, "What did we do before?" Or you could come back to that same doctor and say, "This has nothing to do with that sore throat. Today I'm here for a sore toe."

Gloria: That's good. That's excellent. Okay.

Therapist: Bye. I'll see you whenever.

References

Alexander, L., & Luborsky, L. (1986). The Penn helping alliance scales. In L. Greenberg and W. Pinsof (Eds.), *The Psychotherapeutic Process: A Research Handbook*. New York: Guilford.

Ardrey, R. (1970). *The Social Contract: A Personal Enquiry into the Evolutionary Sources of Order and Disorder*. New York: Antheneum.

Austad, C., & Hoyt, M. (1992). The managed care movement and the future of psychotherapy. *Psychotherapy*, 29, 108–118.

Barbach, L. (1980). *Women Discover Orgasm*. New York: The Free Press.

Bauer, G., & Kobos, J. (1987). *Brief Therapy: Short-Term Psychodynamic Intervention*. New Jersey: Jason Aronson.

Beck, A., Rush, A., Shaw, B., & Emery, G. (1979). *Cognitive Therapy of Depression: A Treatment Manual*. New York: Guilford.

Bennett, M. (1994). Can competing psychotherapists be managed? *Managed Care Quarterly*, 2, 29–35.

Berg, I. (1991). *Family Based Services: A Solution-Focused Approach*. Milwaukee: BFTC Press.

Berg, I., & de Shazer, S. (1993). Making numbers talk: Language in therapy. In S. Friedman (Ed.), *The New Language of Change: Constructive Collaboration in Psychotherapy*. New York: Guilford.

Berg, I., & Miller, S. (1992). *Working with the Problem Drinker*. New York: Norton.

Bergman, J. (1985). *Fishing for Barracuda: Pragmatics of Brief Systemic Therapy*. New York: Norton.

Bischof, G. (1992). Solution-focused brief therapy and experimental family therapy activities: An integration. *Journal of Systemic Therapies*, 12, 161–173.

Blackburn, I., Eunson, K., & Bishop, S. (1986). A two-year naturalistic follow-up of depressed patients treated with cognitive therapy, pharmacotherapy and a combination of both. *Journal of Affective Disorders*, 10, 67–75.

Brehm, J. (1966). *A Theory of Psychological Reactance*. New York: Appleton-Century-Crofts.

Brief Family Therapy Center (1991). Scaling questions. Unpublished document.

Brief Family Therapy Center (1992). Training workshop.

Budman, S., Friedman, S., & Hoyt, M. (1992). Last words on first sessions. In Budman, S., Hoyt, M. & Friedman, S. (Eds.), *The First Session in Brief Therapy*. New York: Guilford.

Cade, B., & O'Hanlon, W. (1993). *A Brief Guide to Brief Therapy*. New York: Norton.

Cheadle, D. (1995). Lessons learned in Denver: A voice from the bullpen. Presentation, Kaiser Permanente.

Chubb, H., & Evans, E. (1985). "Therapy is not going to help": Brief family treatment of a character disorder. *Journal of Strategic and Systemic Therapies, 4*, 37–44.

Chubb, H., & Evans, E. (1987). Clinic productivity and accessibility with the Mental Research Institute brief therapy model. Unpublished document.

Coyne, J. (1986). The significance of the interview in strategic marital therapy. *Journal of Strategic and Systemic Therapies, 5*, 63–70.

Cummings, E., & Davies, P. (1994). *Children and Marital Conflict.* New York: Guilford.

Cummings, N. (1995). Impact of managed care on employment and training: A primer for survival. *Professional Psychology: Research and Practice, 26*, 10–15.

Cummings, N., & VandenBos, G. (1979) The general practice of psychology. *Professional Psychology, 10*, 430–440.

Depression Guideline Panel (1993). Depression is a treatable illness: Patient's guide. Rockville, MD: Association for Health Care Policy and Research.

de Shazer, S. (1985). *Keys to Solution in Brief Therapy.* New York: Norton.

de Shazer, S. (1988). *Clues: Investigating Solutions in Brief Therapy.* New York: Norton.

de Shazer, S. (1991). *Putting Difference To Work.* New York: Norton.

de Shazer, S. (1992). Advanced training workshop. Brief Family Therapy Center.

de Shazer. S. (1994). *Words Were Originally Magic.* New York: Norton.

Dolan, Y. (1994). Solution-focused therapy with a case of severe abuse. In M. Hoyt (Ed.), *Constuctive Therapies.* New York: Guilford.

Duncan, B. (1992). Strategic therapy, eclecticism, and the therapeutic relationship. *Journal of Marital and Family Therapy, 18*, 17–24.

Duncan, B. (1993). Comments and case. *News Of-the Difference, 2*(1), 6–7.

Duncan, B., Solovey, A., & Rusk, G. (1992). *Changing the Rules: A Client Directed Approach to Therapy.* New York: Guilford.

Efron, D. (1994). Editorial. *Journal of Systemic Therapies, 13*, 1–3.

Efron, D., Clouthier, K., & Lefcoe, B. (1994). Developing a focused family therapy approach. *Journal of Systemic Therapies, 13*, 76–79.

Efron, D., & Veenendaal, K. (1993). Suppose a miracle dosen't happen: The non-miracle option. *Journal of Systemic Therapies, 12*, 11–18.

Eisenberg, J., & Wahrman, O. (1991). Two models of brief strategic therapy: The MRI model and the de Shazer model. *Israeli Journal of Psychiatry and Related Sciences, 28*, 8–18.

Elkin, I., Pilkonis, P., Docherty, J., & Sotsky, S. (1988). Conceptual and methodological issues in comparative studies of psychotherapy and pharmacotherapy: I. Active ingredients and mechanisms of change. *American Journal of Psychiatry, 145*, 909–917.

Emard, P. (1991). Strategies for stalemates. Workshop, Mental Research Institute.

Epston, D. (1994). Extending the conversation. *Family Therapy Networker, 18*(6), 31–37.

Erickson, M., Rossi, E., & Rossi, S. (1976). *Hypnotic Realities.* New York: Irvington.

Eron, J., & Lund, T. (1993). How problems evolve and dissolve. *Family Process, 32*, 291–309.

Fisch, R. (1986). The brief treatment of alcoholism. *Journal of Strategic and Systemic Therapies, 2*, 40–49.

Fisch, R. (1992a). Brief Strategic Therapy. Presentation, Kaiser Permanente.

Fisch, R. (1992b). Gender determinants in family problems: Implications for brief therapy. Workshop, Milton Erickson Conference.

Fisch, R., Weakland, J., & Segal, L. (1982). *The Tactics of Change.* San Francisco: Jossey-Bass.

Friedman, S. (1993). Does the "miracle question" always create miracles? *Journal of Systemic Therapies, 12*, 71–73.

Gersten, D. (1988). Psychotherapy of visual hallucinations: A paradoxical intervention. *Journal of Strategic and Systemic Therapies, 7*, 8–15.

Gingerich, W., & de Shazer, S. (1991). The BRIEFER project: Using expert systems as theory construction tools. *Family Process*, 30, 241–250.

Gurman, A. (1978). Contemporary marital therapies. In T. Paolino & B. McCrady (Eds.), *Marriage and Family Therapy*. New York: Bruner Mazel.

Haley, J. (1976). *Problem-Solving Therapy: New Strategies for Effective Family Therapy*. San Francisco: Jossey-Bass.

Haley, J. (1980). *Leaving Home*. New York: McGraw Hill.

Haley, J. (1990). Why not long term therapy? In J. Zeig & S. Gilligan (Eds.), *Brief Therapy: Myths, Methods, and Metaphors*. New York: Bruner Mazel.

Hayes, H. (1991). The "Zen lady": An interview with Insoo Kim Berg. *Australian and New Zealand Journal of Family Therapy*, 12, 155–158.

Heath, A., & Atkinson, B. (1989). Solutions attempted and considered: Broadening assessment in brief therapy. *Journal of Strategic and Systemic Therapies*, 8, 56–57.

Heath, A., & Ayers, T. (1991). MRI brief therapy with adolescent substance abusers. In T. Todd & M. Selekman (Eds.), *Family Therapy Approches with Adolescent Substance Abusers*. Boston: Allyn and Bacon.

Held, B. (1986). The relationship between individual psychologies and strategic/systemic therapies reconsidered. In D. Efron (Ed.), *Journeys: Expansion of the Strategic-Systemic Therapies*. New York: Bruner Mazel.

Hoyt, M. (1994). Single-session solutions. In M. Hoyt (Ed.), *Constructive Therapies*. New York: Guilford.

Hoyt, M., Rosenbaum, R., & Talmon, M. (1992). Planned single-session therapy. In Budman, S., Hoyt, M., & Friedman, S. (Eds.), *The First Session in Brief Therapy*. New York: Guilford.

Jones, C. (1985). Strategic interventions within a no-treatment frame. *Family Process*, 24, 583–595.

Kaplan, H. (1975). *The Illustrated Manual of Sex Therapy*. New York: Quadrangle/New York Times Book Co.

Karon, B. (1995). Provision of psychotherapy under managed health care: A growing crisis and national nightmare. *Professional Psychology: Research and Practice*, 26, 5–9.

Kleckner, T., Frank, L., Bland, C., & Amendt, J. (1992). The myth of the unfeeling strategic therapist. *Journal of Marital and Family Therapy*, 18, 41–51.

Klerman, G., Weissman, M., Rounsaville, B., & Chevron, E. (1984). *Interpersonal Psychotherapy of Depression*. New York: Basic Books.

Kral, R., & Kowalski, K. (1989). After the miracle: The second step in solution focused brief therapy. *Journal of Strategic and Systemic Therapies*, 8, 73–76.

Kreilkamp, T. (1989). *Time-Limited Intermittent Therapy with Children and Families*. New York: Bruner Mazel.

Kuwabara, C., & Tansley, R. (1994). Solution-focused strategic therapy. Unpublished document. Family Counseling Centre of Brant, Inc.

Liddle, H. (1984). Towards a dialectical, contextual, coevolutionary translation of structural-strategic family therapy. *Journal of Strategic and Systemic Therapies*, 3, 66–67.

Linehan, M. (1993). *Skills Training Manual for Treating Borderline Personality Disorder*. New York: Guilford.

Lipchik, E. (1992). A reflecting interview. *Journal of Strategic and Systemic Therapies*, 11, 59–74.

Lipchik, E. (1994). The rush to be brief. *Family Therapy Networker*, 18(2), 35–39.

Madanes, C. (1981). *Strategic Family Therapy*. San Francisco: Jossey-Bass.

Mann, J. (1981). *A Casebook of Time-Limited Psychotherapy*. New York: McGraw Hill.

Miller, S. (1991). Solution-focused therapy. Presentation, San Diego.

Miller, S. (1992a). Solution-focused therapy. Presentation, San Diego.

Miller, S. (1992b). The symptoms of solution. *Journal of Strategic and Systemic Therapies*, 11, 1–11.

Miller, S. (1994). The solution conspiracy: A mystery in three installments. *Journal of Systemic Therapies*, 13, 18–37.

Miller, S., Hubble, M., & Duncan, B. (1995). No more bells and whistles. *Family Therapy Networker,* 19(2), 53–63.

Molnar, A., & de Shazer, S. (1987). Solution focused therapy: Toward the identification of therapeutic tasks. *Journal of Marital and Family Therapy,* 13, 349–358.

Nylund, D., & Corsiglia, V. (1994). Becoming solution-forced in brief therapy: Remembering something important we already knew. *Journal of Systemic Therapies,* 13, 5–11.

O'Hanlon, P., & O'Hanlon, W. (1991). *Rewriting Love Stories: Brief Marital Therapy.* New York: Norton.

O'Hanlon, W. (1994). The third wave. *Family Therapy Networker,* 18(6), 19–29.

O'Hanlon, W., & Weiner-Davis, M. (1989). *In Search of Solutions.* New York: Norton.

Parker, B., & Hart, J. (1983). *Wizard of Id.* Los Angeles: Creators Syndicate, Inc.

Perlmutter, R., & Jones, J. (1985). Problem solving with families in psychiatric emergencies. *Psychiatric Quaterly,* 57, 23–32.

Pincus, H. (1993). Practice guidelines for treatment of depression. Presentation, Kaiser Permanente Psychiatry Symposium.

Prochaska, J., & DiClemente, C. (1992). *The Transtheoretical Approach.* New York: Basic Books.

Quick, E. (1990a). The phobia and panic attack management class. Unpublished manuscript, Kaiser Permanente.

Quick, E. (1990b). The strategic therapy planning worksheet. *Journal of Strategic and Systemic Therapies,* 9, 29–33.

Quick, E. (1993). Case study: The inconsistent overeater. *News of the Difference,* 2(3), 7–8.

Quick, E. (1994a). Strategic/solution focused therapy: A combined approach. *Journal of Systemic Therapies,* 13, 74–75.

Quick, E. (1994b). From unattainable goals to achievable solutions. *Journal of Systemic Therapies,* 13, 59–64.

Randolf, E. (1994). Integrating the strategic and systemic familiy therapies. *The California Therapist,* 40–44.

Resnick, R., & DeLeon, P. (1995). The future of health care reform: Implications of 1994 elections. *Professional Psychology: Research and Practice,* 26, 3–4.

Roberts, J. (1986). An evolving model: Links between the Milan approach and strategic models of family therapy. In D. Efron (Ed.), *Journeys: Expansion of the Strategic-Systemic Therapies.* New York: Bruner Mazel.

Rogers, C. (1961). *On Becoming a Person: A Therapist's View of Psychotherapy.* Boston: Houghton Mifflin.

Shutty, M., & Sheras, P. (1991). Brief strategic psychotherapy with chronic pain patients: Reframing and problem resolution. *Psychotherapy,* 28, 636–642.

Sifneos, P. (1987). *Short-Term Dynamic Psychotherapy: Evaluation and Technique.* New York: Plenum Press.

Simon, D. (1993). Random notes/First word. *News of the Difference,* 2(3), 1.

Simon, D. (1994). Re: Suppose a miracle doesn't happen: The non-miracle option. *Journal of Systemic Therapies,* 13, 16–17.

Stanton, D. (1981). An integrated structural/strategic approach to family therapy. *Journal of Marital and Family Therapy,* 7, 427–439.

Storm, C. (1991). The remaining thread: Matching change and stability signals. *Journal of Strategic and Systemic Therapies,* 10, 114–117.

Strupp, H., & Binder, J. (1984). *Psychotherapy in a New Key: A Guide to Time-Limited Dynamic Psychotherapy.* New York: Basic Books.

Todd, T. (1984). Strategic approaches to marital stuckness. *Journal of Marital and Family Therapy,* 10, 373–379.

Tomm, K. (1984). One perspective on the Milan systemic approach. *Journal of Marital and Family Therapy,* 10, 253–271.

Vaihinger, H. (1924). *The Philosophy of "As If."* Translated by C. Ogden. New York: Random House.

Walter, J., & Peller, J. (1992a). *Becoming Solution-Focused in Brief Therapy.* New York: Bruner Mazel.

Walter, J., & Peller, J. (1992b). Empowering couples: A solution-focused approach. Workshop, Milton Erickson conference.

Walter, J., & Peller, J. (1994). "On track" in solution-focused brief therapy. In M. Hoyt (Ed.), *Constructive Therapies*. New York: Guilford.

Watzlawick, P. (1987). Hypnotherapy without trance. Presentation, San Diego Conference on Hypnotic and Strategic Interventions.

Watzlawick, P. (1991). Brief strategic therapy. Presentation, Grossmont Hospital, Brief Strategic Therapy Conference.

Watzlawick, P. (1992). The creation of "reality" through language. Workshop, Milton Erickson Conference.

Watzlawick, P., Weakland, J., & Fisch, R. (1974). *Change: Principles of Problem Formation and Problem Resolution*. New York: Norton.

Weakland, J. (1978). OK—You've been a bad mother. In P. Papp (Ed.), *Family Therapy*. New York: Garden Press.

Weakland, J. (1992a). In D. Simon, First word. *News of the Difference*, 1(3), 2.

Weakland, J. (1992b). What's the problem? Workshop, Milton Erickson conference.

Weakland, J., & Fisch, R. (1984). Cases that "don't make sense": Brief strategic treatment in medical practice. *Family Systems Medicine*, 2, 125–136.

Weakland, J., Fisch, R., Watzlawick, P., & Bodin, A. (1974). Brief therapy: focused problem resolution. *Family Process*, 13, 141–167.

Weiner-Davis, M. (1987). Confessions of an unabashed marriage saver. *Family Therapy Networker*, 11(1), 53–56.

Weiner-Davis, M. (1992). *Divorce Busting*. New York: Summit Books.

Weiner-Davis, M., de Shazer, S., & Gingerich, W. (1987). Building on pretreatment change to construct the therapeutic solution: An exploratory study. *Journal of Marital and Family Therapy*, 13, 359–363.

White, M., & Epston, D. (1990). *Narrative Means to Therapeutic Ends*. New York: Wiley.

Wile, D. (1981). *Couples Therapy: A Nontraditional Approach*. New York: Wiley.

Yapko, M. (1994). *Suggestions of Abuse*. New York: Simon and Schuster.

Zeig, J. (1987). Ericksonian communication. Presentation, San Diego Conference on Hypnotic and Strategic Interventions.

Zilbergeld, B. (1981). *Male Sexuality*. New York: Bantam.

Zimmerman, T., & Protinsky, H. (1990). Strategic parenting: The tactics of changing children's behavior. *Journal of Strategic and Systemic Therapies*, 9, 6–13.

Index